EROS,
CONSCIOUSNESS,
AND KUNDALINI

DEEPENING SENSUALITY THROUGH
TANTRIC CELIBACY & SPIRITUAL INTIMACY

STUART SOVATSKY, PH.D.

Park Street Press
Rochester, Vermont

Park Street Press
One Park Street
Rochester, Vermont 05767
www.InnerTraditions.com

Park Street Press is a division of Inner Traditions International

Copyright © 1994, 1999 by Stuart Sovatsky, Ph.D.

Library of Congress Cataloging-in-Publication Data

Sovatsky, Stuart, 1949–
    [Passions of innocence]
    Eros, consciousness, and Kundalini : deepening sensuality through tantric
celibacy and spiritual intimacy / Stuart Sovatsky.
        p.   cm.
    Originally published: Passions of innocence. 1994.
    Includes bibliographical references and index.
    ISBN 0-89281-830-1 (alk. paper)
    1. Celibacy—Tantrism. 2. Kundalini. 3. Tantrism—Doctrines. 4. Sex
Religious aspects—Tantrism. I. Title.
BL1283.852 .S684 1999
294.5'447—dc21
                                                                    98-32384
                                                                        CIP

Printed and bound in Canada

10 9 8 7 6 5 4 3 2 1

Text design and layout by Charlotte Tyler and Virginia L. Scott
This book was typeset in Sabon

For Lillian, Jacob, and David

Contents

PREFACE   ix

ACKNOWLEDGMENTS   xi

INTRODUCTION:
THERE ARE UNTOLD POSSIBILITIES   **1**

    A Most Unusual Invitation • 1
    The Possibilities Begin to Unfold • 3
    Celibacy Becomes Provocative: The Tantric Spin • 5
    The Tantric Paradox of an Erotic Celibacy • 7
    Reclaiming Your Vulnerabilities Through Tantra • 9

1

FROM HARRY'S BAR TO THE
MYSTERIES OF TANTRIC SUBLIMATION   **11**

    The Sublimative Sex Drive • 14
    Going All the Way with Tantric Celibacy • 16

2

EROS AS MYSTERY:
THE KEY TO FURTHERING OUR EROTIC LIBERATION   **19**

    The Sexo-Political Burlesque • 20
    More Mystery, Less Liberation and Rules • 22
    Mystery's Inquisition • 24
    Sharing the Wonder • 26

Beyond the Limitations:
    Can the Sense of Mystery Free Us? • 27
Entering the Mystery:
    From Cynical Certainty to Meditative-Knowing • 28

3

MYSTERIES MEET:
THE CELIBATE ENCOUNTER   **40**

Tantric Celibacy in the
    Great Anonymous of Modern Culture • 47
The Shared-Gender Mystery • 50
The Prosthesis of an Owned Sexuality • 59
Homosexual Mystery • 62

4

CHOOSING TANTRIC SUBLIMATION   **63**

Why You Might Choose Brahmacharya • 66

5

THE ARS EROTICA OF YOGA   **73**

Meditation: The Silent Partner to Conventional Sex • 74
Meditation Follows the Mystery:
    The Yogic "All" in Going All the Way • 75
A Moment of Silence . . . • 79
The Yogic Anatomy of Human Potentialities • 80

6

YOGA PRACTICE AS ARS EROTICA   **94**

The Practices • 98

7

RELATIONAL WORSHIP   **120**

The Great Gesture • 122
Nyasa • 125
Mystery of Balance • 127
Pranic Mirroring • 129

The Singular Celibate Kiss ♦ 130
Breathing Mystery ♦ 130
Mantra Chanting ♦ 131
Ritual Worship of Mystery ♦ 131
Problems, Difficulties, and Other Knots ♦ 133

8

GROUNDING IN THE ORDINARY:
TANTRIC RELATING IN EVERYDAY LIFE **139**

Spoken Passion ♦ 139
Commitment and Marriage When Eros Is Mystery ♦ 141
Creating New Life: The Passions of Fertility ♦ 153
The Way of Solitary Celibacy ♦ 160

EPILOGUE
AN OPEN ENDING **164**

APPENDIX 1

WHAT EVERY TEENAGER SHOULD
KNOW ABOUT TANTRIC SUBLIMATION **166**

The Core of Your Body: The Yogic Spinal Pathway ♦ 168
Brahmacharya and Emotional and Spiritual Growth ♦ 170

APPENDIX 2

THE FUTURE OF A MYSTERY:
TOWARD AN ECOLOGY OF THE EROTIC **171**

The Contemporary Sexual Scene ♦ 172
Toward an Ecology of the Erotic ♦ 176
The Fourfold Mapping of the Erotic Mystery ♦ 178

GLOSSARY **189**

BIBLIOGRAPHY **195**

INDEX **206**

PREFACE

◆

Tantric celibacy is based upon a profoundly spiritual understanding of bodily maturation and Eros that includes definitive stages of psychophysical development beyond genital puberty. Kundalini awakening, the first of these stages to become known in the West, involves far more than is now conveyed by the popular, but overly simplistic, definition of kundalini as merely a "spiritual energy."

Given the impact kundalini can have on an individual's identity, sexuality, sense of life purpose, and neuroendocrine alterations, I suggest that such an awakening is, in effect, the long-developing puberty of first the spine and then, later, the hypothalamus and pineal glands, as well as the cerebrum. As a spiritual phenomenon that fully includes the physical body, kundalini helps our basic sense of identity mature from one connected to only our plucky—but lifetime-limited—egos to one that is based in our eternal souls.

This book, previously entitled *Passions of Innocence* and now, more directly, *Eros, Consciousness, and Kundalini,* is my studied—and lived—answer to that most practical of questions: "How do we, living our ordinary, daily lives, reach this place of higher spiritual enlightenment?" The goal of tantric celibacy is not merely to live a contented celibate life (although for some this will prove a worthy enough goal) and to gain enhanced health and intimacy, but also perhaps to reach and enjoy some measure of the safe and gradual awakening of the supremely creative force that for most of us lies dormant at the base of our spines. It is possible that in the coming years these deep spiritual potentials residing silently within us might awaken and come to life, just as the awesome potential of fertility and sexual passion awoke within us when we were teenagers.

As I give you over to the tantric alchemy described in this guidebook, I do so with no small degree of envy. After some twenty-three years of travels upon this path, I recall with fondness my earliest of yogic alchemical experiences, experiences that you will soon read about and, perhaps, pursue. In recalling the tumultuous passions of spiritual longing, the mixture of zealous certainty and utter wonderment, and the ecstatic sensations of transformation themselves, I can only hope that if there is such a thing as reincarnation that this book will be around in the future so that I might take this journey again and again and again.

May those great ones before us who have tread this path—Rumi, Lakulish, Patanjali, Socrates, Buddha, Christ, Hildegarde, Theresa d'Avila, Dalai Lama, Mirabai, Moses, Anandamaya-ma, Thich Nhat Hahn, Saint John, and unknown myriad others—bless all who go this way.

Acknowledgments

◆

This work would not be possible without the lifelong dedication of innumerable yogis, particularly L. Lakulish, S. Kripalvananda, Amrit Desai, Vinit Muni, Rajasri Muni, and Baba Hari Dass; the academic support of Michel Foucault, Meji Singh, Ralph Metzner, Judith Weaver, Karl Kracklauer, Harold Streitfeld, Myron McClelland, Mike Holley, Jim Ryan, and Wayne Richards; the support of my writing efforts by Miles Vich, Georg Feuerstein, Craig Comstock, Keith Hoeller, John Elfers, Thomas Armstrong, and Stephen Bodian; the illustrations of Alex Laurant and the calligraphy of Kartik Patel and S. Chakravarty; the many people whom I interviewed; the personal support of M. Jordan, Katy Wray, Erich Gottlieb, Martha Cochrane, Helen Palmer, Leland Meister, Cheryl Whyatt, Doris Warner, Peter Sutherland, A. D. H., C. F., K. J. R., M. H., L. G., M. S., M. M., Rupa, Nathaniel Gallup, Elena Kuenzel, and Harold Johnson; the staff of Insight Counseling and Blue Oak Counseling and my students at the California Institute of Integral Studies, John F. Kennedy University, and Rosebridge Institute; the Society for the Scientific Study of Sex, the World Congress of Sexology, the Association for Transpersonal Psychology, the Association of Humanistic Psychology and the Eric Berne Seminars for their support of my research underlying this book; Carole DeSanti, my first editor from erstwhile E. P. Dutton, who caught the manuscript as it came in over the transom in 1987 and is due special thanks; the enthusiasm and wise publishing support of Leslie Colket, Lee Wood, Jeanie Levitan, Anna Chapman, and Ehud Sperling of Inner Traditions; the attentive copyediting of Jill Mason; and the insightful editorial contributions of Dan Joy, who brought sensitivity and acumen to the project.

The rallying point . . . ought not to be sex-desire, but bodies and pleasures.

Michel Foucault
An Introduction. Vol. 1 of
The History of Sexuality, p. 157

Always without desire we must be found,
If its deep mystery we would sound;
But if desire always within us be,
Its outer fringe is all that we shall see. . . .

Where the Mystery is the deepest
is the gate of all that is subtle and wonderful.

Lao Tzu, Tao Te Ching

INTRODUCTION:
There Are Untold Possibilities

———————◆———————

"Would you tell me, please, which way I ought to walk from here?"
"That depends a good deal on where you want to get to,"
said the Cat.

Lewis Carroll
Alice in Wonderland

A Most Unusual Invitation

"Going *all* the way," said Rick, dropping the phrase casually into our conversation. His serenely rising pompadour, the confidence he so easily slipped into the word *all,* and especially his knowing glance let me know that, alas, at age ten, I was still a child and that my neighbor, at a towering sixteen, possessed secrets of incomparable power. Although I hadn't the slightest idea what he really meant (it was 1959), I knew enough not to admit it to anyone. Instead, I slinked away to where no one would see me, wrenched my belt buckle off center and onto my left hip, and began Elvising an "I was *born* ready" pucker to some imaginary audience. Eight years later, after slipping out from a freshman college mixer with an equally enthralled coed, I found out what he meant.

On that lower bunk, while Sam the Sham roared on in the gym, veils were lifted and secrets disclosed. A new world of pleasures, precautions, and trepid anticipations surfaced, for I had (finally) gone "all the way." At least, that is what I thought, for another eight years later, a most unexpected event occurred that suggested a realm of even greater hiddenness and secrecy. Suddenly that guiding star of sex that Rick, I, and everyone else I knew were following so devotedly shattered into a pulsing darkness, and "going all the way" began to stretch out before me endlessly.

I had been quietly relaxing at a weekend yoga retreat: healthy food, plenty of exercise and time for reflection in a peaceful country setting. It was Sunday morning, and I was listening somewhat inattentively to our instructor's final talk on the ways of the mind and the needs of the heart and body: meditation, diet, self-acceptance—the usual topics for such an event. Suddenly the lecture took an unanticipated turn, and I thought I felt the room begin to sway:

> *Sigmund Freud was a very brilliant man. He saw very deeply into the sexual nature of man, but he did not see the whole picture. There are many stages of development beyond sex, but if you want to get to them you will have to give something up. Are you ready to go on this journey?*

Beyond sex? It was 1975, the time of sexual liberation and free love, the Age of Aquarius—or at least the age of the Pill. Was this sparkling-eyed Indian yogi serious?

Not only was *he* serious, I too began to sense, as I had at age ten, that something mysterious and powerful was being revealed. And with that question, "Are you ready to go on this journey?," his provocative and fascinating words suddenly became a three-dimensional, outstretched hand that reached for my own. Should I take hold? It was only a lecture, wasn't it? I didn't have to *do* anything, did I?

Over the years I had heard scores of such talks, and I was always able to continue my life relatively unscathed. But this time I wondered, would I be walking away from something that, in Robert Frost's words, would make "all the difference?" If this yogi was right, then was Western psychology wrong? If some "beyond sex" existed, why hadn't I been told about it before? As these questions tugged and circled in my mind, one thing became alarmingly clear. I was actually considering stepping into a world of possibilities whose very existence I had never before suspected.

This step was something called *brahmacharya*—a Sanskrit term meaning, of all things, celibacy! And our confident teacher suggested we "try it" for a year and a quarter! "You mean, me?" I gulped to myself, as a second barrage of feelings whirled through me: disbelief, challenge, fear, a solemn profundity, and then a deeply mysterious churning at the roots of my being.

Trying not to be noticed, I strayed from the group into some nearby woods, comforted to be in nature where things just are and have no pressing questions or provocative invitations. With the snow crunching beneath my feet, I walked up the side of a hill and into the cold silence. I grew calmer.

High above, from the perch where I finally rested, I watched the other retreatants slowly returning to their cars, each one carrying a personal world of relationships, hopes, and concerns into an unknown future. The trees, rocks, sky, and snow—everywhere I looked I sensed a deeper rhythm, an embracing harmony. Within this bluish-white hush of a timeless, almost transcendent wholeness, I heard myself say, "Yes, I'll do it. It's only for a year and a quarter. *Only?* Yes, it will be ok."

THE POSSIBILITIES BEGIN TO UNFOLD

The first six months were the most intense, as I began my daily practice of the meditation, yoga, and breathing exercises I had been taught. An amorphous yearning moved through me as I stretched arms, wrists, fingers, neck, spine, legs, and toes, catlike, from one posture into the next. In some innately intelligent way the yoga seemed to be redistributing my libido throughout my body with each sensation. Even my genitals tingled enigmatically, yet without any focused urge or desire for sexual release. Instead, they seemed to be giving up their somewhat separate willfulness, merging more and more seamlessly with the rest of me.

Indeed, what I had previously *called* sexual feelings began to change in a radical way. Impossibly, or so I had thought until then, the urge to masturbate or have sex just went away. To be sure, I still felt strongly attracted to women, but any desire to have sex, to even have fantasies about having sex, faded into an occasional dream—for years very potent dreams, and later dreams of great serenity, devoid of sexually arousing imagery.

I knew that I could never have caused such changes to occur by an act of will or choice. Why would I have wanted to? But now that they were happening, I could see why: increased emotionality, stronger bodily coursings of the life force, and a boost of creativity were some initial results. I became fervent: a yoga enthusiast by dawn, a county administrator writing grants or counseling youthful offenders the rest of the time; later, a marriage therapist and a researcher of—what else—brahmacharya.

In this research, the writings of Freud, Reich, Kinsey, Masters and Johnson, and Hite no longer appeared so convincing as the welcomed and long overdue bibles of sexual truth but instead were emerging to me as historically and politically determined *theories* of sexuality. If there was a "function of the orgasm," as Reich insisted, there was also a function of sublimation that was far more positive than any of these psychologies had realized. The modern mandate to "have sex, or at least masturbate!" was betraying an element of freedomless compulsivity. As one yoga student put it:

> *I would just push myself over any fear and have sex, and then feel terrified and confused afterwards and wonder, "What have I done?"*

The whole of American society seemed to be caught on a merrily escalating drive for more external stimulation, more consumption, and more and better orgasms, as if an ultimate freedom were in the balance. At times it all looked quite desperate, in comparison with the broadened sensitivities of brahmacharya. Later, in the 1980s, the tragic and conflict-ridden problems of AIDS, greater awareness of sexual violations, and the unremitting abortion debate would cast a troubling grimness over those once liberating hopes.

Through these many experiences and observations, I came to agree with my yoga teacher that although Sigmund Freud was a brilliant sexual psychologist, he had not seen the whole picture. It seemed to me that the liberation he and others had set in motion was navigating with a faulty map. Brahmacharya was revealing that there is much more in the erotic universe to see, feel, taste, do, and love than Freud and his legion of followers could ever have guessed. (Ironically, Freud himself spent much of his life being celibate.) And, although this lifestyle does not involve sexual activity, it was proving to be the opposite of the dry and barren abstinence predicted by their writings. Instead, I found it to be richly "erotic"—in some ways very different from conventional sexuality and in other ways very similar to it.

During the more than fifteen years since that period, I have lived alone celibately for years at a time and have been both serene and lonely. I have been in celibate households and in fully celibate and semi-celibate love relationships and have been both joyful and disheartened. In my personal research, I have experimented with various forms of brahmacharya, and in my professional studies, I have interviewed many other brahmacharins.

Like Eskimos who are capable of discerning numerous shades of white, I began to see a variety of celibacies. Some focused on purity or psychic development, others on humanitarian service or theological commitment. Some allowed for sensual contact, while other forms were strictly reclusive.

CELIBACY BECOMES PROVOCATIVE: THE TANTRIC SPIN

The version of celibacy I have found most interesting is *tantric sublimation,* which is the focus of this book. It is based upon the yogic philosophy of paradox known as *tantra,* which fosters individual development through the integration of seemingly opposite aspects of life. It describes a mundane world, which is at the same time a sacred world. If we have lost the sense of the holy in our everyday lives, then tantra can serve as a corrective; if we haven't lost this sense, tantra preserves things for us as they are: filled with alluring mystery and wonder. Tantric sublimation (literally, eros become sublime) shows us that even *good* sex can become limiting within the broader expanse of erotic possibilities.

Nevertheless, tantric sublimation is not utopian. It is a way of being in which we accept our difficulties as something sacred; thus our mundane problems regain the spiritual depth that can be too easily trivialized in our daily routines. Instead of a promised land of "new and improved" popular solutions or analytic belaborings of one's past, it leads us forward on a tried and winding path of honoring our joyous achievements, stumbling efforts, and painful failures with equal appreciation; we learn about life from all the situations we encounter.

And, unlike other forms of celibacy, tantric celibacy requires a sex-positive, body-affirming attitude, for it is a path of sublimation, not repression. As we see in the following description of Lianne's experience of the partnered practice called Hearts and Backs (page 111), the body remains very involved in tantric sublimation:

> While balanced on Andy's back, I felt supported, but not forever. I learned that his steady holding of me was a two-person project. I really liked switching to support him and learned not to compare but to just share the differences between us. In each posi-

tion, I feel close to him in a different way. Here, I feel a pleasurably tingling reliability trickle up my back and down my legs that makes me feel very connected with him. Finally, my whole body would feel awakened.

In short, the many practices of tantric celibacy reveal a post-Freudian world of passion and meaning accessible to practically anyone—from the hot and horny to the natural renunciate; from the preteen who is just beginning to learn about the ways of sexuality in a sexually confusing and dangerous world, to the sexually sophisticated urbanite who is beginning to question life in the fast lane; from the newlywed couple whose marriage could take them into these uncharted lands, to the silver-anniversaried couple whose maturity has unearthed passionate rhythms deeper than those of desire. Karen, twenty-nine, discovers a closeness with her partner hidden in the resistance between them:

The meaning was just going out of our relationship. After two years of living together, the routine of it all, even in sex, made me doubt our love. Tantric celibacy reconnected us, first through helping us to actually share the frustration we were experiencing in our isolation. While in Twin Boats (page 113), pressing against each other's ankles to brace ourselves, I thought, "Is this why we fight over small things? Just to feel this connecting resistance between each other?" When I just let go of even these musings, I felt we got even closer. A surge of heat went right into my chest.

Mike, sixteen, finds tantra to be a most helpful pathway through his adolescence:

I took some yoga classes and went on a few meditation retreats. I started to like them better than what most of my friends were into—partying, drugs, and sex. The brahmacharya part, I guess I started it to be cool, in a weird sort of way. Now I'm really glad I did because I'm understanding myself and girls in a better way. I think it's helping me to like myself just the way I am, without having to prove anything.

The purpose of this book, then, is to reexamine the basic elements of sexuality—lovemaking, gender, passion, the body, relationship, and pro-creation—from the tantric perspective. In this reexamination, uncharted aspects of the erotic universe emerge—ones that might be able to help rebalance our currently disturbed erotic ecology. For the individual, the results often happen unnoticed until suddenly one realizes an easefulness has entered one's life, as Mark, forty-four, notes:

> *After six months of this lifestyle, I suddenly realized I no longer worry about contraceptives, accidental pregnancies, or getting diseases. So, my mind is that much freer.*

For some, this book can serve as an arena in which to consider their own sexuality without ever leaving the precincts of sex-desire. For others, however, the words of this text will begin to feel like an outstretched hand inviting them to venture forth into these perhaps unsuspected domains of sublimation—whether for three months, three years, or three decades.

It is my sincerest intention that none of these reformulations and how-to instructions eclipse the inscrutable erotic mystery that glows deep in all human love, hope, and possibility. I feel protective of that innocence. Instead of converting tantric sublimation into yet another mechanistic system of erotic practices and theories complete with their own performance anxieties and false confidences, I hope this book will help to celebrate, revere, and reawaken (if necessary) that original sense of erotic wonder, unpredictability, and enthralling discovery.

THE TANTRIC PARADOX OF AN EROTIC CELIBACY

Tantra (from *tan*, to stretch or expand, as in the process of weaving strands together) is an ancient Indian system of practices and mental-emotional attitudes that weaves the wholeness of spiritual truth and ultimate satisfaction into the often problematic and fragmentary experiences of daily life. Thus, such ordinary activities as dating, the pursuit of personal well-being, or even the struggle of who does the dishes can become arenas of spiritual discovery. As Ellen notes, a simple homemaking chore can be evocative of deep longings and their fulfillment:

I guess I don't take having a home for granted, ever since my parents'
divorce when I was a kid. When I saw my husband, Bill, putting
up new shelves in the pantry, I started to cry. It was like watch-
ing some kind of workman from God's staff come to help build
me a home—something I had secretly doubted for over twenty
years. Through this tantric perspective, my long-held resignation
was dashed in this utterly mundane, yet moving, experience. I even
began to suspect that "I" might be more than my remembered
history—I might be capable of a faith in life that can make more
possible for me than I ever expected.

If mundane activities and spiritual resources are the threads this *yoga*
(from *yug*, as in *yoke*, a way toward union) weaves into a whole cloth, then
paradox is its loom. Paradox is a midwife to meanings that otherwise remain hidden in seemingly contradictory pairs of phenomena—pairs that
ordinary logic would view as irreconcilable opposites. Thus, in Christianity we have the paradox of the God-man, Jesus; in Taoism we hear of the
Tao that, paradoxically, cannot be named; while in Zen there is the silent
sound of one hand clapping.

Through the paradoxical lens of tantra, opposition and conflict gradually
reveal an underlying unity. The sacred is found hidden in the obvious—
love buried in anger, dignity disguised in shame, and oneness masquerad-
ing as irreconcilable differences—while the goal of all desiring can be obtained through the utter desirelessness of an "erotic celibacy." But to our
modern ears, "erotic celibacy" is not just another poignant paradox. It is,
at the very most, an impracticality and a rather unpersuasive euphemism
for "doing without."

Yet, even in the realm of conventional sexuality, the ever-expanding
plethora of new ways to "keep it hot" that leap off every *Cosmo* and even
Reader's Digest cover may be betraying an unguessed ruse: We are over-
looking how much *more* there is to know about sexuality by continually
reworking the same quadrant of a much larger erotic universe. Maybe it is
our ignorance of the vastness of erotic sublimation that restricts us to seeking
all of our erotic satisfaction in the more familiar realm of sex-desire. Perhaps it is time to approach sexuality with more questions than answers and
with questions of a different kind.

RECLAIMING YOUR VULNERABILITIES
THROUGH TANTRA

In pursuit of a "zipless" (in Erica Jong's sense) or uninhibited sexuality, our psychologies of personal assertiveness have come to view certain poignant feelings—shyness or bashfulness at one's own beauty or foibles, fearfulness before great possibilities, silencing awe, interpersonal reverence, humbling gratitude, baffling innocence, thought-provoking guilt, self-protective shame, and rectifying contrition—as emotional chastity belts. Tantric sublimation sees an erotic depth in these many "vulnerabilities" that raises them from the level of, literally, "valued weaknesses" to that of sublimative fulfillments. While Freud called blushing a "mild erection of the head," tantric sublimation goes further to reveal what amounts to various "orgasms" of purely emotional vulnerabilities.

Thus, in the tantric erotic vocabulary *orgasm* becomes an *adjective* or *general quality* that characterizes various kinds of culminating breakthroughs rather than being a specific and all-too-literal physiological event. Through partnered meditative practices, shyness, embarrassment, need, and even longing itself intensify into their own particular sublimative fulfillments.

Furthermore, since our fluidly alive emotions, in contrast to our theoretical definitions of statically specific emotions, are constantly shifting and interactively changing, tantra holds to an alchemy of emotional transmutation. In agreement with psychological researcher Jerome Kagan of Harvard, in his renaming of emotions as "unstable ideas," or with what jazzist Charlie Parker called "the notes within the notes," tantra holds that our feelings for each other interact so quickly that we are transported from the leadened communication of language to the mercurial intimacy of ever-changing sentiments and wordless communions. As Karen notes, an often overlooked world of emotional resolutions lives just outside our typically distractable gaze:

> *We learned to pause with each other, slow down, and simply sustain*
> *eye contact while we were arguing. My anger would begin to melt*
> *as I saw its immediate effects on Tony, beneath his defensiveness,*

where I could see he was already starting to feel apologetic. He would see my need for him beneath my anger, which, as I said, was already melting. And, by the look on his face, I could see that Tony saw my anger melting, which made me feel really seen. We were able to work out the logistics of my upset in a few minutes. Our typical embattled escalations were cut short by this gradually developed, meditative regard for these living emotional subtleties.

Similarly, through its many meditations and rituals, tantra gradually brings us to intimacies of reconciliation, respect, and even reverence toward each other, not just for the things we may have done but for the erotic mystery that each of us is. Instead of a primarily sensualistic sexuality, an erotic art based upon feeling and profundity is uncovered. We peer into another domain of the erotic universe, hidden within the energies and molecules of sexuality itself.

1

FROM HARRY'S BAR TO THE MYSTERIES OF TANTRIC SUBLIMATION

◆

People who achieve access to the deepest roots of their freedom can completely change.

Peter Koestenbaum
Existential Sexuality

Harry's Bar, said my fortyish friend Clark, is the number one pickup bar in San Francisco: low-key jazz, a set of red-cheeked ex-rugby players for bartenders, a decor of dark, money-green walls and lightly tinted mirrors reflecting the images of intent people, all having a great time.

From our corner table we looked out and wondered: Were they really having such a great time? A closer inspection revealed a more flickering image. Behind the ready smile, a private loneliness; beneath the flourish of vitality, the tiredness of the hunt; within the friendly ambience, a fear of contagion. Yet at an even deeper level there was an undeniable hopefulness for something that could really work; the belief in a chemistry with a special someone, somewhere—(maybe this evening); a desire to give and create with that someone—passion, love, a fullness, a life together, or at least the night.

As we looked around, we recalled the madcap sexuality of the sixties, the Harrad Experiments, Woodstockism, and the search for deeper values that inspired those times. The goal was to have more sexually rewarding relationships than we imagined our parents had had. Freed from their re-

11

pressive beliefs, we assumed that we were on the brink of a new age of peace and enlightenment; and the ground of this utopia was sex. Our battle cry? "Make love, not war!"

This "new sexual freedom," conceived in Freudian thought, born in the sixties, and struggling to survive in the nineties here at Harry's seemed in need of more enduring spiritual guidance. But guidance from where? Clark asked me if my study of Eastern philosophy had provided me with any clues. Should I tell him about tantra? Would he really be interested? Clark had been breast-fed on the sexual values of the sixties, and I had never before heard him consider weaning himself.

In his travels, Clark had heard about the exotic sexual positions of tantric yoga, the mythic reports of powerful aphrodisiacs and hour-long orgasms. But those are the exterior aspects of tantric sexuality. As I told him about the hidden side of sublimative tantra, his pensive gaze made me wonder if there might be many other people, even here at Harry's, who would like to know about these mysterious facts of life.

The recent interest in Gabrielle Brown's "new celibacy," Germaine Greer's call for re-honoring virginity, and George Leonard's insights into the end of casual sex and the beginning of "high monogamy" could be the swing of the pendulum away from an anything-goes attitude. And from loftier heights, there is Michel Foucault's scholarly exposé of the sheer grandiosity of the sexual liberation movement, his critique of its more materialistic *scientia sexualis* (our biomedical science of sex-desire), and his call for a more aesthetic and spiritual *ars erotica* (art of bodily pleasure). Foucault jars his readers by saying that "sex-desire has become more important than our soul" (*An Introduction*, p. 156).

If we turn this carousel back a century, we find it was "hysterical women" who led Freud to tout the now-famous sexual solution: "The sole prescription for such a malady," Freud (1977) quotes the eminent Viennese gynecologist, Croback, "is familiar enough to us . . . 'R. penis normalis dosim repetatur!'" (p. 938) (one normal penis, given repeatedly).

Enough dosims. With a little tantric sex education, the crowd at Harry's could very likely discover this tantric dimension of intimate rapport with one another, a rapport that taps that energetic spark, yet provides "nonsexual" satisfactions of the need for closeness that one would otherwise only expect or hope to achieve in bed. As Gary comments:

I would never have believed it before I tried it. As I was holding Beth, we started breathing together, and my concentration got ab-

sorbed with our synchronized breaths. We were like one living organism, and when we moved apart, it got more intense.

In considering an erotic celibacy, we approach something that is new to most of our culture. Some people might think of it as "flakey," although it has been practiced for thousands of years; others might think of it as emotionally barren, although its literature is filled with passionate accounts of bliss. To make any personal contact with the realities of brahmacharya, nonjudgmental openness is essential.

Judgmental thinking is difficult to drop, and, in a general sense, sex will tend to feel more desirable than tantric sublimation, not because the former is preferable to the latter, but because sex deals with the emotional gradients of desire. If a comparison were to be risked, we could say that sublimation deals more with the emotional gradients of profundity.

For some, the vignettes in this book describing sublimative erotics will pale in comparison with the desirability of conventional sex, but in terms of profundity, they will hold their own. This is not to say that sex can't be profound or that brahmacharya is deficient of passionate yearnings. The passion of sublimation can often prove no less heated and invigorating than the passion that enacts sex. Tim describes yoga animated by sublimation:

I had been holding the bow pose and I felt this shaking, so I gave in to it and started moving from one pose into another with a rhythm of its own, like in sex, but there was a calm within this moving. I wasn't thinking of anything, just watching it all happen.

To understand what is happening inside these tantric experiences, we must sense them through slightly different feelers than those that detect sexy desirability. We must use feelers that can sense the perhaps "less desirable" but more profound erotic experiences of utter desirelessness, such as spinal arousals of deeply slumbering energies or tearful heart orgasms that can arise in breathless meditation.

In a culture such as ours, so heavily based on identifying, satisfying, and even creating desires, profundity will be further marginalized. We see an ad with some sexy person driving a sleek Mercedes off into a glowing sunset, and we remember the car, longingly. We forget the haunting profundity of the sunset and even the full humanity of the driver. Only those features that appeared desirable to us linger in our thoughts. The unspeakable beauties and qualities served merely as window dressing for the sexy, red machine. We want the things that make us feel desire; that is the nature of desire. Maybe it is time to yearn for the profound as much as we pant for the desirable.

Since we are trying to learn something new about a topic—sex—that we may feel we already know a lot about, openness is doubly important. Without an innocent beginner's attitude, we merely continue to interpret what is truly a new experience by making it fit in with what we already know. One can think "Oh this is *just yoga!*" and with that very telling vocal inflection end up discovering little, if anything, new. Every page of this book will require open curiosity.

The provocative questions that guide our tantric ars erotica are these:

- How much closeness, enjoyment, and intensity are we willing to experience as an ever-deepening end in itself without interpreting it as a desire for sex and orgasm?

- If we persist in this mode alone or with someone for very long, what can we expect? As we take up the many physical and meditative practices for months or even years at a time as a general approach to our erotic attractions and feelings, what of value might we discover?

THE SUBLIMATIVE SEX DRIVE

The seeming paradox of desires that diffuse into their own fulfillment, of being *filled* with longing to the point of devotional fullness, is at the heart of tantric sublimation. But we must note, too, that the way of filling spiritual needs is inverse to the way of filling physical needs. While the former matures the soul by increasing our capacity to yearn faithfully and receive gratefully, the latter asks us to end the pang promptly with the right thing.

Although contemporary theories and research claim that sexual feelings denote a biophysical need that *requires* frequent orgasmic ending, the theory of brahmacharya reinterprets most of this enigmatic need to be of the spiritual sort. As Jan, thirty-eight, says of her first sublimative experience:

> *[After the breathing practice] I felt in touch with . . . a love, I mean a huge, great big, monster love, everywhere; it filled everything. This infusion of spiritual overwhelm changed my perspec-*

tive of what's possible . . . sexual energy isn't purely sexual. It's sexual and it's not sexual because I wasn't having sexual contact with my partner.

Jan's word struggle denotes the contradiction of a "biological sex drive" that is no longer driving her biology. If we read "biological" as "unavoidably real," the term will trap us. But biology is just one of many possible conceptual systems that can be used to understand the phenomena of human life, and it is a rather young and changeable one at that. While fertile heterosexual intercourse is necessary for reproduction, sociologists have hypothesized a purely *sexual* need that, in Desmond Morris's bioevolutionary conjecture, developed in our prehistoric ancestors as a behavioral adaptation to strengthen family stability.

Although it is risky to speculate about the evolution of any human behavior from its conjectured prehistoric origins, anthropologists, sexologists, and sociobiologists have continued to hypothesize how sex was *decoupled* (as the scientist terms it) from fertility cycles to become a separate "reward mechanism" to pair-bond ancestral "naked apes." Donald Symons (1979), in *The Evolution of Human Sexuality,* reasoned differently than did Morris:

> If one views the matter in terms of ultimate causations, and assumes that permanent group-living is adaptive for some reason, then, all other things being equal, selection [Darwinian natural selection] can be expected to favor the most economical of the available mechanisms that results in permanent sociality. One possible mechanism is for a formerly episodic reward to become permanent, but in terms of time, energy, and risk this seems to be a very expensive solution if the reward is sexual activity. It is much more economical [from a biological perspective] to alter the reward mechanism of the brain itself, so that the sight, sound, or smell of familiar conspecifics [those of the same species] come to be experienced as pleasurable. (p. 102)

Symons is suggesting that even from a biological perspective, direct perceptual bonding would have been a more efficient behavioral adaptation to ensure primeval pair-bonding than coital sexuality. His scientist's speculation is remarkably consistent with tantric psychospiritual developmental theory. The sublimative enhancement of consciousness itself (altering "brain reward mechanisms") is a perfect example of the Symonsian alternative evolutionary course for human pair-bonding behavior.

Tantra notes a spiritual sublimative drive that satisfyingly bonds couples by enhancing their aesthetic and emotional sensitivities (those enigmatic brain reward mechanisms again). Furthermore, given our culture's pervasive difficulties at this time with all manner of uncontrollable drives, including drug and alcohol addiction, workaholism, overeating, gambling, shopping, TV viewing, and so-called sexual/love addictions, the tantric evolutionary alternative of less is better appears even more broadly relevant.

GOING ALL THE WAY WITH TANTRIC CELIBACY

Tantric yoga, as a system of rituals, exercises, and philosophical teachings, was developed over the past 2,500 years in a practical search for profound feeling and awareness. Just as a modern scientist might spend years on a single research problem, tantric yogis might dwell on a certain feeling for hours a day, plumbing its every nuance and what it told them about existence. They became experts in the arts of feeling and concentration. As their explorations took on devotional qualities, known as *bhakti,* their erotic practices became acts of worship. They became worshipers of the entire range of emotionality, and when mature, they enjoyed a consciousness that reached from the despairing depths of the horrific to the heights of divine ecstasy. Thus all of life's potential could pass consciously through them with unfathomable acceptance.

Through prolonged appreciation of genital or other sensual feelings and fleeting emotions, they discovered a natural progression from sexual feelings to profound ecstasies. This continuum of feeling and the bodily process that supported it was named *urdhva-reta,* literally, the upward flow that refines the juice-current of life. As they entered the subtleties of these feelings, they came to know a further essence within each bodily essence.

Ultimately, urdhva-reta revealed that *bindu,* the substrate of the gamete itself (analogous in modern terms to reproductive DNA), could actually be experienced as a bliss that could be refined to a pitch so exquisite, it leaped into the spiritual range. *Ojas,* or radiant life energy, was the name given to this profound essence within the essence of future human life. Ojas was so brilliant that it illuminated consciousness itself and, through worshipful appreciation and a life of high integrity, was deepened yet further into a quintessential distillate known as *virya*, the spiritual force of virtuous or heroic and even saintly character. From desire to virya: such is the erotic continuum these yogis discovered.

First, any sense of genital desirousness, bodily tension, or emotional yearning was followed with rapt awareness as it moved throughout the body. At a certain point, the energies would become so intense that the yogi's body would begin to move as well, stretching into the now familiar yoga *asanas* (postures). Even emotional expressions like sorrowful or joyful crying, reasonless or delighted laughing, a victorious or wild roaring, or devotional singing and various uncanny alterations in breathing would occur.

Gradually such sensations, longings, and urges were refined into a singular passionate feeling that moved more or less up the spine. The yogi grew still. In amazement he saw the passion blossom into glowing, blissful radiance at seven spinal locations called *chakras* or "wheel-flowers." After many years of devoted nurturing of the distinctive tonalities of each chakra, this passion dissolved into a primordial brilliance of indescribable beauty and fulfillment. As an inward "orgasm of consciousness," it exceeded the yogi's every expectation. His sense of body and self was that of a cathedral housing a spark of divinity.

While all agreed that sexual activity could generate a temporarily invigorating ecstasy, most of these yogis felt that meditative sublimation, with or without a partner, went further. Some who had partners, however, broke with sublimation and moved with each other into orgasm; others tried a sublimative form of coitus without orgasm; and still others rested spellbound in touchless eye contact or merely holding hands with their partner. Many meditated in solitude, spreading their love more and more equally to all things and all people.

There was much divergence of opinion among the yogis on how best to guide the energy through the chakras. Numerous meditative techniques, physical exercises, and rituals were devised. Some concluded that nothing could be accomplished through individual efforts alone, that divine grace guided all. Such pronouncements also expressed their profound gratitude and amazement over the magnitude of the tantric bliss and the beauties of the divine creation.

The paths that included orgasmic and coitus reservatus sex, being more similar to conventional sexuality, have already made their way into many popular books on "tantric sex." Those books can be considered partial bridges to sublimative erotic life. In this book I will hold to nonsexual sublimative ways in pursuit of the *hidden* mystery of eros, fulfillments that are found through entering the evermore desireless depths of body and soul.

The differences in paths notwithstanding, all the yogis agree that the desires of the human body and ego-personality are but pointers to our true identity, the utterly vulnerable Self, forever conscious and desireless. The wandering holy person, or *sadhu,* was the outward appearance of this eternally vulnerable Self, while a profound sense of innocent freedom was its inner hallmark.

To this day, the vast and varied cultures of India find honor in supporting those who enter upon this path of the eternally vulnerable life. Thus, Mahatma Gandhi could have a profound political impact while possessing virtually nothing. In fact, anyone could live as this Self—male or female, married or single, wealthy or impoverished. In rare cases, we are told, this ecstatic sense of Self even transmuted the sting of death into a permanent sense of immortality and blissful infinity. Thus, legend has it that certain yogis followed the path of brahmacharya for thousands of lifetimes.

As the yogi matured, the desire or *need* for sex apart from procreation was rendered vestigial, not through moral proscriptions but through gradually deepening sensual and supersensual fulfillments. Too much sex, more than once per lunar cycle, proved sublimatively nonecological and diminished the yoga, or union with life's nourishing harmonies. The yogi would lose his or her fulfillment, and desires would arise forthwith.

Thus, the brahmacharin eventually renounces even the desire to be celibate and instead follows the inner rhythms of this sublimative process in two phases: a half hour to several hours each day of yogic meditation and exercises, known as *sadhana,* literally, the gathering of spiritual power; then, during the rest of the day ferreting out this evermore primordial fulfillment, often hidden in the feeling states we call frustration, emptiness, or even desire. As one American practitioner told me with a smile, "Brahmacharya is a very special form of hedonism, just with pleasures and practices of a different sort."

2

EROS AS MYSTERY:
THE KEY TO FURTHERING OUR EROTIC LIBERATION

---◆---

In 1985 I published a study of the sexual experiences and beliefs of people who saw themselves as sexually liberated or who were practicing noncelibate or celibate yoga. As I listened to my interviewees, I heard how each one was being allured by something hidden within her- or himself, within another, or within the greater universe. I concluded that drawing-closer-to-something-hidden is the essential erotic act, whether by means of conventional sex or sublimative yogas.

Thus, the concealing-while-revealing powers of the double entendre and the discretely veiled gesture serve erotic intentions very well, for they all deftly convey that *something* hidden is going on. The sense of a double-taking ambiguity inherent to such communications signals alluringly and undeniably that we are moving from nonerotic to more *intimate* domains. A tingle here, a spark there—from the suggestive smile of a lingering stranger whose eyes stir our secret hopes, to the Buddha's trace of a smile hinting at a spiritual bliss barely veiled by the play of worldly illusions.

The question "What exactly is this hiddenness?" led me more deeply toward the essence of eros—into the feeling of Mystery itself. Sex feels hidden from us not because any authority or moral code has hidden it but because it *is,* intrinsically, archetypally, and ontologically, of the Hidden. For eros is not a thing but an essential quality-that-allures. It is the Secrecy within any secret, the Hiddenness within anything veiled, and the Mystery within anything suggesting further revelations.

For example, a movie's timely blackout is no less erotic than an explicit scene, only differently so. The latter obeys the scientific rules of empiricism, verification, and disclosure; the former obeys the aesthetic rules of reserve, imagination, poetics, ineffability, and hiddenness. The history of movies, from *Forever Amber* to *Deep Throat,* tracks the empiricist's trajectory of willingness to show a little more. But this bare-all trajectory leaves another side of hiddenness farther and farther behind.

The primal mystery that we approach, however, is not the confused mystery of unknowability or obfuscation, nor is it the histrionics of an eerie mystery. It does not belong more to the feminine—the right brain, menstruation, and pregnancy, than it does to the masculine—the left brain, spermatogenesis, and fatherhood.

Certainly mystery is not merely one aspect of eros among many others, as in "put excitement, pleasure, and *mystery* back into your sexuality," for mystery creates the other two attributes and never the reverse; nor is it a heading for a category of sexual phenomena, as in "the three mysteries of sex are orgasm, fertilization, and love," for mystery is not a category but the ultimate essence of eros. The mystery of a darkly seductive and steamy sexuality is not its best example. Neither are we voyeuristic tourists looking for it in the faraway exotica of Eastern yogis. Primal erotic mystery is as accessible in the most conventional as in the most underground and seemingly exotic of sexualities.

THE SEXO-POLITICAL BURLESQUE

Bringing erotic phenomena into the bright light of day, however, will never make their nature obvious. On the contrary, when we actually draw closer without reducing or converting them, we experience an even greater sense of mystery and awe, even reverential fear or dizzying arousals. Erotic experiences spellbind and humble while simultaneously energizing and exalting us.

Spiritual authorities, both Eastern and Western, are commonly accused of hiding sexuality from us. But that is like getting angry at the proverbial

Easter Rabbit (a symbol of fertility) for "repressively" hiding Easter eggs from us, when that is exactly consistent with erotic mystery and creates the excitement of the hunt. Such accusations miss the mark, for, at the deepest levels, eros will always remain enfolded in hiddenness. No theologians or parental figures hid sex from us in such a way that psychologists must later reveal and liberate it. That "history of sex"—its repression and liberation— authored rather self-servingly by modern psychology is a sexo-political shadowplay on the outer surfaces of eros and part of our historical bur- lesque, not a record of some definitive, at-long-last discovery. Those struggles trace the spiral of actions and overreactions of cumbersome institutional- ized authorities trying to fathom a mercurial and utterly intimate mystery, looking only where their assumptions and counterassumptions lead them— not in the hiddenness itself. Perhaps a story will help.

> *Late one night a young man saw his neighbor walking in circles under a street lamp looking down rather intently at the pavement. The young man went over and asked his neighbor what he was doing and was told, "Oh, I lost my keys and I'm looking for them." The young man offered to help, and so they both combed the area several times, finding nothing. The neighbor, however, just kept on looking until the young man asked, "Are you sure you lost them over here?" And the neighbor replied, "Oh no, I lost them in my driveway, but there isn't much light there, so I'm looking here where there is more light."*

Erotic mystery lives glowingly in a dark place, to be sure. Moving deftly by its own mercurial rules, it is always seeking to preserve something of itself, its hiddenness, outside of the limited foci of each morality, porno- graphic image, laboratory measurement, or judicial liberalization that seeks the key to its truth. Like the tail of some snakes when caught, eros gives its captor what it grasps for while elusively slipping into an elsewhere freedom.

Suspenseful urgings on, alluring uncertainty, awe—such are the un- canny pleasures unique to opening to a mystery. The fact that sex makes us feel these things should be a tip-off. But even so, our scientific worldview sees mystery as merely grist for its one track, demystifying mill. In one posi- tivistic sweep, psychology explained eros away: Erotic feelings are not mysterious; they are merely the physiological urge for orgasm. Procreation is not a mystery; it is merely gametes and DNA.

Traditional moralities have been no less reductive and damaging. Not trusting us to be guided by our personal sense of the alluring mystery, they fashioned their overcontrolling codes, making us feel we were in perpetual danger of doing something wrong. The snake? It's the devil. Reproduction? A fall from grace.

For a century, the moralists and the liberators have been pulling and thrusting at each other and now polarize violently on issues such as abortion and homosexuality. Their passionate squabbles erupt predictably, with each side fighting the other as if the truths of life and freedom rested in the balance, a vicious circle that seems to justify the serious need for further fighting.

Even the descriptions of the erotic maps of other cultures are often biased by our Western sexological perspective. As Germaine Greer and others have maintained, the West has been waging a war of sexual imperialism in third-world cultures for decades. Our interpretation of their sexologies have the final say, and so we learn nothing that we didn't already know. For example, in India, Greer (1985) notes:

> The great erotic sculptures of Khajuraho are not depictions of daily life but emblems of the union of Shiv and his Shakti, which result in the creation of all that is. The tourist is titillated by the linga [phallic symbols] that he sees around the temples; his guide, who is likely to be a divinity student, tirelessly repeats that they are emblems of universality, but his earnest insistence falls on deaf ears. The tourist assumes that the Hindus are as lecherous as he is. (p. 119)

What we need now is to return to the experience of eros as sheer mystery.

MORE MYSTERY, LESS LIBERATION AND RULES

Knowing mystery will always reveal the limitations of the opinions and certainties we gather via science, religion, and our mundane, workaday interactions. As Beth, thirty-two, muses:

I worked with Gary for two years before he ever asked me out. He was just one of the guys in our office. Then I found out about his adventures living in Spain, his family, and pet quirks. After we slept together, seeing him in the office was never the same. How could I have even thought of him as the nondescript figure I passed in the hall? After we got married a year later, those images seemed even more bizarre. When Gina was born, I wondered if she had been hiding somewhere between us in the halls or at the watercooler. It's all so unpredictable. I wonder what is yet to come.

Whether through sex or meditation, eros makes us, like Beth, wonder if matters are not other than they first appear, if they will lead us into aspects of life that, perhaps, we didn't plan on. And the suspenseful allure to go on, to want more, is the allure of the mystery itself. This ominous power of intrinsic secrecy resolves the sexo-political debate of whether sex is to be sought or avoided, for in an utterly paradoxical way both appraisals are true—just as the awesome brilliance of the Burning Bush induces our whole being to look and be filled while simultaneously compelling us to cover ourselves humbly and turn away. (Such overwhelming brilliance leaves the metaphoric to become literal experience in certain meditative awakenings. See page 89.)

What awes and seduces us is Mystery itself, not its naked resolution. Even the pleasure we feel is best described not as aroused nerve endings or sated desire-needs but as contact with hiddenness. The cloaking taboo, the hushing secret, the covering shame are all sexy in themselves and make anything else erotic (that is, mysterious) by their very touch. Hence the finding of sex researchers that scantily clad people have more erotic appeal than those who are totally naked—veils heighten the sense of mystery, of something yet to come. Cries to "take it all off!" are part of the theater of sex; the dancer who comes out nude deprives the audience of exciting expressions of sexual passion.

The word *fuck,* for example, had the most purely erotic potency when it was taboo; in modern repetitive usage it falls farther and farther away from mystery into the pejorative heap of nonerotic explicatives. The power such words originally held came from their proximity to a mystery so hidden it was unspeakable. Likewise, the reason Victorians covered the legs of their furniture was not because they were repressed prudes but because to them a mystery was visible there and, according to the erotic economy of their times, modest coverings were called for. Now, when everything tangible that can be exposed has been exposed, a different erotic economy prevails and we lament the lack of erotic intangibles like intimacy and commitment.

Efforts to make sex speakable shift the allure of hiddenness into First Amendment political passions, and the judicial trysts of avant-garde pornographers with conservative magistrates become a burlesque of erotic ideologies. Pornographers are the provocative dancers, and the conservative, then liberal, judges are their fans of (im)modesty, concealing and revealing before the catcalls of the public. But what about this more enigmatic eros?

MYSTERY'S INQUISITION

That eros is essentially alluring hiddenness, rather than sex-desire, presents us with a problem of a most elusive sort: How do we preserve and participate in the enigmatic nature of erotic mystery without reducing it to its opposite, the known, fixed commodity? Our success rests upon a most subtle quality, a matter of nuance: the very tone we use in raising the question.

The more serious and too exacting intonation speaks of a serious problem. It asks questions with a furrowed brow, hoping for scientific certainties, statistical norms, expiating confessions and strident outcries against sin, or unambiguous demands for choices and pleasures. Do I need sex? Should I masturbate? Is our sex good enough? Is this desire normal? Will I go to hell if I do? Coupled with life's frustrations, such serious questioning can lead to cynical certainties: "What's love got to do with it!" "Men can't be trusted!" "A woman will turn on you every time!" "Sex will ruin you!" "Sublimation? Yeah, sure!"

The consequences of such interrogations of eros inevitably reduce it to a demystified thing—a sin, a reflex, a goal—for we are dealing with realities too amorphous and vulnerable for such severity. Through the so serious inquiries and dialectical debates of each generation, the phenomena of erotic mystery are continually reshaped into a "sex" that is alternately something fallen, something utterly natural, something that can trap us, or something in need of liberation that, in turn, frees us.

A second voice, however, is less inquisitional and far more paradoxical, enlightening into sheer wonderment. For eros is not a problem in need of a solution or a drive in need of freedom but a suspenseful yearning and a reaching that is felt as mystery, awe, and profundity—a yearning that never asked for scientific certainty, encyclical decrees, factual answers, or even the satiation-answer of a completed physiological reflex.

Certainly, we enjoy an exquisite erotic tension however we question ourselves about sex, for inquiry begins the dialogue with hiddenness. Whether we soul-searchingly confess, as does the "sinful" penitent, or move heatedly into sexual activity as a libertine, it is the same sense of mystery that triggers our action. The exquisite sensations of confessing a sin or having an orgasm come from approaching and releasing something hidden. Repentence and confession poignantly release the hiddenness of one's private remorse (and thus are erotic processes), while orgasm releases hidden fantasies, arousals, and secretions. The tantric sublimator, however, is not seduced by the alluring passions of ferreting out hidden sinful feelings or by the literalness of any specific desire for sex. He dwells in mystery itself.

Innocent wonder, whether in the domain of sex-desire or sublimation, is the only attitude transparent enough to approach erotic mystery. It is the prerequisite for any truly nourishing sublimative or sexual practice. More accurately, if it were not for certain powers inherent in innocent wonder, we would quickly tire of erotic experiences, as our problem-and-answer, "thingified" modern sexuality clearly demonstrates. We substitute endless sensational "new ways" for our lack of innocent wonder, an addictive strategy that works only for a while. Jan, thirty-six, describes being single and looking:

> *I had gotten into picking up any man that I was attracted to, mostly in bars or classes. Forty or fifty men in a year. I wore shorter skirts and more make-up and saw that I could have exactly the effect on a man that I wanted. Then I got a sense of how exploitation works. I would play upon this sort of vulnerability between men and women, the attraction-thing. It would be fun for a while, and the choice was getting to be: would I go even deeper into these one-night stands to keep my life exciting or would I admit how shallow it really was? It really was like a drug that feels so good you don't want to stop, you only want more; yet there is this feeling that I'm losing more and more of myself . . . but does it matter? Yes, no, yes, no. Was this promiscuity something I needed to go through? I don't even know how to answer that question.*

The "problems" of eros, of needing, wanting, and seeking love, are not a matter of sin or purity, nor, as Jan saw, are they even a matter of expression or repression. They are matters for an attitude of enduring awe and wonder that, rather than succumbing to the allure of certainty or conclusivity, remains innocently open and devotedly follows a mystery, instead of a convincing climax—a sustained threshold, an ever-opening gateway.

SHARING THE WONDER

Consider that feelings across a dark, crowded room might constitute an invisible and satisfying communication rather than an incomplete tension that must be consummated or repressed. As an exercise, while on the bus or in the mall or club, you might try responding inwardly to any attractions that you feel toward the passersby by breathing rhythmically and thinking thoughts like "fulfilling," "appreciation," or "great just as it is" with each breath. After perhaps twenty or more such responses of evermore desireless appreciation, you might begin to sense the transmutation of conventional fantasy images into the image-free sublimity of contentment. When sex-desire dissolves into alluring mystery, orgasm diffuses into a quiet secret of being with each other that is shared everywhere as an ever-growing sense of oneness. Even the concept of flirting is inaccurate, for it implies that a flavorful taste is only a tease or, more hopefully, an hors d'oeuvre.

The concept I am suggesting is that of sharing mystery. Sharing is a way of perceiving one's erotic relationship with another that is immediately fulfilling. One's current feeling of attraction is not being used as a means to pursue some further end, some later and more convincing union. No one is doing something manipulative to another. Only the sense of a shared, living mystery lingers. As another exercise, try sitting across from your partner for about ten minutes, repeating alternately, "We are sharing *this* now," on each slowly exhaled breath. See how each repetition unveils a new degree of fragile wonder.

It becomes more and more apparent that the experience of mere sharing both clarifies each partner's individuality and unifies the couple in this place, at this time. When this perception deepens over the course of a few minutes with no hope for a later climax as a postponing distraction, profound arousals can result, as with Lisa and her partner:

Seated in the Cornucopia practice [p. 111], our legs spread completely open and holding hands, we began the slow rotating stretching. And it was like a cornucopia, originating in our genitals, spiraling up around both our bodies together, with each circular stretch. Bill's back relaxed, and my shoulders. After about ten minutes, it was like being in a vortex. We were sweating, and my whole body started to shiver. Every cell of me felt "woman, woman," and Bill felt "man, man." Then I noticed the swirls of sensation were interacting with one another, merging. I couldn't speak if I tried. My body was too filled with vibrations, blending together with our stretchings. Yet, by this time, sex or fondlings of any sort were the farthest thing from my mind.

Such experiences suggest how vast the forms of sublimative sharing can be.

BEYOND THE LIMITATIONS: CAN THE SENSE OF MYSTERY FREE US?

Clearly, the sexual liberation movement had one mission: to promote sexual activities as the primary means of contacting erotic hiddenness. Imagine someone telling Columbus, "You are free to explore the entire earth, just don't go over the edge, for there is nothing beyond the horizon." That the sexual liberation movement's concept of erotic freedom could have limitations has rarely been considered by its proponents.

Since modern sexuality promotes and requires giving up one's innocence for a knowing attitude of sexual sophistication, it seals its own fate perhaps more hermetically than any other aspect of modern life. This is the collective sense of Freud's observation of a "genital tyranny" over the polymorphous sexuality of the whole body-personality and culture. And all the while we can still hear the moralists' whisperings that wantonness will invariably lead us to hell.

The redefinition of eros as mystery gives us a gateway out of this contentious struggle. It adds the living touch of mercurial and multilayered nuance to a sexual liberation that has been painted in broadly political strokes. Within this context of an ever-broadening mystery, a sexuality of great secrecy emerges—not because any person or dogma has repressively kept it away from us in spite of all liberating efforts. The sense of a secret being shared everywhere is eros and only secondarily sex or tantric sublimation. The mystery grows deeper as we step out of the too familiar grooves and conventions of current sexual knowledge. As D. H. Lawrence noted in *The Plumed Serpent,* "How wonderful sex can be, when men keep it powerful and sacred, and it fills the world! Like sunshine through and through one!" To understand eros we may need to leave the realms of certainty to study on its own terms everything we can about mystery.

ENTERING THE MYSTERY: FROM CYNICAL CERTAINTY TO MEDITATIVE-KNOWING

Sit quietly with your eyes closed and feel the many pulsings in your body. Become aware of your most immediate erotic sensation; feel the sensation pulsate, shift, and move throughout some bodily locale. Go more deeply into the details of this feeling without doing anything about it.

As sexual-love fantasies come and go, sense one nuance or tonality of sensation arise, throb, stir, and pass in loins, penis, vagina, testicles, womb, ovaries, prostate, anus, legs, chest, gut, throat, eyes, fingertips, toes. Feel the warm rushes and their fleeting evaporations, the currents of excitement with their cresting heat and their withering falls, lighting up again in some other, deeper visceral dimension. This seething flow of feelings, when traced to its subtlest levels, is the elusive erotic mystery about which we articulate our numerous and divergent interpretations and opinions and from which we enact our manifold ways of love and pleasure.

From smitten allurement and well-meaning plans to reverential awe, and then to disappointments and cynical bitterness and back again, such are the meandering moods of the passions of our innocence. In the next sections, we will trace how erotic mystery appears within five of the many possible moods of its passion:

- the bitterly opinionated passion of *cynical certainties* nursed on personal resentments and the media's magnification of our culture's more lurid desperations and tragedies;
- the more hopeful, temporarily useful but over-generalized *demystified certainties* of sexological science, popular psychology, and traditional

moralities that in strangely divergent ways try to guide us toward better or healthier habits of living;

- the pulse-quickening and alluringly alive waters of *suggestive ambiguities,* which will always rock our demystified, pat certainties and crack even our most cynical rigidities with their siren calls of possibilities hidden betwixt and between more decisive erotic viewpoints or theories;

- the profoundly shuddering and captivating flickers of *evanescent subtleties,* which make us feel quite awesomely that right NOW, you and I are the inexplicable, living, aging, creating, and dying-away mystery itself;

- the meditatively spellbinding hush of the innermost *intimus* (as in *intimacy*), where eros-as-sheer-mystery unfurls in a shimmering sanctity and where all love, struggle, failure, hope, and preparation are mercifully redeemed and, in exquisite complexity, fulfilled.

I have charted this fivefold approach to mystery in Figure 1. Each mood is guarded from the next by the dubious warning "Beware! That next mood is too wondrous to be true!" This attitudinal gatekeeper of our wavering

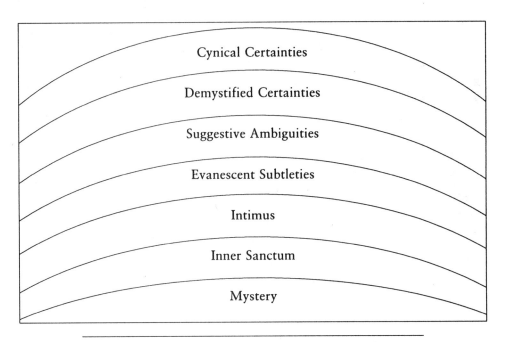

FIGURE 1: Entering the Auras of Mystery

hopes and credulity must maintain certainty in our current erotic knowl-edge and skepticisms, for maintaining our orderly and familiar beliefs is her job. But at the same time, she wonders, she knows better, she suspects there is more.

So, risking her job, she opens the first gate, and we proceed. Then, having given up her grim outpost in cynicism and, after that, her persua-sive, authoritative uniform of demystified certainty, she nakedly flings herself into suggestive erotic ambiguities, evanescent subtleties, and, fi-nally, into the wonders of mystery itself. The gatekeeper, we find, is our own focusable yet oft wavering ego-mind (endearingly called "the mon-key-mind" in Buddhist literature). And our pathway to her erotic free-dom? The ever-deepening concentrations and meditations of tantric sub-limation.

Cynical Certainty

On the outer edges of eros, estranged from perceiving our own innocence and that of others, is where we sometimes stand, grown cold, bitterly so, and cynical in our too certain pronouncements about the subtle, now dis-tant warmth inside. With privately resentful grumblings or loudly strident sexo-political railings and counter-railings, the cynical ones scoff, "There is no mystery. The real truth is on tabloid TV, the hard copies; it's all sex and power, and it's a damn mess! And remember, the wages of sin are death!" In heterosexuality, misanthropy and misogyny have tango-danced them-selves into a litigious-like frenzy of distrust and hopeless passivities or re-taliations. Regarding homosexuality, both homophobia and homosexual self-hatreds preoccupy. Intoxicatingly passionate, such cynical certainties can come to ruling one's life for decades.

"There is no love! Just take what you want!" or "Just forget it all, go celibate!" "The fallen gurus and priests prove that celibacy is an impos-sible pretense! Or maybe they just can't perform!" "Trust no one, for they'll use you every time!" Such are the pained and soured pronouncements of cynical certainty.

But perhaps some day a curiosity arises; we read a self-help book or we take up yoga classes in a church basement. Perhaps a Bible is looked at or a liberating report is published, and our eyes are opened. We shed tears of remorse, and our lives turn toward more alluring radiances. Something "too good to be true" is glimmering as a "maybe so." With innocence renewed, we enter demystified certainties.

Demystified Certainty

Inside the portico it is a bit warmer. We feel more hopeful, willingly guided by an expert voice with clear definitions about good habits and exercises, the "good news." We learn of "natural drives," "four-phased orgasms," scientifically verified differences (or similarities) between men and women.

We are inside the sociocultural system now, collectively rooting for our particular left, right, or mid-road sexo-political agenda. Regarding abortion, for example, liberals take to the streets, knowing it to be rightful and necessary, while conservatives form human barricades, convinced it is unquestionably evil. Regarding a more solitary matter, masturbation is celebrated by one group as a self-loving relaxation and shunned opprobriously by the other as a wasteful vice. Such demystifying certainties about everything erotic impassion and guide each adherent, as best as one could hope, given these demystified, constrictive circumstances.

Lists of discrete "emotional needs" are drawn up by the popularizing psychologists, and the healing way of the inner child is outlined in step-by-step fashion. All of the difficulties of erotic life seem to be easily explained by one morality or school of therapy or another or by the proper sociopolitical analysis. Insightful, compassionate, and encouraging, but still far too certain, these generalizations and formulaic approaches to eros refresh us but are overprocessed. If we do not move on to greater mystery, we outstay the usefulness of these recovering, rehabilitative ways.

Like the strict certainties of moral codes of an older vintage, such clarity can become well-intended help that binds. Becoming too confident, we can even find ourselves using the pop formulas—"All love is an addiction; everyone is a codependent"—against ourselves and others when, even given their oversimplifications, they don't really apply.

As in the demystified certainty of the scientist, the partisaned conviction of the politico, and the coolness of the sexual sophisticate, an aloof confidence lets us know we have to go farther than unambiguous generalizations to enter the living currents of erotic mystery. We must surrender more of our certainties and uncover the ever-shifting subatomics of the erotic matrix of suggestivity, evanescence, and the well-guarded intimus. Indeed, we are allured by the very mention of such things.

Suggestive Ambiguity

The lecture hall is packed, with all eyes enrapt upon the gesturing figure at the podium expounding on the demystification of the ways of love. As the speaker's words, "mystified relationships cannot stand up to the natural pressures of reality . . . ," resound boldly, that strikingly attractive individual in the fourth row catches your eye and your heart begins to swell, and everything else fades away.

When he turns in your direction and your gazes meet in a stunning shyness and with quiet, eyes-dropping smiles, only the throb of a mystery stirred brims in your every cell. What does this mean? You imagine your first date with each other, moving in with each other (will we have the same tastes?), even the hair color of your children is dreamed of in tousled delight. Simultaneously, the lecturer's amplified words of demystified certainty drift high in the air: "Too often we engage in relationships based in some form of romantic fantasies. . . ." But you are only awaiting the break when you can go down to the fourth row.

Suggestive ambiguities, given their greater proximity to mystery, are indeed far more powerful than demystified certainties. This class of ever-beckoning erotic communications includes double entendres, vocalized innuendos, veiled gestures, synchronous coincidences, and foreshadowing dreams. In their inherent ambiguity they imply and allure with suspense and excitement but not without also radiating daring moods of uncertainty and trepidation.

Even during such a well-meaning lecture as sketched above, the suggestive power of erotic ambiguities overwhelms us, and no doubt during the break any single and adventurous person will walk down to the fourth row to gambit an ironically veiled, "Don't you think our speaker is just great?" Or she will sit impatiently through the rest of the lecture wishing that she had.

From endless tabloid exposés to the latest anatomical discoveries, we muse endlessly about eros, not because we are so liberated (or because we are addicted) but because suggestiveness grips us, as if in a page-turning mystery with always another page to turn. The ambiguous come-up-and-see-me-sometime and have-you-seen-my-etchings? serve as covert invitations into further invitations into the intimus, where the more intimate of rites might be revealed.

Every checkout-counter magazine (as well as those kept half hidden behind the counter) stirs us with another and another ploy: "What Women/ Men *Really* Want!" "Ten Ways to Better Sex!" "Checklist Quiz to Improve Your Self-Esteem!" Or, in days gone by: "Repent, the End is Surely Near!" "Give Up Thy Sinful Ways! Get Saved!" Why, like old wine in new bottles, do such lines reappear unflaggingly? Because ads (for sex, salvation, or personal growth), like estral cues, are essentially tantalizing promises of sheer promise, the hopeful possibility of new, future possibilities. From that magnetically suggestive glint in your parents', grandparents', and their parents' and grandparents' eyes when each couple first met, all else is the (un)winding spiral of your lifetime.

As an exercise to unveil suggestive ambiguity, listen to the dialogue in a movie to hear the vocal inflections and the half-hesitating silences beneath the words spoken. In these lilting innuendos and intonations you will hear a subtext of ambiguous meanings that imply but cannot convince. The one *sounds* trustworthy, but is he? She *seems* interested in him, but only if he is willing to sound interested in her. But will she hear and believe what you think you hear in his voice and see in his lingering looks?

Or try looking in a mirror at the end of a long day. As you gaze at your face, repeat each of these phrases a dozen times and watch how your face changes each time: "true dignity," "quietly courageous," "sad weariness," "persevering strength," "irrepressible sparkle." See how each phrase brings a different nuance to your own face. This can show you the interactivity between the domain of suggestive ambiguity and labeling, thus the importance of eventually leaving the oversimplifications of demystified certainties. If we stay there too long, we are in danger of assuming the identity of a particular label.

Suggestiveness is the ambiguous fabric of hiddenness and possibility. For if there isn't enough veiling, sex brashly gives itself away and isn't so sexy anymore. The terms for an even more secretive eroticism will then, invariably, be sought: "g-spots," "ESO's," "supersex," "exotic tantric sex," "joy of" and "more joy of. . .," in hot, "buy me" models, sleek and new.

Thus, the language and images of advertising don't merely exploit sex; they are themselves seductive forms of eros. And each season's hip, new fashions owe more to the inexorable seasonal rhythms of erotic mystery than to a designer's label. For a designer or an ad writer is merely someone who attempts to feel the pulse of the next moment and then schemes to suggestively harness it, often "hormonally," to some product.

And then there are the nuances of love's ever-shifting promises, as made most famous by Shakespeare's langorously romantic Duke Orsino:

> That strain again! It had a dying fall;
> O, It came o'er my ears like a sweet sound
> That breathes upon a bank of violets,
> Stealing and giving odor! Enough, no more!
> 'tis not so sweet now as it was before.
>
> (*Twelfth Night,* I. i.)

These fickle ambiguities allure by twists and unpredictable turns, forming the moment-to-moment currents in which we create, uncreate, and re-create our erotic meanings and choose our erotic actions.

The details of our internal dialogue with suggestive ambiguity go on and on, down to the wire: "Can I say this, ask for this?" "Will it last afterward?" For when you put your body in the hands of another, even by the fingertips as in tantric sublimation, you are giving over a whole delicate web of hopes, possible embarrassments, and dreamed-upon images that, through the passions of your innocence, have made their way into your body, into your dreams, feelings, and thoughts. Can we begin to see, it is never really "sex" or "tantra" that we are having with each other? We are exposing, receiving, and touching, tentatively or boldly, each other's innocence.

And the evermore desireless passions of tantric celibacy, being so well hidden, will always be the most frightening, elusive-sounding, and mysteriously suggestive. The alluring invitations to this secretive domain range from the spare Zen koan of "What is the sound of one hand clapping?" and the occult exhortation of "Arise, Oh Kundalini! Mother of the Universe coiled at the spine's base!" to the most lyrical:

> My beloved spake, and said unto me, Rise up,
>   my love, my fair one, and come away.
> For, lo, the winter is past, the rain is over and gone; . . .
>
> (Song of Solomon 2:10–11)

If we try to ignore such alluring subtleties during tantric sublimation, in whatever form they may arise, we risk cutting ourselves off from mystery and each other to enter a barren abstinence. Then the ars erotica practices of yoga devolve into cut-and-dried how-to exercises. To be sure, the techniques are well-traveled gateways, but we must pass through them into these landscapes of wonder, profundity, and the refining allure of pure suggestivity and happily suspenseful uncertainty. And we must become even more devotedly attentive; we must enter the living waters of evanescent temporality itself.

Evanescent Subtlety: The Living Passage of Erotic Life

The hopeless certainties of cynicism, the championing certainties of demystifying simplifications, the shimmering allure of suggestive ambiguity, and now the fleeting-in-this-moment, reviving-in-the-next scintilla of innocently erotic wonder. Chief celebrant of these elusive living mysteries, of the ever-renewing springtime revelries (which, contrary to modern opinion, were not "sex orgies"—yet what if they were?), God-Dionysus warns Pentheus, representative of demystifying order and accusational authority, not to try trapping his primordial vitalism in Pentheus's stultifying grip.

> Pentheus: Seize him! This man is taunting me and Thebes.
> Dionysus: Don't bind me I tell you. You need control, not I. . . .
> He was binding me—he thought—yet he neither grasped me nor touched me. Hope was all he fed upon.
>
> (Euripides, *The Bacchae*)

In our next movement toward mystery, the ambiguous yet compelling communications of suggestiveness dissolve into the allure of the unknown future and fascination with living impermanence. The mundane temporality of sexual physiology, with its time frames of spasms per second and outlets per week, is left far outside these Dionysian gates. Even the exciting realm of erotic fantasies and beguiling innuendos seems like a dreaminess compared to these more vivid yet imperiled beauties, mercurial charms, and mortal longings.

In the opening stanzas of the *Tao Te Ching*, Lao Tzu describes this entranceway, deeper and more refined than the suggestive innuendo:

Where the Mystery is the deepest is the gate of all that is subtle and wonderful.

Wholly temporal, erotic mystery is in the infinity of details and nuances revealed in our ever-changing, unfolding-into-the-yet-to-be contact with each other. No wonder we want to hold onto each other; no wonder we reproduce ourselves in "sexual embrace"—the mortal urgencies of time passing, not some bio-instinct, is in our very blood and marrow.

Walk up a flight of stairs and then look into a mirror, or sit across from a partner and allow your heartbeat to pulse freely in your relaxed face and eyes as you gaze out. The visual world will pulse, pulse with your own living currents. In a few minutes, you will begin to see the pulsings of life in your own face in the mirror or in your partner's face. Think, "This moment goes, another comes, this moment goes. . . ." Spellbound, realize, "This is the passage of each unique moment of our ever-moving-into-the-unknown lives." Note how this comment brings out a poignant beauty in your mirrored self, or in your partner, who sees you likewise. Thus your partner's face, like a living, interactive mirror, reflects your poignancy back to you.

It is in our constantly deepening, temporalized perceptions, not through some unconscious drive, that we experience the intimate and spiraling mystery of beautifying and recreating each other. Erotic intimacy is a matter of penetrating all generalized perceptions, opinionated characterizations, excited fantasies, and, finally, our distractions to enter the unbroken flow of impermanence NOW. For shared impermanence, not sex-desire or sublimation, is the serpentine fundament of the erotic: that which allures us mysteriously by seeming to slip away from us while also beckoning us anew. Such soul-stirring intimacy is the result of touching beneath the stories, issues, and patterns of the relationship to each other's utterly unique, aging, re-creating, and one-day-dying presence here.

Thus we find that sex-desire is a derivative begotten of the more primordial temporal urgencies. In these living waters we want to hold on to someone or something stationary who will be there for and with us. From these mysterious rhythms and suspenseful urgencies of time passage we reach out our hearts and bodies to each other with our hopes for a "forever," together. Thus, even sexual reproductive acts must be understood as impermanence's way to continue the human passing of time together infinitely beyond ourselves and not as a mere "biological instinct." For the generation of new life is a common result of shared suspenseful, temporal urgencies and mysterious rhythms.

In tantric meditative rapport, we can recover, share, and explore many such primordial temporal passages. Through its sustained energetic transmutations, we can awaken "post-genital" bodily puberties with their erotic longings and capacities to feel the cosmic rhythms of the eternal. Thus we come to see that eros is the ever-broadening love of existence felt as mystery, and we perceive how very limited and limiting our modern sex-desire psychology really is.

Try sitting across from your partner, lightly touching fingertips, and begin to gaze at each other. Think to yourselves: "This person cannot be explained. His presence is a living miracle. This is the only one of him there is, and this, now, is the one, evanescent passage of our life-mystery together. That look of tender awe in his eyes is living vulnerability and innocent courage. He sees me seeing this in him; his eyes wince. My awe is tinged with fear of unknown possibilities of each and all the next moments. My fear is soothed by the sharing. I feel tingling in us, an echoing into the future of new lives. We are singular mortals and, yet, possibly more."

Even as you separate and close your eyes, perhaps you will vow to stay in the mystery. But be careful not to misinterpret the experience of slipping-by impermanence as "abandonment," especially at times of saying goodbye to someone you love. Impermanence is heightened at such times, but no one is causing it, discarding us, or abandoning us. All moments pass and, blamelessly, we are always saying goodbye to the impermanent present and hello to the unknown future. Such are the constant poignancies of erotic evanescence.

To see someone following the shifting glimmers of our never-happened-before self will always present us with a daring and blamelessly difficult paradox. We are both totally allured and hardpressed not to turn away in shy trepidation or sudden awe of what we see and of being seen so profoundly. Like any mystery, erotic intimacy seems elusive, softly beckoning us with no little quaking, for evanescent subtlety is the entrance to "where the mystery is the deepest." Beth describes the heightened closeness that she and Gary discover in the subtleties of feeling that, ironically, live most poignantly in the moments when they turn away from each other:

We were talking about moving in with each other, marriage and family. At first, I was angry and disappointed in Gary because he seemed afraid to really commit to the relationship. Then I saw that it was because he had invested so much meaning in our possibly having a future together that he was sort of overwhelmed by the possibilities, as was I. When he told me of his roller coaster of feelings, I realized how very involved with me he was. I started to feel, we really are in the same uncertainty of life, together.

I realized that I had been shyly turning away from him at the very moment his feelings of hopeful uncertainty would be the strongest because in seeing him that way, my own similar feelings would seem unbearable. And the same was true for Gary. He would see my hopes and fears rise and would bashfully turn away in the moment just as they peaked.

Then we began sharing these "turning point feelings" without turning away at the last moment, not as listeners and speakers but in a silent meditation. We began experiencing this amazing flow of feelings that, ironically, was always being disrupted by our talking about our feelings, or in that most critical moment when we would actually turn away from each other. I felt a spiritual quality, a faith in each other, that the divine is real and eternal. We were in some kind of time flow.

Through the meditation, we shared the ride we were already on, rather than fighting about who was to blame for the hilly parts of the ride. Sharing our fears this way converted our blamings and differences into precarious yet intimate unions.

In this vignette, what is often pathologized as a fear of intimacy emerges under closer examination as a plethora of fluctuations and innuendos that, fortunately, no amount of "clear communication" or assertiveness can dispel. Only by devotedly paying attention to each fleeting moment do we deepen this kind of intimacy. We see and share this existential-erotic mystery in our quivering, not in spite of it or by subduing it and certainly not in our personalized guilts and blamings. That we are mortal is no one's fault.

The endearing blush of self-consciousness as we just look at each other begins to reveal this fragile yet utterly charming rapport. Somewhat uncomfortably embarrassed, we want to look away and have often used a seductive move, or even an argument, to do so. But if we refrain, we can begin to share these feelings of the impermanent, more vulnerable self, stirring myriad unnameable passions before our most heartfelt meditative regard.

In this phenomenology of impermanence, that most innocent of feelings, shyness (and its pink nuances of embarrassment; azures of an alluring coyness; silvers of over-delight; rosy, hoped-for acceptance; brazen, yet trepid curiosity; and, once purged of popular pejorations, many dark-velvety folds of shame) is the wavering eminence of the now concealing, now revealing soul and serves as the emotional illuminant for all greater being-in-the-world.

By this point, the spellbound gatekeeper has given up all of her cynicisms, demystified certainties, and exciting imaginings. To continue, she gives up even her rapt wonderings that sparkle and fade, again and again. She now aspires toward the hushing awe of wordless meditation and surrendered worship.

Meditative Knowing: Entering the Intimus

In the steadied gaze resulting from spellbound rapture in the heart of our existence, even courage and vulnerability sublimate themselves. Some might say, "We are in the hands of deity." Others will merely grow silent. For having fulfilled its guiding mission, verbal description now passes the torch of explication to pure faith and unconfirmable truths, or, rather, to the truths that need no further confirmation, that grow profusely and wildly (that is, innocently) within sustained silence.

Like the softly arriving first light of morning stars that soothes this wrinkled earth unfailingly just before each dawn, the etheric glow of the soul emerges as the undying and merciful sentience within each other's eyes, and yet is beyond that. For this primordial witness to all realities is both within and beyond sight, hearing, touch, and life and death.

Infinities of impossibly weathered times and immeasurable joys have left their mark as the muted receptivity just behind the eyes' sparkle. But behind, before, and after all the events of life that have affected us—in the eyes and souls of the newborn, to be sure, but also in those of the aged and dying, the quiet neighbor, the impassioned artist, and even the sullen criminal—are dark pools of eternity; this is the inscrutable liquidy depth from which all lives emerge and into which all converge. In this inner sanctum, a meditative intimacy yields to reverence and worshipfulness, and sublimative, desireless passions begin in earnest to flower.

3

MYSTERIES MEET:
THE CELIBATE ENCOUNTER

---◆---

Return with me from the subtleties of devotional attention to a dimly lit Harry's Bar and my old friend Clark. At first you might sense an incongruity of erotic mystery, chakras, and yogic sublimation with martinis, BMWs, and heavy flirtation. That would be understandable. But look again, for beneath all the Cardin, Gucci, and Lancome is a nearly invisible energy that breathes everywhere.

It glimmers in every eye, radiates in the shadowy creases of every silky dress and from every half-opened collar—a mixture of promises, invitations, and alluring hopes of something suggested yet hidden. That "something" is not a thing but the essence of mystery. Harry's crowd only *think* they know what it's all about. For Clark and me, it is all very tantric. In this sea of suggestive innuendos and elusive hopes, Clark had come to meet me with something rather important to discuss. That something was named Roxanne.

Like many San Francisco searchers, Clark is in the habit of reading the personal ads in the *Bay Guardian*, a weekly column known locally for its matchmaking powers. He is a man looking for love, to create a home and maybe children. Although I explained to him a few of the basics of tantric celibacy that other night at Harry's, he said that he had forgotten our whole conversation by the time he answered Roxanne's ad:

Single, attractive, active, and alluring. Longing to share the mystery with someone without an end in sight.

When Clark showed me his response, it was clear he *had* remembered some of our talk:

Dear Roxanne,
The more we will know each other, the more will emerge yet to be known.

Please call,
Clark

She did, about one week after Clark mailed this missive. They agreed to meet for a walk by the ocean on a Saturday afternoon. It was a most unusual meeting for both of them. Mixed in with the more typical expectations and swirling desires was an uncanny, calm sense of just belonging with each other. It was a subtle feeling you might otherwise discount and dismiss in favor of more exciting ones, like the lull between waves.

Clark was, in spite of everything, really hoping that he would score. Yet he couldn't figure out why he was beginning to want something else as well—something he couldn't put a name on, much less his hands. When he and Roxanne looked at each other or touched, which they did increasingly as they walked on the edge of sand and sea, the strangest thing would happen. Their fantasies would escalate and then evaporate. By the time they had turned around to walk back, Clark noticed for the first time in his life that he wasn't having any fantasies, that he could have one only with an uncomfortably contrived sense of making it up. Instead he felt, "It's really all happening right now." It made him dizzy.

Roxanne, it turned out, had been aware of the mystery for some time. She was quietly thrilled because she saw that Clark was sensing this mystery. Mostly, she would meet men who would get all engrossed in their own fantasied desires of her, and they missed *her* and the sense of mystery completely. She in no way felt superior to Clark. For, although she had been with the mystery for several years, it gave her no sense of superior knowledge, sexual expertise, or prowess. She was just as amazed about the sense of mystery then as she had been the first day she felt it—maybe more so.

Clark was aware that he was being accepted by Roxanne in a way that was very different from the way most women responded to him. Usually he would feel empowered by sensing himself to be the object of a woman's desire. This was not the case with Roxanne. It was more as though she was aware of the possibilities that were in him. He felt both appreciated and humbled.

Clark was attracted to Roxanne in a different way, too. He couldn't put her on a pedestal, which is what he liked to do with women, whether he admitted it or not, for it made him feel he had really lucked out. At other times, he felt either superior and somewhat rejecting or insecure and rejected in the presence of overshadowing beauty or perceptivity that would eventually detect all of his shortcomings. Instead, there wasn't any shopping list shaping their first date into little checkable "desire boxes." Their relationship was more like a sunrise than a silent auction, and they felt more like wondrous natural mysteries to each other than like scrutinized items on the block.

So they agreed to have dinner that night. As Clark got in his car, he wondered whether Roxanne might feel insulted if he didn't try to seduce her. Then he wondered if he would feel the coward if he didn't try to seduce her or the boor if he did; maybe he should just talk with her and make his move when he was sure she was ready, or maybe she wanted a "real man" who "knew what he wanted" and went for it. Then he wondered if these jumpy analyzings weren't just some sort of certainty-seeking habit that had him thinking about his "next move." He smiled, shook his head, and drove off. For the first time in his adult sexual life, he really didn't know what to do, and, even more befuddling to him, he was beginning to enjoy it.

At a deeper level, we could say that Clark was living some of the important parts of the preceding chapters, that he was veering from the certainties of desire to the uncertainties of sublimation. He was being attracted by mystery rather than turned on by imagined scenarios orchestrated by the desire for sex. Still, the question remained somewhere drifting in and out of his mind: Would he get laid?

Well, after their dinner together, Roxanne and Clark just said a long goodnight, in case you're wondering, but after two more dates, they had a talk. Roxanne put it on the line: Would Clark be interested in pursuing the tantric mystery? Clark felt a little controlled, and Roxanne claimed that she too felt controlled—by a mystery greater than herself. She told him that she was learning something about "surrendering" to the unknown and allowing herself to become a follower. She was no longer so afraid of being controlled in matters of following the mystery.

True, she could no longer do everything that she once felt she wanted to do. In fact, her whole relationship with the world of sexuality had become concerned less with what she wanted or desired and more with following a kind of seething fulfillment that seemed to always be there if she would but follow it. An ongoing flow of subtle feelings of fulfillment seemed to develop as she let go of her agenda of "getting satisfied." And then there were the practices, or "arts," as she put it.

Clark was enchanted by the many moments of Roxanne's shyness in telling him about these experiences. Yet she also spoke with a quiet conviction that one can feel in someone who is really onto something, even if it is something that the listener does not entirely understand. He found himself intrigued and drawn in to learning more about this mystery of tantra.

It sounded very natural but slightly strange and a little disappointing. It was clear now that he was not going to score with Roxanne. Although they did sleep with each other that night, it wasn't like anything either of them had ever experienced. Electrical feelings just passed between them all night, without either of them making any effort to "do something" with them beyond holding hands or cuddling. These feelings were refined and refined until the two of them awoke, around sunrise. They could actually feel the effect of the rising sun on their bodies, and it seemed to Clark that he was understanding something about surrender to cosmic harmonies that was usually overshadowed by desires of one sort or another.

Roxanne got up and led Clark to a room that opened to the sunrise. They sat on the floor across from each other, Roxanne reached over so they were hand in hand, and they began to stretch forward and back in slow circles. No words were exchanged, and, as naturally as the wind, they fell into this circular movement together, gradually synchronizing it with their breathing. Clark had experienced a similar sense of unity with a woman only in sex. But in this flowing, shared stretch, the chronic tension in his shoulders, a certain rigidness he had gotten over the years from trying to do too many things at the same time, vanished. He smiled, seeing Roxanne's enjoyment. He wondered why he had never considered doing this before.

They were sighing now, making small sounds of delight, punctuated at times with a groaning stretch. They spoke not a word as they separated. Roxanne silently showed Clark a rhythmic breathing meditation, and they closed their eyes to begin it. Needless to say, Clark was a little baffled. First he felt that in closing their eyes they would be ignoring each other. Then, when he closed his eyes, he was surprised to feel as if they were together in the same dark silence of their psyches. Finally, he got antsy and opened his eyes, and she was gone. "Shit," he thought. "I've been dumped. No, impossible. What a knee-jerk reaction—abandonment anxiety at the slightest suggestion!"

He tried to get back into the breathing practice, but with each breath he felt a pang in his chest, a kind of inward sigh. Although he stayed with the breathing practice, all he could think about was how much he missed Roxanne. The feeling in his chest grew stronger and stronger and consumed his entire awareness. He felt like an abyss of yearning. Without knowing it, Clark was becoming a bhakti yogi, a follower of devotional longing. And Roxanne felt the same way in the next room, where she was practicing these arts. Then, for about five minutes, a most uncanny phenomenon occurred. They both began to see in their meditative state the image of a satin cord of longing that was connecting them, that was pulsing with their hopes and concern for each other. The feeling and image became more and more radiant, and, as they became more anxious to verbally confirm this experience with the other, they both began to smile.

When Roxanne returned, they were both instantly very happy. They sat across from each other, reached their arms up over their heads, and joined hands in a pose called the Mystery of Balance. After four minutes, Clark started to try to hold up Roxanne's arms, which he knew to be tiring. He was the man, and that is what he figured he was supposed to do. Then he remembered feminism and stopped. After ten minutes, his arms were getting tired. Could he rest against her? No way! He would lose all respect.

On and on his mind ambled and danced, like Gabby Hayes at the foot shots of Dirty Dan's six-shooter. She thinks I'm a wimp; no, she thinks I'm trying to be macho; no, she's trying to control me; no, she thinks I'm trying to control her; she's competing with me; no, I'm trying to compete with her. On and on and on he went, until he just looked over at Roxanne, their eyes met, and he saw in her face a mixture of joy, struggle, longing, and fulfillment, shifting and changing from moment to moment. They fell into a wordless conversation about the difficulties of their lives, their hopes, the struggle to trust each other, and about their limitations, fears, shames, and embarrassments. In a matter of minutes they felt as though they had known each other for years.

Their arms were getting very heavy, but each time they silently shared these many truths, a rush of energy would come through them and lighten their arms. Sure, Clark got aroused from time to time, but each time it felt as if that cord of sexual desire that reverberated upward through his body from the root of his penis—the whole structure of his sex-desire—was melting into the rest of his body and being blended with all sorts of other body sensations and emotions. It was as if his genitals were dumping their arousal into the rest of him and giving up their separate identity for the sake of the whole.

In Roxanne's face Clark saw the faces of women he had once loved, had once rejected, or had once been rejected by. Roxanne began seeing many faces in Clark: his confusions, his sorrow, and his longings, and then his innocent brilliance glowing behind it all. Clark looked more carefully and started to see Roxanne's sorrow, her longing and loneliness, and then her irrepressible spirit. It was like a candle flame deep in her eyes, a glow from her breasts, a radiance all around her. He suddenly felt the same glow in his own eyes and chasing through his heart and arms, as if they were two living mirrors, enhancing each other's reflection.

They stayed locked in this gaze as their breaths deepened and deepened. Fifteen minutes passed, and their arms were occasionally very heavy and trembled from time to time, but their communication was so spellbinding that they merely shared the difficulty as well. It was all ok, their strength, pain, humility, and pride. Wordlessly they saw and knew. More, they felt a flow of energy throughout their bodies that tingled with heat, pleasure, and release.

It felt as though years of tensions and illusions were being washed out of them and that some new and almost eerie energy was stirring within them. The room seemed to glow, and the orange of the sunrise felt as much within them as outside. Slowly, they lowered their arms, became mutually very shy about it all, even blushed a little, and could only bow slightly in response to seeing each other. Clark wanted to give Roxanne something. He motioned that she should stay, and he got up and went to her kitchen, rumbled around (which ruined the surprise he had in mind) and came back some minutes later with a breakfast of breads and fruits. Even doing the dishes was just another part of it. Something had happened between them.

When he looked at Roxanne, Clark quivered a bit, because he was beginning to realize how much bigger this tantric mystery was than he had previously thought. He quivered because he was sensing how easy it could be to let go of conventional sex once this other door started to open. He remembered some lines from a poem:

> The way is suspicious, the result uncertain,
>   perhaps destructive,
> You would have to give up all else, I alone would expect
>   to be your sole and exclusive standard.
> Your novitiate would even then be long and exhausting,
> The whole past theory of your life and all conformity
>   to the lives around you would have to be abandon'd. . .
>
> Even while you should think you had unquestionably
>   caught me, behold!
> Already you see I have escaped from you.
>
> (Walt Whitman,
"Whoever You Are Holding Me Now in Hand")

Clark figured Whitman was talking about the ways of mystery.

In these scenes from Clark and Roxanne, we see the successful negotiation of some typical problems in beginning to explore tantric celibacy with a person who doesn't know anything about it and, even if told, would remain skeptical and incredulous. First, there must be a willingness to admit that there might be something other than sex-desire that attracts two people to each other and can draw them closer and closer. The power struggle about who is going to be in charge must be set aside at an early stage. In other words, we need trust, openness, and a willingness to believe in these immediate wonders and fulfillments, even if they contradict our conventional sexual expectations.

This problem of struggling over who is going to set the direction of the sexuality in the relationship may be more difficult to negotiate than the actual practice of tantric celibacy. As Roxanne put it, she had to give up the idea of trying to control the mystery and instead surrender to it. Clark understood what Roxanne was saying, even if it meant surrendering his fantasies of the conventional way of surrendering through orgasm. When Roxanne brought up the subject of erotic mystery, she did so without a sense of superior knowledge, for one gets to know mystery through awe, not through boldness. Whoever first suggests the topic enjoys no advantage over the one who just listens, for, in the matter of erotic mystery, we are all perpetual beginners.

By inviting others to share the sublimative passions with you, you will be making yourself quite vulnerable to their skepticism and judgments. You will be extending your innocence to them, and if you observe carefully, you will see that in their efforts to understand you, they will be extending their innocence to you. Thus, even before you think you have begun, you will already have started to share the mystery. You will see their innocence in their confusion, their fear of not knowing, and their curiosity. You will feel your own innocence in the sense of approaching as yet unknown erotic possibilities. Perhaps the two of you will grasp that you are sharing exactly the same uncertain adventure. Then the enthusiasm takes over.

Certainly, tantric experience speaks louder than words. If you raise the issue before there has been enough shared tantric experience (even experience that hasn't been named by either of you as "tantric") or without enough attention to the possible fears your new partner might have, the potential appeal of tantric celibacy can invert into an intimidating unknown. Some inevitably will think, "Just as I have mastered the art of being a good lover, I am being asked to start learning something completely new." Let a second adolescence of "beginner's mind" guide your discovery.

Let's take a look at four arenas of life in which you will have to establish your bearings as a new brahmacharin: first, the *anonymous contact* with strangers and neighbors experienced walking down the street, on the bus, or in the mall; next, the *meeting of the genders* and the *private arena* of one's "own" sexuality; and finally, the *homosexual mystery*.

TANTRIC CELIBACY IN THE GREAT ANONYMOUS OF MODERN CULTURE

We have already redefined the subtle phenomena of erotic innuendo, sensation, and allure in terms of tantric sublimation and erotic mystery. Now we must extend these revisions to the authoritative and more informal beliefs about gender, homosexuality, and sexual rights and dangers that circulate in modern life.

Danger or Excitement?
The Tightrope of Overdetermined Erotic Meaning

We live at a time when a lingering moment of anonymous eye contact often provokes a turning away, not in the shyness of too much delight in seeing and being seen but out of a fear of making contact, for suspicion and insecurity now consume the innocent moments of anonymous rapport.

If the gaze of two strangers filled with indeterminate mystery should meet, there are no longer myriad possibilities, nuances, and exchanges. The longer their eyes linger in these uneasy liberated times, the more only one possibility, one excitement, and one danger seem to exist. How many times in a day does something like Tim's experience happen to you?

> *I see someone on the bus and we catch each other's eye and half smile at each other, as if it almost didn't happen. I spend the next five minutes afraid to look in her direction for fear of looking like I'm coming on to her. How has so much nervous fear entered my life?*

Through our overdetermined erotic assumptions, we, like Tim, have come to believe that anyone and everyone knows what those looks mean. So that, in the wink of an eye, in the most peripheral of contacts, it is all established. We just need walk down the street, and it is all there: the preparation for danger or excitement in a sea of sexual searchers. The specific hopes, the adventure, the cynical or bored certainties are all laid out in advance.

Perhaps in some strangely intensifying process accelerated by the media (beginning with Gutenberg and culminating with tabloid TV), the assorted fears of having "sinful thoughts" or possibly sexually repressing oneself; of being "inappropriate" or getting harassed; of being homosexual or being homophobic; of venereal diseases, sexual addictions, and, most chillingly, AIDS have all spun together into an inchoate double-binding narrowness. Thus, more and more, we find ourselves walking a tightrope on the edges of restricted erotic meaning.

Yet, in a culture where the nuances of mystery, more than desire, are the fundamental erotic language, the lingering eye contact between two strangers becomes an evanescent honoring of something wondrous, alluring, and uncertain—"owned" by no one. The only trepidation that arises is the shyness one feels in the precincts of beauty. Think of how you respond when someone looks warmly and deeply at you as you pass on the street.

What if such "mystery-based" contact were the norm? Would we get spoiled, confused, repressed, or would we, over time, lose those hungry hopes and guarded looks? Would we experience another wave of erotic liberation in which mystery nourishes all and sex is but one specialized option? No doubt this is what Herbert Marcuse envisioned in 1955 as another sort of sexual liberation based upon a "spiritualization of the instincts" rather than a "hyper-repressive desublimation" of our longings and urges into the channels of desire.

And certainly, this is what Norman O. Brown hoped for in 1966 with his "erotic sense of reality," a sensualized consciousness awakened to symbolic, multilayered subtleties of meanings. When the idealism of "Make love, not war" met Eastern yoga in the sixties, it might have gone a little deeper. "Make *sublime* love, not war"—*that* would have been quite a revolution!

In a society where eros is preserved as mystery, anonymous contact could be safer than the safety that any morality or antirape law might ever hope to provide. In certain third-world cultures this innocence is still viable and visible, and the looks one receives fill one beyond belief. Often, however, the mystery is either overprotected and heavily veiled or struggling against modern images. While I explore ascetic caves in India, my teenage local guide pores over the latest Indian movie gossip magazine, trying to be "with it," like his fantasied image of the American he leads.

Naïve as it may sound, for several years of my tantric celibacy I forgot that sex was so popular. I thought Hollywood was making it all up. I felt so many sublimative sentiments that I no longer grasped the singularity of our culture's interpretation of erotic mystery as sex-desire. Walking down the street celibately is like being in another world; suddenly I am reminded of the wise saying: "The reason we do not find God is that we do not look low enough."

It is in the small, subtle details of life—the many kinds of tears, the immense blue silences when no thought arises—that eros drifts desirelessly, like summer heat in the arching trees. Perhaps such innocence will lead you into ways of desireless love that those of the great anonymous cannot yet believe. But perhaps, someday, they also will.

THE SHARED-GENDER MYSTERY

Of the many provocative sexological redefinitions that emerge from an understanding of eros as mystery, perhaps none is more challenging than the notion that gender does not exist except as a shared elastic interdependency. Thus, we will be discussing gender as the fundamental condition of erotic embodiment that men and women find themselves in, not as a way to differentiate one from the other nor even to distinguish the specific behavioral patterns each displays toward the other. We will be entering gender as a mystery being shared.

Gender names that class of human phenomena that includes friend, partner, rival, and enemy. Like friendship or rivalry, gender reverberates *between* people, not in them. Gender always implies (with infinitely more cogency than the less alluring term *selfhood*) a mystery of ever more subtle rapports going on with another and with the world.

Gender is also a subject heading, as in "gender issues." Only one other heading grasps as fully the integration of all constituent elements under its rubric, and that is the heading "ecology." For example, while *forest* is a one-dimensional name for "an expanse of wilderness," the term *forest ecology* is a multidimensional name that denotes an exceedingly dynamic interactivity and ever-refinable relatedness, even synchronous oneness. Change one branch, and the change ripples changes throughout the entire forest ecology.

Likewise, people may share many things (history, language, religion, culture), but as we call them *gendered people*, their dimensionality suddenly and exponentially ramifies. Suddenly the sense of an elusive, shared mystery drifts among them (as it does in the ecology of a forest community). To understand gender, watch the more suggestive, subtle, and mysterious sharings among people (or any other life forms).

Gender is like the water two fish swim in that makes visible and possible their play with each other. It is the play or shared interaction of any two or more people regarding erotic mystery. Even our physiologies change distinctly and sometimes dramatically when we live with, or separate from, a lover. A definition of *gender* that distinguishes the composite traits of male-bodied persons from the composite traits of female-bodied persons (that is, *gender* as specifying gender *differences*) is very persuasive but is insufficient to deal with the interactive reality of gender.

Male and Female as Starting Points

The terms *female* and *male* are merely starting points in the life of gender and imply a relatedness between a man and a woman or between two women or two men that is different than the relatedness between a twenty-year-old person and a thirty-year-old person. Reading a story about a person, rather than about a man or a woman, provokes scant erotic mystery in the reader (except in the way that the term *person* is itself an alluring veil).

But as soon as we say that a woman reads a story about some person, a little more of the erotic mystery begins to stir. And then the person in the story turns out to be a man. But then the woman reader is a lesbian, while the story-male, as in a Shakespearean drama, is really a woman. A woman who is attracted to . . . and on and on we track the crests and falls of shared-gender permutations in which *male* and *female* are purely suggestive of something or other but are meaningless in themselves—in an inevitable and inescapable process of shifting nuances, possibilities, and plot swervings.

Gender is the Sharing of Mystery

Gender is itself the sharing of mystery. Gender is something we are immersed in profoundly, and mystery is the experience of profound immersion in an alluring uncanniness. This is the particular beauty of the term *gender:* It points to the erotic immersion that all share. Just walk down a busy street and feel the interactivity of gender mystery. Feel the awe, suspense, curiosity, and spontaneous allure—cues that we are immersed in a shared mystery.

As we shall see, our erroneous conventional understanding of "separate genders" or gender as gender *differences* is the faultline of anguished tumult between men and women in our contemporary erotic world. Our problems with gender are fundamentally conceptual and then perceptual; we have expunged sharedness from the concept of gender and have expunged mystery from our too certain perceptions of sharing and being. Only a contacting of one another in careful wonder can re-reveal "sharing" and "gender" as indivisible.

To understand sharing is to understand gender, but it is not the active-voice transitive verb, as in "He shared his seat with her" or "She shared her ideas with him" or even "They shared their resources with each other." The sharing I have in mind is not wielded by anyone, for the sharing of gender is a fully interactive *condition* that we, as men and women, find ourselves in, not a set of stable traits or behaviors inherent to one or the other.

Sharing is the realization or perception that with reference to gender, men and women are in an ecological or "same boat" situation with one another—an *African Queen,* as it were. It is this realization that provokes a sense of awe, dread, relief, or respect, for shared interactive gender makes us inherently committed to one another. The *inescapability* and the *equal degree* of being in this gendered condition are what make it a shared condition. Gender, like procreativity, is an inexplicable trust given to us. It is a trust in the sense of being a reservoir of possibility, as in a trust fund. As well, it is trust as a magnetlike, inherent, holding together felt as an uncanny connectedness, an allure, a hope, and, most certainly, a need.

Sharing Lost . . .

Even if men and women speak and act as if gender is not an utterly shared trust, we are still in it as our given condition. We then share the lack of this recognition. We share it just as blacks and whites, Arabs and Jews, rich and poor must share any lack of recognizing certain truths regarding the shared human trust called specieshood. The problems that emerge in such contradictions breed in the contorted but unavoidable sharedness that remains anyway.

If one boat mate says to the other that she is not getting what she needs from the other, what she is doing with the shared condition is seeing a problem and announcing it. The two now share (intransitively) and interact regarding the complaint "My needs aren't being met."

The deeper problem for this pair is that the sense of sharing the same boat on the same deep waters is in jeopardy of being swamped by the emotions stirred by the complaint. What if they lose sight of the irrevocable sharedness of their situation and think the *single* thing they share and now must do something about is the declared problem of an unmet need. What happens? The way of differences unfolds.

Gradually they will come to believe that they are not in the same boat at all or even clinging to its turned-over sides together. They begin to think and feel and speak to each other as if they are in different universes. Instead of sharing this dubious feeling of being in different universes, they start to measure and dogmatize their observed differences, perhaps as gender-based, irresolvable differences, and wonder if they have ever shared anything but differences! They then start to live as if they are in two separate universes, reaching over the wall to make any contact. Thus devolves the vivisection of the shared-gender mystery. In the gaping expanse of this preoccupation with differences, dark fears seem to look back at us. What Jung termed our own "shadow" meets us.

Disparities in societal opportunities solidify; moods of superiority-inferiority infect. The beauties and risks of flirtation become suspect, exploited, and compromised. The significance of gender itself feels so insufficient that men and women resort to exaggerated mythic images—the "wild-men," the "wolf-women." Love itself feels so dangerous, authorities apply the concepts of addiction to much of romantic life—and they are believed, as the proliferation of (gender-based) support groups testifies. As the fluid play of shared gender rigidifies, we lose some of our sense of humor, and our sexual icons take on a Madonnalike harshness.

Homophobia emerges where compassion fails regarding AIDS. Not a single new thought on the abortion debate emerges; instead, battle lines are drawn more deeply. A symptomatology of divorce, rape, batterings, misanthropy and misogyny, and victimhood precipitates. Forty or fifty million people recount painful memories of childhood incest, numberless incidents of sexual harassment and abuse occur, and, in this confusion, others lodge specious complaints of sexual abuse.

. . . Sharing Found

Certainly the final mapping of the phenomena of gender (and the solutions to the above conundrums) will not come through yet another investigation of the differences between men and women. The map, and solutions of any depth, will come only through the comprehensive study of gender as a conjoint and mysterious sharing of erotic powers, for that is what gender is. Positivistically framing the research question in terms of contrast, such as "What are the differences between men's and women's abilities, linguistics, or attributes?" ruptures the in vivo phenomenon that is being approached.

To secure inviolate data, the method of this study itself must be one of sharing.

The study must become what Michel Foucault called an ars erotica and no longer a scientia sexualis. The former requires and takes place in the intimate relationship of those who are moved by one another and are guided by that feeling; the latter involves a peculiar subject-object separation and (supposed) neutrality in which the observer derives data *about* the other, the object of study.

Adherents of these findings on why women are thus and men are different at first feel empowered by their "verified" specificity. They enjoy the explanatory power of the discovered differences and employ this information in daily life with hopeful conviction. Later, which for our culture is now, they begin to feel the limitations of these gender objectifications: the stereotypes are discerned and resisted; the panacea fails to deliver. From the onset, and in spite of all the best-selling reports and studies, the demystifying method guaranteed as much, for these findings are often little more than shadow measurements in the proverbial Platonic cave.

Those who would study gender as a shared reality, like those who would attempt to feel the heat of the Burning Bush, struggle with more mysterious problems outside the cave, in the dizzying radiance of living gender powers. In the ars erotica, every solution to a problem of gender spirals into a more intricate sense of sharing.

The question must be asked, Why might individuals want to define genders based on differences? The answer will inevitably imply difficulties with sharing, over-determining theories of "individuation," entrenched cynical certainties, and a fear or denial of even fleeting spiritual responses to the other. Such difficulties are not a function of gender differences but of the uncanniness of sharing uncertainty, suggestivity, subtlety, and mystery. Questionings intoned one way will seem to lead us to convincing literal answers, or intoned another way, to awesome experiences of the incomprehensible. The former emerge from scientia sexualis, the latter from ars erotica. We must recover through intimate and artful means the wonder *of,* not information about, one another. Awe, not certainty, signals that we are gaining knowledge about gender.

Even our "own" gender is inextricably rooted in the combination of our two parents' gametes, while the seeds of our children's possible lives tingle mysteriously in our bodies, awaiting deeper contact with the seed of some other. The biological believe-it-or-nots of gender amorphousness—

the hermaphroditic phase of normal embryological development, the rare but real adult hermaphrodites, and the various gender transmutations of the greater plant and animal world—should give us some pause. Heterosexuals fail to learn anything new about the fluidity of gender from homosexuals, transvestites, and transsexuals. One wonders if we will ever leave the shallows of "sort-and-file" gender enframement for the more mysterious depths of an utterly shared gender.

Even our observations of other cultures and species have been made through these gross lenses. Monkeys grooming and preening one another, the vast array of animal mating behaviors and rituals, and the cross-cultural diversity of social-erotic customs are best described as an ever-changing, interactive play of gender, not as "male behavior" and "female behavior." But the scientist of gender asserts, "The female always does the x behavior, and the male always does the $1/x$ behavior; therefore, there are two distinct genders." No: x and $1/x$ are functions of each other; they are mutually variable with regard to each other and thus determine each other at unfathomable levels of delta-x subtlety.

Even the idea of each person being peggable on some kind of continuum from ultra-masculinity to ultra-femininity is only relatively useful. Androgyny, the synthesis of masculine and feminine qualities in any person, still locates gender within a sort of psychic bisexuality and is only a symbol for the living condition of shared gender. The principles of social systems theory, in which roles and meanings are understood as group phenomena, can provide some insight into the fact that the significance of a person's gender is shared by the group, but not strongly enough to make the radical leap we now approach.

What we are looking for is a fundamental ecology of gender and a romantic and erotic sense of this ecology in our relationships. For shared gender is not just a partnership, as Riane Eisler proposes in *The Chalice and the Blade*. This cooperative, same-team metaphor misses the profundity of how deeply and indistinguishably the roots of gender entwine and tendril into the ground of our existence.

Partners who cooperate together, who get paid equally, and who worship goddesses as well as gods might never know in their bones how very *shared* the condition of human gender is. The kind of knowledge of each other that I have in mind is different from all of that. It is a knowing that is verified when it *provokes* a spiritual response of each to the other: a mood of devotion and reverence that trails into shy astonishment.

While give-and-take partnering and cooperation is a common understanding of sharing, it falls short of, first, perceiving gender as a shared *mysterious* reality and, then, living up to that perception. All such concepts as give and take belong to the materialistic realm of economic exchange and fail to settle into the more ontological potencies from which gender manifests—the spiritual economy: *nemein,* a disbursing sharing, within the intimate place of sharing, *oikos,* the home.

Instead of wonder and awe at the reality of shared gender, we usually seek literal answers to our questions about this mystery. We believe knowledge comes from demystification, which, in the domains of eros, can be fatal. In our current world—where eros is demystified as ultimately meaning a well-defined desire—gender definitions turn out to be what we want genders to be like. Gender gets caught in desirability, and its mystery is shaped likewise.

For we do not relate to gender as shared mystery but as specific need-fulfilling commodities (we are to "meet needs"), explanatory resources, and vested-interest groups. We think of gender as a given that can be used to explain why things are the way they are; it's this way because of men, because of women; the one must change; the other; no, both must change.

The historical record reveals our difficulties with gender and the sharing of social power but not the more subtle spiritual history of the fall of gender-as-shared-mystery into gender-as-assignable-differences. In "tantric genderosophy," we see that we do in fact call forth or limit the possibilities for one another's gender (for any particular time span). Yet, tantra takes its stand upon gender as a shared mystery, the recovery of which provokes an inherent awe and spiritual respectfulness of one another. Such provocative spiritual knowledge can form the basis for social and political revisions, just as the plea for a "deep"—that is, spiritually provocative—ecological vision can provide the internal motivation for needed environmental protections.

Gender Awe

The inequities between the genders, currently discussed as the history of patriarchal dominance and sexism, cannot be reversed merely through scholarly research, as some might hope, nor through political initiatives as many demand. Spiritual problems, even if they also foster material inequities, require spiritual solutions. For sanctity can be neither proved nor legislated and lies beyond anyone's political agenda. Reverence is always an unrequested response to another who is perceived as being beyond all of our concepts and estimations. We must let the other mean that much to us. Typically, forgiveness, contrition, and reconciliation wash through worshipers in these moments as well. Such is the transformative potency of a spiritual resource.

Certainly, reverence does not belong more to the one gender than to the other, nor does it belong to those who worship gods rather than goddesses. For it is not the form or gender of the deity that matters but the depth of the reverence its devotees bestow upon it.

If reverence be profound and ever-spreading of its blessings, one can worship a cobblestone—humility may, after all, be divine. We can recover the birthright or trust given us as gendered creatures only through the holy recognition of an utterly shared gender.

These feelings are not some kind of rare luxury that only a few select individuals deserve, nor are they rarefied emotions to be reserved for special occasions. The situation is in fact the reverse: Reverence is the *only* sentiment we do not earn. It is the universal response to the other as the mystery that she or he is just for being "the other."

This is the deepest erotic opportunity we provide each other: to be humbled and exalted reciprocally. Quietly watch the other's sleeping face for one minute. The mystery is not far away. This overlooked nearness is our tragedy.

As for reverence being a luxury, would that were true, for whatever we shy away from worshiping inevitably atrophies and lives on in an ever more withering state. Thus the future of gender is itself at stake, and it shows. We have turned away from the deep beauty of one another and no longer worship one another or the earth we walk on. Instead, we rest upon the "surface" tumescences of desirability, shying away from those arousals of awe and surrender. Only worship of one another is profound enough to call forth the deepest of human possibilities, and only the depths of possibility provoke our awe. In erotic reality, possibility and mystery stand higher—have more alluring "life" in them—than actuality and certainty.

Admiring one another, struggling and accomplishing together come and go as talents, crises, and projects come and go. These are responses to life's actualities. They are well worth exploring with one another. But more alluringly mysterious is the reverence for another essentially because she or he is *other*, because dawning in the other are living, yet uncertain possibilities. Self-worship is viable, but only in the same way another can worship us: We must stand back in awe, humbled by the dignity we bear.

Gender Worship

Worship is what even the immortals long to do, and they willingly relinquish their immortality in order to find something to bow to. What they long to worship is the other, not themselves. Thus, the immortals become the other—that is, mortals—in order to carry out their sacred rites. They become us, we become them, over and over again.

यत्र नार्यस्तु पूज्यन्ते तत्र रमन्ते देवताः

"Where man/woman is worshiped is the play of the Divine."

This is the crowning touch to a recentering of eros with mystery: We discover through a devotional meditation, or other such means, that, erotically, we are in a shared mystery together; that all the psychological interpretations, desires, fears, and expectations we have about each other merely circulate around the inexplicable mystery that every man or woman is.

If we are unsure whether our devotion is authentic, we must take it on faith that it is, for it is greater than us at those times. Our worship of each other will frequently be a mystery to us, particularly when we don't believe this is possible. In such uncertainty, the mystery has a chance to grow, our faith has a chance to grow.

We also allow ourselves to be worshiped, not as a great person but as mystery, that is, for reasons we may know nothing about and must therefore take on faith. Meditative worship is the opportunity for each of us to transcend our conditioned beliefs about each other for some moments, even amid the most trying times of a marriage or relationship, and to experience the mystery that lives in spite of the dramas and crises. It is a return to the possible as real and to the hidden as a promise. Thus we recover the reverence that can be obscured by fearfulness.

Spouses who worship each other might not save their marriage in so doing. Worship is merely the response to the perceived erotic truth of the other and not a strategy to some further ends. It is certainly not a requirement, like routine church attendance. It is the most profound and enigmatic expression of the shared-gender mystery.

Whether the privilege of worship rests with the worshiped or the worshiper is altogether unclear; it is even unclear whether there are such distinctions at the core of the shared-gender mystery. As you will see, the love-making practices of tantric sublimation hover in this uncertainty, in the partners' ever more vulnerable and empowering intimacy with each other. As you discover worship of each other in some mundane moment, such as when doing the dishes, watching TV, or feeling resentful, you will go even deeper into this tantric paradox of holiness hidden everywhere.

The seeming risk is for the partner who makes the *first* offering to the other, without any concern for reciprocation but merely as the *immediate recognition* of the holy mystery of the other and the opportunity this holiness provides for us, originally and eternally. When we contact the erotically worshipful in each other, we must face the ironic fact that it has always been there and in ourselves as well.

THE PROSTHESIS OF AN OWNED SEXUALITY

Even the notion of one's "own" sexuality is a politicized derivation or appropriation of eros, a personal act through which one hopes to attain a sense of being an autonomous agent. As a collective, public act, the proclamation of an ownable and owned sexuality is intended to redress previous inequities by producing socially recognized personhood, as in the inspirational slogans "Woman Power" and "Gay Power."

We would like to own various powers, and popular psychology supports these aspirations with its encouragements to "reclaim" or "own your sexuality." But the erotic powers of sexuality—love, attraction, arousal, fertility, and surrender—are entrusted to us or, rather, among us, and are not "owned." Such slogans are merely transitional metaphors or therapeutic word-tools to help us recover from depression, social-political abuse, or low self-esteem.

Such terms belong to the technologies of recovery and rehabilitation. Although the image of an owned sexuality can be a temporarily effective prosthetic word-tool, it should not be used in mapping the intimate contours of erotic space, for prostheses and maps serve entirely different functions. After we have recovered, we must put away such prosthetic devices, for we cannot pass through the eye of the needle of intimacy carrying our own sexuality with us.

It might be just as helpful for some people to hear that they needn't worry about owning a sexuality or not owning one. Often in such cases when people have suffered abuse, they need merely to learn how and when to say no or yes to others within the context of the shared-gender mystery. The deeper goal implied by this quest for "personal power" or "reclaimed sexuality" seems to be respect.

Respect for each other is most authentic when it is a secondary response to feeling the awe of the other or oneself. Respect for our own erotic nature is a matter of being moved by the lyrical romanticism—the spirit— of life that we, as humans, are entrusted with, as our collectively shared and interactive nature.

No one owns any part of nature's spirit or its powers and beauties. If we can discover the poetry of nature (human-erotic and otherwise), what it is we seek through "owning" it or "reclaiming" it will have been accomplished: a kind of ecological—that is, respectfully shared—balance of self-and-others, of humanity-in-the-world, that will always remain somewhat beyond our control, as mystery.

In the rough-and-tumble world, arming ourselves with the idea of an owned sexuality and gender may feel like an attractive strategy. But, as Rilke has said, "In the end it is our unshieldedness on which we depend." Unshieldedness is a sufficient stance only when we have grasped our final essence as being infinitely resourceful—that is, in our discovery that humans are souled beings. We have an ultimate meaning and innocence that cannot be taken away, for it is inseparable from us, even by death. Merciful and ever-forgiven, we ring with soul.

Under even the most tortuous of conditions, the soul replenishes us, not omnipotently but inexhaustibly. Thus, the higher spirit of tragedy: The strange capacity to endure and live through untoward and even cruel hardships is part of the human condition. Often it is tragedy that surfaces the soul-sense as being deeper than the personality-self, the soul's everyday agent. We discover that we are more than our personalities ever thought. Popular psychology's concept of the "survivor" of past abuse is further cleansed of victimistic overtones within the spiritual psychology of soul. The soul as our essence radiates an inherent dignity untouchable by worldly abuse.

A dread accompanies grasping the awe of the soul's capacity to endure all, for the implication is that if the dreadful were to happen, we are capable of enduring it and thus we would go through such unthinkable fires, unavoidably. Such strength is not good news for the limited personality-self of psychology, and rightly so. For the limited personality-self "knows" with great terror that it cannot endure the most dreadful of possibilities. We must know the soul to grasp the depth of such fortitude, a knowledge that would radically transform most of contemporary psychology.

Lost from a sense of the enduring spiritual resources of the soul, our demystifying psychology has come to believe that the personality-self is best restored by creating strong boundaries around its periphery and "owning oneself." But *boundaries* is merely another prosthetic word-tool, a crutchlike means to some end; certainly it does not accurately map erotic reality.

As Martin Buber has stated, "Every *It* is bounded by others; *It* exists only through being bounded by others. But when *Thou* is spoken, there is no thing. *Thou* has no bounds" (*I and Thou*, p. 4).

The goal is not to build boundaries but to feel respect and share it with others. This goal is better obtained by fathoming the spiritual fortitude and uncanny resilience of the awesome soul that is our essential nature.

The recently coined metaphor of "soul murder" is a particularly costly overdramatization used to emphasize the horrifics of interpersonal mistreatment (and perhaps to deter future perpetrators). Unlike the body, however, the soul cannot be murdered, nor can it be "wounded" to later "survive" such blows. Devastations, abuses, and crises are obstacles that, when dealt with from the integrity of the soul, will mature and soften us—sometimes even unite us in a transformed relationship with our adversaries.

While the concept of wounding provokes a kind of pathos that leaves us less than we were, that of an encountered "obstacle" engenders a daring and suspenseful response in which we remain whole and challenged to continue to participate in our lives. Thus, on one hand is the labeling of our difficulties as a wounding or a murdering, requiring a shoring up of boundaries (against the "other") and an owning of one's power (taking it back from the "other"). On the other hand is the seeing of our difficulties as obstacles that draw out the more hidden powers of our souls in unshielded living within the strangely vulnerable mystery of reciprocal awe for one another. The differences between these two linguistic routes through adversity could be all the difference in the world, for each leads to the creation of a different kind of world of selves and others. For, as the great linguist Ludwig Wittgenstein noted, "to imagine a language means to imagine a form of life" (*Philosophical Investigations*, p. 8).

HOMOSEXUAL MYSTERY

From the perspective of erotic mystery, we are *homosexual* as soon as we like another man or another woman. It is only through the reduction of erotic mystery to sex-desire and, perhaps, to fertility that homosexuality becomes difficult for many heterosexuals to fathom. Why are men attracted to other men with a sex-desire, why women to other women? For that matter, why are men and women attracted to one another?

The answer again is a matter of wonder and amazement, and psychological, biological, or religious concepts merely obfuscate the uncanniness of erotic attraction with their interpretations, research findings, and judgments. The path that seems to lead one to the persons he or she loves is as many-layered and enigmatic as the currents of the oceans.

The capacity to see beauty in another to the degree that passion arises is a sign of individual sensitivity, for it is our surrendering that makes the other attractive, as much as it is another's beauty that induces us to surrender willingly. Two men or two women can even feel the home-building passions of fertility stirred by each other within the context of their sharing of gender, as well as the passions of desire and sublimation. They may partially or openly grieve that as with an infertile heterosexual couple, the mystery denies them conception. They share this limitation.

Coded cues of seduction and drag disguises that reveal the "true self"; ultra-guarded privacies where one's home has been a closet; one's lovings as a private struggle to accept and then, hopefully, to enjoy; a "difference" from others described by them but hidden from oneself: Such are a few of the ambiguities of hiddenness in the homosexual mystery.

There may be something unremarkable about same-sex tantric celibate love and lovemaking. Groups of men or women—gay, bisexual, or straight—can share many of the sublimative practices to find that, like desire, preference can be sublimated.

4

Choosing Tantric Sublimation

◆

The path toward exploring the sublimative side of eros can be rather unpredictable.

Ed and Marcie had been on other sexual adventures together, enacting favorite fantasies and going away for frequent romantic weekends. One day Ed had a more curious idea and asked Marcie how it would be if they built up their desire for each other for two or so months before expressing it sexually. Four months of being exquisitely attracted to each other went by before they made love. Then they discovered tantric sublimation, which fitted naturally into their new sexual rhythm.

Mike, sixteen, went to a yoga retreat with his mother and heard how brahmacharya contributes to one's personal development. He liked yoga and meditation, so he decided to try it.

Mary was fed up with dating, with not being called back the next day, and with how much sex had come to rule her life. IUDs, the Pill, and abortion left her feeling uneasy. Tantric sublimation gave her a positive way out of her withdrawal. Now she feels she has regained her openness, she has thrown out her contraceptives, and she has choices she can live with.

Father Tom found that yogic breathing exercises helped balance his bodily energies and thus supported his priestly vow of celibacy. He felt less distracted, and his daily prayer life deepened.

Jan was so afraid of the health hazards of sex that she overreacted; tantric celibacy was merely a strategy to make her abstinence easier. Then she started having some unexpected experiences in her yoga practice. Tim was impressed, and they started going out together. Their brahmacharya now has nothing to do with safe sex; it has a life of its own.

A broken romance, a penchant to be different, a tiredness of the sexual merry-go-round, a search for something deeper, curiosity, fate—what brings a person to consider celibacy for a few months or years cannot be easily explained. In erotic actions, we enter a mystery, and often we only discover afterward the real reasons we got involved. In a yogic cosmology, which includes reincarnation, one might find out only a *long* time afterward. According to the theory of karma, our psyches are literally reborn from the seeds of our inner motives, stirring us to live them out in the next moment (or in the next lifetime); this is how the mystery of our relationships develops its circuitous plot.

If you decide to try tantric sublimation, I recommend you set a minimum duration of three months. It will take some time for you to live yourself into the choice that you have made and to reap the results of greater tolerance for sexual feelings without needing to act on them in conventional ways. During these first months, the yoga practices will be opening channels in your body to facilitate the sublimation process, giving you a basis for celibate erotic fulfillments. Sex will become more of a choice than a need after this degree of opening has been achieved.

You may or may not find a great deal of anxiety in setting the duration of your practice. Should a period of more than a few months shock you, I would advise you to think again about what you want and what you believe about your sexual situation. Brahmacharya is more than a weekend workshop. It requires a sincere and devoted application of oneself to develop its potentials.

My first commitment was for fifteen months. After that, I stopped counting and thus added another dimension to my practice, an almost frightening sense of freedom. Before I reached that point, however, I saw more subtle, ambivalent feelings taking the form of the thought "When is this going to be over!" At this point, I feel I must raise a question for you to consider: If you really start to enjoy tantric sublimation, on what basis would you decide to stop?

You might insist that you'll know exactly when to return to conventional sex. Ramakrishna, an Indian saint who went deeply into the practice of brahmacharya, described his experience as "one in which it seemed that all the pores of the skin were like female organs and intercourse was taking place over the whole body." Such experiences, which may emerge only after years of development, can make the decision to stop or continue far more thought-provoking than you might imagine.

Not setting a specific duration can help make your practice less self-conscious and studied. You might even begin to feel a sense of freedom in having no predetermined limit. On the other hand, if you have trouble establishing yourself in your commitment, a preset duration could give you support to pull yourself through the first months of practice and uncertainty. You need some time to reorient yourself within the everyday world of sexual attraction from the tantric perspective.

Another formidable consideration is how tantric sublimation fits into the idiosyncrasies of your personality. Are you a perfectionist, expecting to get it right the very first time and more and more right as you go along? Or are you spiritually competitive and think sublimation will make you "more" spiritual than others? Are you from an older school of sex and feel that celibacy is a proper way to restrain waywardness? Do you tend to go to extremes, expecting to swing from sublimation to utter sexual abandon? Perhaps you consider yourself overly dependent and feel you might be doing this to win someone's approval. Another possibility is that you may be angry at someone and want to inflict your celibacy on them as a revenge. As you might guess, all such motivations can severely narrow your experience of sublimation, at least initially. As you progress, however, more positive motivations based in your new experiences might arise.

Consider whether you might not be trying to avoid the challenges of social interaction by going celibate. Not only is such uneven growth unsatisfying; the high degree of intimacy that tantric sublimation works toward will not allow it.

If you intend to practice with a partner, observe the manner in which any problems you ordinarily have while talking about sex emerge during your conversations on trying celibacy. Notice which partner wants to practice it more, who acts as though he or she knows more about it, who is taking it more seriously, and so forth. By returning to the foundation of eros-as-mystery, you will be aided in dislodging yourself from these hierarchical and polarizing dynamics.

Finally, you may be concerned about AIDS, problematic relationships, being rejected or getting committed, or sexual performance. It is important that you be as honest as you can about such concerns as you set out on your celibate path. Your tantric practice might even help resolve some of these nagging worries of the ego-mind as you discover moments of the self-acceptance known as "the peace that passeth all understanding."

WHY YOU MIGHT CHOOSE BRAHMACHARYA

YOU ARE GOING TO BE INVOLVED IN A PROJECT FOR SOME TIME, AND YOU THINK TANTRIC SUBLIMATION WILL HELP YOU TO FOCUS YOUR TIME AND ENERGY.

Celibacy has long been part of certain traditional lifestyles of service and personal development. Mother Teresa, Mahatma Gandhi, and United Nations Secretary-General Dag Hammarskjöld are three well-known exemplars of chosen celibacy as a support to work and service. It was her doctoral research on creativity that led Gabrielle Brown, author of *The New Celibacy,* to draw a correlation between unusually creative people and celibacy.

Meditation, which we will discuss in chapter 5, becomes particularly useful in conjunction with brahmacharya for a creative project. When the mind becomes still in meditation, currents of energy begin to flow up through very subtle pathways, invigorating consciousness. As you return to thinking about your project, new, lively ideas may emerge, so you might want to keep a pad and pencil near your meditation cushion—but not so near as to distract you.

The principles of karma yoga, the yoga of life activities, might be particularly relevant to a celibacy that serves a creative project or activity: to enjoy the process of your work at each step, rather than focusing too much on the gratification of completion.

YOU ARE FEELING SECLUSIVE.

As one of my teachers used to say, brahmacharya is discovering the love in yourself that you usually reserve for falling in love with someone else. He claimed it was an ideal preparation for a relationship or a satisfying lifestyle in itself, based on discovering one's inner source of happiness.

Meditative peace is itself an inner form of being alone, for we are free of that crowd of chattering thoughts that can endlessly distract us. Such inner quiet holds the possibility of discovering a profound paradox: We are each singularly alone in the world, yet, in this undistracted silence, we feel even more intimately related to one another and to the world. If you are single, you might choose to use your personal time to practice three or four hours of yoga almost daily, while maintaining your other involvements. For some single brahmacharins, sadhana might become "the love of your life"—at least for the months or years of your practice.

YOU HAVE A SEXUALLY COMMUNICABLE DISEASE, AND YOU WANT SAFE WAYS TO EXPRESS LOVE, PASSION, AND AFFECTION.

AIDS, herpes, chlamydia, and other sexually transmitted diseases are demarcating the limits of a territory that earlier sexologists depicted as an idyllic paradise. You might be feeling unjustly backed into this seemingly claustrophobic corner of "no sex" for longer than you expected. Tantric sublimation will reveal many alluring gateways out of that boxed-in place.

YOU WANT TO DEVELOP NONSEXUAL FRIENDSHIPS, AND YOU ARE BEING MORE SELECTIVE THESE DAYS.

We are used to seeing one another either as possible sexual partners or as "just friends" (that is, "There is no way I could be turned on to you!"). An inner yes/no switch automatically catalogs everyone we see as sexually desirable or undesirable. In tantric sublimation, we can operate beyond this binary narrowness via the unprepared openness of "nonattachment."

Though nonattachment may sound austere, it simply refers to an experience of intimacy without agendas. We learn to see others without appropriating or grasping at them for some personal end. Our friendships with the other gender often take on a freeing and relaxed intimacy when the expectation of sex has been put aside.

YOU WANT TO DEVELOP A DEEPENING SENSE OF INTIMACY WITH YOUR PARTNER.

Intimacy is a matter of one person being moved by another. The rustle of her robe, the shyness of his gratitude, the heat of her disappointment, the bitterness of his losses, even possessions can be mediums through which we are moved by one another. For it is not the "things" that move us but the way our love brings them to life with the individuality of the beloved. In Saint-Exupéry's *The Little Prince,* the fox speaks of such intimacy, which he calls "taming":

> "If you tame me, it will be as if the sun came to shine in my life. I shall know the sound of a step that will be different from all others. . . . And then look: you see the grain-fields down yonder? I do not eat bread. Wheat is of no use to me. The wheat fields have nothing to say to me. And that is sad. But you have hair that is the color of gold. Think how wonderful that will be when you have tamed me! The grain, which is golden, will bring me back the thought of you. And I shall love to listen to the wind in the wheat. . . ."
> The fox gazed at the little prince, for a long time.
> "Please—tame me!" he said. (p. 83)

So often, however, the impatient desire for more intimacy is what obscures the subtle phenomena of intimacy presently alive, as, sadly, the little prince responded to his fox:

> "I want to [tame you], very much," the little prince replied. "But I have not much time. I have friends to discover, and a great many things to understand." (p. 83)

To which the fox responded in parting:

> "And now here is my secret, a very simple secret: It is only with the heart that one can see rightly; what is essential is invisible to the eye."
> (p. 87)

The art of seeing with one's heart is what tantric sublimation is all about.

YOU ARE TROUBLED BY THE DIFFICULTIES IN LOVE RELATIONSHIPS AND WONDER HOW TANTRIC SUBLIMATION AND PSYCHOLOGY MIGHT HELP.

If you are not currently in a love relationship, the practice of solitary sublimation can give your life a satisfying fullness of emotionality, commitment, and passion typically thought available only to coupled people. Thus, your longings for a partner can be freed of the desperation that being alone sometimes breeds. Instead, should you meet someone you are truly interested in, your longings will have a welcoming freshness.

Since tantric sublimation is a transformative art, its approach to difficult emotions is far more paradoxical and poetic than most conventional and popular psychologies of love. Instead of a vocabulary of semidiagnostic terms, like codependency, emotional wounding, or fears of abandonment and commitment, tantric terms like *viyoga*—the union that lives in even the most painful struggles—grasp the ambiguity inherent in erotic difficulties.

Thus, you will learn about the hidden rectifying powers within apology and forgiveness, how to miss someone romantically instead of thinking of yourself as abandoned, how to protect "the awe of great possibilities" from being misinterpreted as fears of commitment. Fear and awe are close cousins in erotic matters, and it is an ironic tragedy that the same *awesomeness* that inspires feelings of total possibilities in the beginning of love and family life will claustrophobically close down possibilities when misunderstood as *fear*.

In this more intimate world, we encounter the paradoxical and lesser-known erotic passions of joys that seem too good to be true, of being ourselves more than we ever thought, even as we awaken to other possibilities that seem too tragic to be endured. We uncover the too common irony that sometimes it becomes easier to fight over personality issues and mundane problems than to get all choked up with one's gratitude. We spare each other our gratitudes, for the ensuing intimacy is more than we can readily bear.

YOU WONDER IF YOUR MARRIAGE CAN BE ENHANCED IN CERTAIN WAYS BY A PERIOD OF CELIBACY.

Marriage exists because we need the time of a lifetime to bring forth more completely the deeply hidden potentialities that begin to emerge when people are in love with each other. Commitment is merely the natural and immediate response to perceived, yet hidden, possibilities. Commitment is the sustained and suspenseful allurement of mystery.

For example, newlyweds will argue over the color to paint a certain room to camouflage the awesome and perhaps unbelievable experience of knowing and feeling that they are actually creating a home in which they will live, share, create life, and die. In tantra, money problems, household chores, and parenting responsibilities must all be placed in a larger context of living. For older couples, the tantric perspective can reveal a long-developing passion that attains its climax only after a lifetime of sharing.

Phyllis, fifty-eight, and Jason, sixty-two, have been married for thirty years. Their lives have been busy with dual careers and family life. "Too busy for a mid-life crisis," says Jason. Yes, they have been committed to each other for over thirty years, but their commitment has been to expectations, and their satisfaction has been in attaining them. Uncertainty was something to allay with plans and success and has never been a gateway to the trepid and alluring awe of the unknown future. Since they are "almost celibate," they turn to the philosophy and practice of tantric sublimation. During their newly learned eye-contact meditations, they share their amazement at what now comes out of hiding from behind the daily routines of thirty years: They are giving each other their lives and receiving the same as well.

In uncovering erotic rhythms longer than sex-desire, tantra reveals an organic basis for lifelong monogamy known as "the householder's path," commitment allured onward by the fullness of a lifetime.

YOU FIND THE VARIOUS ARTIFICIAL METHODS OF CONTRACEPTION TO BE UNDESIRABLE, AND YOU WONDER IF THERE ARE "OTHER WAYS" TO MAKE LOVE.

When Wilhelm Reich was formulating his basic principles of sexual liberation for fertile heterosexuals, he concluded that, since sex was necessary thrice weekly, contraception was "absolutely necessary for sexual health." Within the conventional biological model of sex, this may be true. Yet this solution is not as utopian as Reich and the rest of us had hoped—as our abortion rates and problems with contraception can attest.

Kristin Luker's abortion research in *Taking Chances* concluded that unintended pregnancies weren't best explained as "contraceptive failures" but as a kind of sexually enflamed willingness to "take a chance, just this once." Fertility just slips slyly through the cracks of sex, not through our irresponsibility but because of the exhilarating power of erotic mystery.

Contraception, unintended pregnancy, and abortion, and the debates surrounding them, are rendered obsolete for the tantric celibate. Conceptions, when they occur, are always sought rather than being varyingly regretted side effects of sexual intercourse. And, as R. D. Laing (1970) noted in reference to the significance of being a welcomed conception, "The difference between being welcome and unwelcome . . . is all the difference in the world" (p. 31).

Furthermore, if we had intercourse only when we were hoping to conceive, we might recover the actual experience of procreation. Rob, forty, describes his surprise of "discovering" that sex is also the procreative process:

> *After several years of tantric celibacy, it was easy to feel the procreative aspect of sex. When we did conceive, it was one of the most profound experiences of my life. I had lost all my sexual associations with the act of intercourse, and all that I was aware of were the sensations of conceiving this unique, new human being with my wife.*
>
> *On one hand I was amazed—this is a miracle! On the other hand I felt convinced—so this is what sex is about. I could see why some religions have tried to keep sex just for reproduction, although I doubt they had this sort of experience in mind. It felt so real, so meaningful, that it has changed my understanding of what human life is all about, of how much spiritual power we have as human beings.*

The sublimative way of erotic expression could also be particularly useful to teenagers, whose sexual curiosity forever outsmarts even the most well-schooled efforts of our sex/contraception education. Originally, the term *brahmacharya* referred to preadolescence through young adulthood, when, in the wake of genital puberty, we learn and grow at a rapid pace. An open-minded teenager might find brahmacharya very fulfilling, rather than being one more nagging parental injunction against which to rebel. I have included an appendix for teenagers who might be interested in tantric sublimation.

YOU HAVE BEEN CELIBATE FOR SOME TIME NOW, AND YOU ARE WONDERING WHAT MIGHT BE GOING ON IN YOU AS A RESULT.

Having a vocabulary to apply to your celibate experiences can be most helpful, especially in a culture where celibacy is generally understood as an absence of experiences. Yoga gives you a detailed mapping of the subtle physiology of sublimation that grounds its processes and unique arousals in the body. The many physical and meditative practices help you to derive the greatest benefits from your celibate time.

If you have been celibate for some time, the mere publication of this book may be important to you. I remember that in my third year of practice I could readily identify with many of the pains common to any minority—sexual or otherwise. People might not accept a person's being gay, but they now at least admit that homosexuality exists. Most people don't think that a viable sublimation can exist, which can be a uniquely difficult social pressure to be exposed to.

YOU WONDER WHY CELIBACY AND SPIRITUALITY ARE STEREOTYPICAL BEDFELLOWS; YOU WONDER IN GENERAL ABOUT THE SPIRITUAL SIGNIFICANCE OF SEX AND TANTRIC CELIBACY.

Throughout history, many people have become celibate spontaneously, not as a cultivated practice to become a better, happier person or couple but as a consequence of self-realization. If you are always feeling love, then you always feel as though you are making love. Sex becomes rather redundant.

Tantric sublimation begins with the feelings a person currently experiences and helps trace them toward greater subtlety. At some point, even the subtlest feelings come to an absolute limit, and one will need a leap of faith into the spiritual aspects of human life, a leap into unverifiable truths that our faith knows to be true anyway. There one is awed by how endlessly real God is and how refinedly innocent are all the passions of innocence. This unparalleled awe has, for thousands of years, remained the spiritual possibility of which brahmacharya is only an outward sign.

5

THE ARS EROTICA
OF YOGA

◆

Dharmaviruddho bhutesu kamo 'smi. . . .
(I am the passion in beings aligned with universal harmonies.)

Bhagavad-Gita

In this chapter we will become acquainted with the yogic approach to eros, including its unique anatomical map of the human constitution as a gateway to sublimative arousals and the "post-genital phases" of our "psychosexual" development. But to discover this dimension of our being requires a wordlessly rapt concentration that, from the tantric perspective, is engendered naturally by our own erotic nature. The sensations we feel captivate our attention, and that very captivation is meditation.

Thus, another reason that we, as followers of Western sexology, have no inkling that such a sublimative eros exists is that we have not yet meditated on our own mystery. We have used only laboratory devices or questionnaires to query the range of the life passion, and the passion that we enact and query has always been "pre-meditative." If we follow the moralists, we merely try to avoid sex. And even during sex, our minds typically wander in uninhibited delight.

Through eros-enthralled meditation, the chakras, kundalini, *samadhi*— all the phenomena of the ars erotica to be discussed in this chapter—are revealed.

MEDITATION:
THE SILENT PARTNER TO CONVENTIONAL SEX

Even sexologists note that a primary reason conventional sex feels so good is that we become expectation-free "sensual meditators" during that time, and it is the receptive focusing of our attention upon the stimulations of sex that makes the pleasure available to us. Who can tell what the innovative sexologist John Money (1980) is referring to in the following description?

> The two minds drift into the oblivion of attending only to their own feeling, so perfectly synchronized that the ecstasy of the one is preordained to be the reciprocal ecstasy of the other. Two minds, mindlessly lost in one another. (p. 119)

Although he refers to sexual intercourse, he could just as well be describing what sublimation and meditation expert Swami Kripalvananda has called, in a verbal teaching, "the embrace of love-drenched minds" of celibate lovers.

In clinical sexology, desire-filled thoughts that aim too strenuously into the future, better known as "performance anxieties," can sabotage even the most passionate encounter. Sexual dysfunction is often merely a result of the anxiety one can feel if distracted from the "now" by the *expectation* of impending failure. One is preoccupied with the approaching orgasm, and suddenly and "as usual" it happens too soon. Or, one expects the orgasm or requisite arousal *not* to happen, and those bracings for failure impede tumescence and release.

The clinical remedy? "Sensate-focused attention," that is, a little nonattached, meditative regard for subtlety. Partners touch more slowly, breathe and move with greater relaxation, and even drop the agenda of sex and orgasm-seeking. Unwittingly, sex therapy has moved them toward sublimation! Sensate focusing, at least in its preliminary stages of nonsexual relaxation and contact, could be seen as the beginning of a bridge to tantric practices, yet only if the less "desirable" but more profound shimmers of sublimation glow as the "other shore" that allures our traverse.

MEDITATION FOLLOWS THE MYSTERY: THE YOGIC "ALL" IN GOING ALL THE WAY

The abstinent run away from what they desire
But carry their desires with them:
When a man enters Reality
He leaves his desires behind him.

(Bhagavad-Gita)

One decisive point on this bridge from sex to tantra is in leaving orgasm and sex-desire behind, allured by hopes and pleasures of a more subtle nature. This, of course, has a tremendous impact on couples when partners must work together to proceed in this new direction. It's as if a couple went to a sex therapist for one session, learned sensate focusing, and forgot to go back for more sessions, or even to go back to sex.

The steps across this yogic bridge from sensate focusing's more conventional erotic truths to the subtler erotic truths of what we call *consciousness* itself were first put into an ordered format by the great meditator and semanticist Patanjali (200 B.C.). In his *Yoga Sutras* (yoga aphorisms), he noted six ever-deepening degrees of sensate focusing: *pratyahara, dharana, dhyana, sabija-samadhi, nirbija-samadhi,* and *kaivalya.*

Pratyahara, "attention that reverses the scattering," gathers us from our wandering opinions, spinning worryings, and jumpy reactions to the myriad external stimulations. The happy or sad story of our relationship or life—constantly replaying itself in our minds with its voice-over analyses, fantasies, and occasional cynical eddies—begins to drop away. What Richard (Ram Dass) Alpert fondly called our "mellow-drama" quiets down, and we are more "being here now."

As an experiment, sit quietly and breathe in and out while making a smooth, hissing sound deep in your throat. Just listen to the sound and let it fill your awareness. Your thoughts will vanish for at least a few moments. This is the beginning of pratyahara.

No longer so tossed about by thoughts, we become capable of a more unbroken perception of each other and ourselves. We pass through the gates of cynical and demystified certainties toward suggestive ambiguity. We hear the songs of inflection beneath speech. We feel the greater whole coming together, previously obscured by our habitual fragmenting preoccupations. Drawing back from the rush, we feel the quieter emotions of shyness, charm, and trepid vulnerability as the graceful but uncertain romanticism of life. As R. M. Rilke asks us:

> Is it not time that, in loving,
> we freed ourselves from the loved one, and, quivering, endured:
> as the arrow endures the string, to become, in the gathering
> out-leap,
> something more than itself? For staying is nowhere.
>
> (*Duino Elegies*)

In early pratyahara, even mundane activities approach the sense of being sacred rituals, as Ellen (in the introduction to this book) discovered, and formal ritual practices leave the pejorative for the truly revelatory. Experience itself becomes more "religious" (from *religare,* to bind together or re-align), because our heartfelt attention is more continuously aligned and devotedly undiverted.

Pratyahara sustained will intensify, further revealing the finer gradations of evanescent subtleties glimmering within the more dense, suggestive erotic innuendo. This more smoothly alive, impermanent world of self and others appears as if one were experiencing it for the first time, yet repeatedly so. We find one response, feeling, or perspective transmuting into another and another; simultaneously, we know that none of this has ever happened before. The sung mantra reveals myriad shifts in rhythm and sentiment; the in-and-out breath surfaces its manifold textures and inexplicable origin. Thus captivated, our meditation deepens naturally.

Try sitting quietly and practicing the hissing breath, alone or in close synchrony with your partner. Consider: "Each breath is unique, my life is this series of breaths, just like this one, and this one, and . . ."

We may want to linger, to stay, to arrest the flow and talk about it, photograph it, lyricize it. Yet, this beauty is mercurial and we must let go, for it is already slipping away to be replaced by the new. We are getting into the stream-of-living-time. We must find what Heraclitus ("You never step in the same river twice") called *ek-stasis,* freedom from static attachment to these most moving perceptions.

When we step into this temporal flow, our listening gets smooth. We begin to hear sheer hearing itself, the silent sound of one hand clapping; our eyes even close, and we see the light of seeing itself; in the movement of breath, we feel bare touching. Something that feels like an underlying profundity is drawing us easily away from the many specific images and thoughts that would excite us with desirous eroticisms.

We arouse instead into the concentration of dharana, "holding toward unwavering-focus," a nearly continuous nongrasping awareness of the flowing evanescence of mercurial subtleties. A trusting faith holds us to the world, and we find a new sort of elusive confidence from which to prepare our thoughts and plan our actions. We discover faithful spontaneity:

> . . . take no thought how or what ye shall speak: for it shall be given you in that same hour what ye shall speak. For it is not ye that speak. . . .
>
> (Matthew 10:19–20)

The "intelligence" within our intelligence that precedes language breaks through our familiar sense of our "knowing-speaking self." Preoccupying thoughts loosen their grip, and the ensuing silence feels ecstatic. As the fourteenth-century Eastern Orthodox monastic Nicephorus the Solitary advised in a Christian version of dharana:

> You know that our breathing is the inhaling and exhaling of air. The organ which serves for this is the lungs which lie round the heart, so that air passing through them thereby envelops the heart. Thus breathing is a natural way to the heart. And so, having collected your mind within you, lead it into the channel of breathing through which air reaches the heart and, together with this inhaled air, force your mind to descend into the heart and to remain there. Accustom it, brother, not to come out of the heart too soon, for at first it feels very lonely in that inner seclusion. But when it gets accustomed to it, it begins on the contrary to dislike its aimless circlings outside . . . so the mind, when it unites with the heart, is filled with unspeakable joy and delight. Then a man sees that the kingdom of heaven is truly within us. (Kadloubovsky and Palmer, 1977, p. 33)

As dharana blooms into full tumescence, one falls devotionally in love with undistracted devotion itself, and the "kingdom within" begins to emerge like a slowly dawning sun. In this unwavering appreciation, a further threshold of wonder opens as dhyana, "fathoming, unwavering attention." Here, the constantly poised wordless intellect, freed of grasping, worrying, and commenting, begins to fathom directly or intuit something of the soul or essence of things: sheer suchness, I am This, core teachings, That Which Is, bare haiku presence, YHWH, the moral—or, literally, the manner—of things.

If dharana is a devotional attention like a sometimes smooth, occasionally shifting flow of water, dhyana (meditation proper) is like an unperturbed flow of warm, sacred oils, deep and rich, motionless in its motion. In this depth one begins to feel, as in any ominous first meeting, "*This* is really it! Here it all begins and ends!" We feel the underlying unity of all being, all time, and all people that differentiates into the poignancies and drama of existence.

Thus the Buddha's great enlightenment began one day while he merely watched with pained concern the quiet struggles of an oft-pausing old man laboring his way down a bustling Indian street.

A poignancy so singular and true awakens dhyana to the essence of loving commitment: the constant following of eros-as-mystery unfolding in sometimes magnificent, sometimes tragic twists and turns. Subjective attention and all objective manifestation come to a steadiness at their conjoint omphalic source. The solemn sanctity and breathless bliss of this union are exactly that of an engagement for marriage, known as sabija-samadhi, "complete togetherness with origin-consciousness (with seeds of future wavering)."

After a long-developing engagement of innumerable hours of secret liaisons (thousands of hours a year, often for decades), this meditation-marriage of sabija-samadhi dissolves all prenuptial seed-waverings and consummates in nirbija-samadhi, "complete togetherness with the origin-consciousness (without seeds of future wavering)." Sheer consciousness, known now as omnidirectional, desireless love, or *prema,* opens in a vast embrace. All the arguing opposites, demystified certainties, suggestive ambiguities, and evanescent subtleties light up with this singular love song. The scaffoldings (of this book) come down; the entire mystery of consciousness, love, and existence has been revealed.

Finally, after many years or lifetimes of ever-deepening intimacy in this meditative marriage of nirbija-samadhi, the wisely innocent child kaivalya, the "natural state," is born. This state of fully liberated erotic life is the utterly new beginning, unencumbered by the laborious and consuming processes that have borne it—sheer trust, a gift, a "virginal-born" spirit, living without reservation in self-world intimacy, where mystery *is* the deepest, for even the seeming terminus of death has yielded to the endless mystery. As the ultimate erotic liberation, kaivalya is (finally) the conclusive, if not also rarely attained, "all" in the tantric version of "going all the way."

> 399. Worship of Me is the ladder by which this state is reached; from this it may seem to thee that I am a means to that end,

> 400. but do not let this thought enter thy mind, for Brahma is not different from Me.

> (*Jnaneshvari*, 1987, p. 428)

A MOMENT OF SILENCE . . .

Since these advanced stages of development may take many decades or even lifetimes to unfold, it is fitting to pause for a moment and feel the awe of what we are approaching. As Malebranche said in the seventeenth century while considering the most interior aspects of human fertility, "One [is rightly in awe] that we penetrate too deeply into the smallest works of God."

Without such awe and pause-taking, we race past the aura of profundity that looms heavy whenever great erotic mysteries are approached. Instead of humbling us like some rarely seen velvety orchid, these deep yogic teachings blur pejoratively into apparent new-age jargon or are lost to us as another lifeless philosophy of rarified abstractions and practical impossibilities.

Through humbled reverence, the half-understandings of arrogance and the demeanings of cynicism wither. Or, rather, humbled reverence is the response that denotes we have touched the hems of mystery, while its absence guarantees we are as yet too assuming, and thus too distant, from its powers. "For Beauty's nothing but beginning of Terror we're still just able to bear . . ." (Rilke, *Duino Elegies*). If yoga makes you shudder, then you are feeling its true depth.

The fact must startle us that we are touching truths and practices rooted in humanity's first religious searchings, perhaps twelve thousand years old. This needs to be felt in one's bones. The millions of individuals, no different from you or me, who spent whole lifetimes experimenting with these practices and beliefs, at first on faith alone, are due our respect. Their parents, children, husbands, wives, and supportive friends and teachers must be remembered and honored as well. The challenges we will face, surely these yogis also faced, and the encouragement they received from others, we most certainly will equally need.

But when the wondrous results came, the generations of yogis continued and continued, so that today we have an unbroken heritage that says, "This way is good. By your own free choice enter here and use of it as you will."

THE YOGIC ANATOMY OF HUMAN POTENTIALITIES

Through exceedingly detailed meditations over thousands of hours, the yogis determined that the human body is far more than a configuration of fleshy organs, bones, and fluids. Composed of five gradients or *koshas,* literally, "sheaths," with each one more interior and more subtle than the previous one, we are the actual "bridge" from the physical to the spiritual. Each sheath exerts a guiding intelligence over the next more dense sheath in the following order: the individual soul and causal body (*jiva* and *anandamaya kosha*), the reflective-intellectual body (*vijnanamaya kosha*), mental-emotional body (*manomaya kosha*), vital energy body (*pranamaya kosha*), and the physical body (*annamaya kosha*). Through this anatomy of increasingly interior bodies, yoga maps the emotionality and sentient capacities of the intimus itself and thus the way toward deepening our intimacy with one another and the world.

The Subtle Bodies

The *physical* and *vital sheaths* operate together, forming the densest of our dimensions, the biological body. The erotic phenomena of sheer sensation, physical-emotional warmth, the various orgasmic reflexes, and hormonal rhythms are based primarily in these two interacting bodies. Erotic pleasures and intimacies of the physical and vital bodies operating together constitute the "realm of the senses," the ideal of a pure sensuality.

The *mental-emotional* body holds the cognitive intelligence by which we identify and attribute a socially agreed-upon meaning to the events and sensations that occur in the two preceding bodies. People who thought they were going to "just have sex" who later feel emotionally involved with their sexual partner have aroused this more intimate sheath during the otherwise seemingly casual sex. Here is where fantasies, desires, joys, jealousies, angers, hopes, and sorrows reside to be shared with those whom we trust.

The *reflective-intellectual* sheath takes the erotic sentiments and meanings of the mental body one step further. Here we grasp the value of the other and his or her emotions and thoughts, as well as our own. Thus, the reflective-intellectual sheath provides the even longer-lasting erotic pleasures and intimacies of loving admiration, the feelings of sincerity and respect, the romanticisms of love, gratitude, apology, and forgiveness. Thus, vijnanamaya kosha is the domain of human character, or integrity.

Continuous appreciation of these deeply human sentiments and capacities is a meditation that reveals the next underlying *causal* or *bliss body,* the most intimate abode of the individual soul, jiva, or *atman.* We have penetrated mundane concerns and changing ways; now we glimpse beyond body, emotion, and character into the eternal glow of the Self, the unconditional love of the Soul. The utter uniqueness of each individual has a sense of the remarkable to it, of being a singularly nuanced spark of the divine.

Located in an etheric space within the heart, this bliss body is in intimate rapport with *brahmarandhra,* the subtle center of mind and intellect. Together and in balance, they manifest what the great Dutch philosopher Baruch Spinoza called "the intellectual love of God," thought and love combined.

In anandamaya kosha, the Blakeian "fearful symmetry" emerges—the inexplicable original pulsations of life into all the bodies. Erotic pleasure is permanent, and, independent of efforts or stimulations, it feels of the "miraculous." Fulfillment in the causal body can be so great that complete dispassion or nonattachment to sense-objects, desires, and thoughts results. One has attained a profound balancing of both the internal and external realms of "needs" and "needing." As the yogi Vyas Dev says, "This is an indescribable state, beyond the pairs of opposites. . . . This is the highest limit of individual knowledge" (*Science of Soul,* p. 225).

Through "self-ishness," that is, the self's clinging to experience, the clarity of such knowledge diminishes, imbalance emerges, and the ego-self (known as *ahamkara,* also in the heart) gets confused. Using the reflective and mental-emotional bodies, it thinks and feels itself into a fictive separate identity.

Cut off from anandamaya kosha, it becomes (falsely) convinced by the obviousness of the physical body that annamaya kosha is its only basis in reality. The solutions it then seeks to dispel its confusions and satisfy its "needs" can become even more egoic, that is, cut off even further from the otherwise powerful spiritual resources, which now appear to exist only as impossible ideals or rarified abstractions.

When the resources of all the bodies are functioning in balance and the ego-self is able to grasp its more modest place in relationship to the subtler bodies, sexual (and many other) desires arise like small waves upon the deep ocean of our being. They do not sway us but slip into our depths, gratifying us as they dissolve into a simple joy and contentment of the remarkable.

The Chakras

To effect this balancing of all the bodies, tantra attends to the septenary system of chakras, or energy regulatory centers, located approximately along the spinal axis. These include *muladhara, svadhisthana* and *manipura chakras* (presiding primarily over the physical body); *anahata* and *vishuddha chakras* (presiding primarily over the vital body), *ajna chakra* (presiding primarily over the mental-emotional and reflective bodies); and *sahasrara chakra* (presiding primarily over the causal body). Each chakra also generates a specific locus of longings and pleasures associated with its particular properties.

MULADHARA CHAKRA

Muladhara, the root chakra at the base of the spine, holds the power of fundamental survival and the primal erotic passion to live. Its element is earth. It is closely related to the adrenal glands and is attuned to our basic survival needs. In meditation it appears as an earthy, ruddy, red glow.

Concerned with elimination, muladhara has a gutsy feel and a strength that is "not afraid to get its hands dirty." Dependable and earthy, it might be considered the "Ernest Hemingway" or "Mae West" of the chakras. Concerned also with the sense of smell, muladhara's instinctive powers can, literally, "smell" trouble, truth, or deception; it is the source of the proverbial nose for news. Pheromones, of course, are biology's name for the way the shared-gender mystery affects muladhara.

At the more esoteric level, the wise "serpent power" called kundalini rests coiled within muladhara, as a residue of the primeval force responsible for the creation of the physical universe. It can be aroused by yogic or other spiritual practices to enter a subtle channel in the spine *(sushumna),* causing a blissful tumescence throughout all the bodies and inspiring a deep sense of reverence and humility. The Holy Ghost and other charismatic phenomena have been compared with kundalini activity. Gopi Krishna, author of *Kundalini: The Evolutionary Energy in Man,* maintains that all forms of genius involve some degree of awakening of this essence of revelatory intelligence.

SVADHISTHANA CHAKRA

Svadhisthana chakra is located a few inches above the root chakra in the general area of pelvic sexual arousal. Its element is water. It is associated with the endless seeds within seeds for all future incarnations and is the primary basis of conventional sexuality.

Svadhisthana also governs taste and the world of "good taste," which displays itself in fashions as the play of taste and sensuality. Raunchy, sexy, alluring, classic, monastically robed—all are manifestations of svadhisthana, via dress. "Juicy" people with a kind of "chemistry" also reveal something about this chakra but only suggestively so, for that is the manner of svadhisthana. Sexual fantasies and scenarios, as internal adult entertainments, are also stirred by this center, and stir it as well. Thus we might say it is the "Elvis" and "Marilyn" of the chakras.

MANIPURA CHAKRA

Manipura chakra, the solar plexus center, is where the fire element presides. The whole gamut of heated emotions of jealousy, anger, vanity, belly laughter, and willful assertiveness is based here. Manipura is associated with the navel, and feelings of dependency and autonomy relate to it, as well as the psychological ideal of "emotional honesty."

As the most elevated of the three physical body chakras, this is the site of existential struggles to believe in "higher realities." The loss of one's "groundedness" can also happen in manipura via the "flight to the light," or "flakiness" phenomenon, whereby a thin veneer of spiritual development is mistaken for a more mature attainment. Ken Wilber has referred to this foible as the "pre-transpersonal fallacy." To achieve spiritual growth, one needs to have gutsiness, juice, and "stomach" as well as heart and soul. Perhaps Amelia Earhart, Fritz Perls, and C. Everett Koop are manipura types.

In tantric sublimation, manipura holds critical importance, for it is the actual site of transmutation where bindu, the seed force from svadhisthana, is sublimated by the heat of this solar center into ojas, a nonphysical constituent in the radiance of consciousness. The beauty of this radiance also allures kundalini to rise from muladhara.

ANAHATA CHAKRA

Anahata chakra, the heart center, is related to the air element. Here the language of emotional needs is replaced by that of devotional needs, which is to say, "I need" has become "I love" or "I feel devotional yearnings." The soul is reaching beyond the ego's hopes for self-directed autonomy and emotional closeness and senses the fulfillments of a shared reality. Indeed, the limited and fictive sense of the separate-self ego is coming to light.

In anahata, compassion opens toward "there but for the grace of God, go I." Love shows us that the happiness of the other is our happiness and the mystery of giving is like receiving, or better. Thus, we face various contradictions among value systems in moving from the first three chakras, which oversee the physical body, to the heart, the first chakra that governs supraphysical resources and realms of erotic meaning.

When we feel love for someone attractive to us, anahata and svadhisthana can both be stirred, and we can feel pulled in two directions, one familiar and lush, the other more airy and distant feeling. To continue in tantric sublimation at such times, we must let go of the seeming certainty that the lushness of sex would be *so right* with this person we love. Instead, we must take the leap of uncertainty. Through such faith, ojas intensifies and the unexpected can occur, as we see with Lianne and Andy.

Lianne had been living in a yoga community, practicing brahmacharya, for five years when she met Andy. He moved into the community mainly to be near Lianne but was interested enough in yoga to take on the various practices. During the first year their friendship grew and so did Andy's understanding of brahmacharya. They saw each other only in larger group settings. Lianne was moved by Andy's dedication, and during the second year of his residency she was falling more in love with him. On one of their morning walks Andy reached out to Lianne.

The moment of awkwardness lasted about one second and they embraced. All of a sudden it was as though she had never practiced celibacy; she felt like a "teenager in love." A rapid succession of sexual images raced through her mind as she hoped both that they would surrender to this passion and that they wouldn't. Andy thought that after two years, now they were together, but he, too, was of two minds, not knowing where his sexual feelings would lead him.

As their embrace continued, first Lianne, then Andy, started to laugh. It was so funny thinking about how impossible it was to know what to do with each other. Their embrace took on the warmth of a shared, unexpected discovery. They were still laughing when they kissed each other and fell down together.

As they looked up, the sky and the air everywhere seemed pink. The trees seemed to be visibly breathing, in a kind of oceanic harmony with their breaths. It was as if their love had carried them to some hidden space where even the air was alive with love and magic. They were there together and had preserved the essence of their celibacy.

Such sublimative discoveries on the brink of desire are not unlike the feelings you get when you have approached a deeply inviting pool, seemingly too wide to jump across, but you jump anyway. Through the tantric leap of meditation, conventional images of a lush sexuality and a pejorative sense of an "airy" one no longer appear as unequivocally accurate mappings of the ways of love and erotic freedom. Instead, the images of sex-desire can seem to be metaphorical, instead of literal, suggestive of something yet unknown and quite "real."

To get to this new place, we need faith and the light of ojas. But how can we make subtle discernments between gradations of loving passion when frequent sexual activity quickly raises, then dramatically lowers, ojas levels? Thus we have the many wily tantric strategies of "half-orgasms" and occasional orgasms for both men and women or only for women. Less wily is the heart's own way through the alchemical heightening of ojas to virya.

For it is in anahata that the soul abides with its finer sensitivities and courage (from *couer,* "heart") that often exceed good sense and sensual familiarities. Sustained by the gutsiness of muladhara, the daring of svadhisthana, and the willingness of manipura, anahata can become inspired.

Virya, the further distillate of ojas, precipitates like sweet butter from fine cream. Felt as a sublimely rectifying forgiveness that keeps stretching and encompassing more and more, or as a courage that follows only its own star, virya sparkles with virtue. Strategies and plans to "find love" become unimportant. Heart-felt faith prevails, and one is able to take leaps of faith.

While ojas clarifies the more aesthetic subtleties of emotion with its light, virya ignites the compassion of "heart-consciousness." With virya, one tastes of the evanescently poignant and even anguished human hopefulness that lives in challenging or distressing situations. With ample virya, virtue appears hidden (perhaps in convoluted or even deranged forms) in human acts, everywhere. Beyond the din of despondent or unconvincingly optimistic demystifying opinions, virya *really* understands.

While ojas heals the effects of injury, physical or emotional, the empathic forgiveness of virya lives a deeper understanding of what is really needed. Instead of healing the symptom or the painful effect, virya's selfless forgiving heals the cause of the injury. It forgives others and oneself any commissions and omissions in unreasonable poignancy and mercy, as the ideal of *kshama*—loving forgiveness—becomes real.

As a side effect, one's own pain mysteriously transforms; bitterness and cynicism are obviated. The harshly tragic aspects of human life have met their match—compassionate love—and the soul matures the ego-personality through these difficulties. Thus, forbearance, sacrifice, anger without vengeance, courageous action, and, at times, a distracting humor ennoble us and deepen our characters with the softened gnarl of experience. Albert Schweitzer, Mother Teresa, and perhaps a certain person you know well embody the qualities of anahata chakra.

VISHUDDHA CHAKRA

From sexual passion to compassion to spiritual dispassion: such are the refinements from svadhisthana to anahata and now vishuddha, the throat chakra.

Words are, literally, "shaped currents of air" (the heart element); thus, "the word become flesh" is found as the opened heart. The elemental ether that lives in vishuddha is even more subtle than air and is thus "more than words can say." Vishuddha permeates words with their spirit, their near-ineffable meanings, nuances, and innuendos often lost in a too-literalness. In other instances, subtle meaning is lost to us because we are in too much pain or fear or, worse, because we are blinded by greed or vengeance.

The waverings of the heart receive a whispered steadying from the dispassion of vishuddha, quickening the words of the heart with the Summative Word, prema, unconditioned love. Thus King Solomon discerned the foundling's true mother from the false. Thus marriage vows and final vows ring ominously.

The legendary artist's, orator-statesperson's, teacher's, or poet's heightened perception of a transcendent beauty or a cosmic order in the phenomena of life involves the sensitivities of vishuddha. (Perhaps, therefore, the special license given to artists regarding the erotic?) Sublimity has been refined yet further.

As Sri Jnaneshvar (1987) stated, "The sentiment of tranquillity will be found to surpass that of love . . ." (p. 235). Such deft tranquillity, supported by the other chakras, approaches all of life's possibilities with unperturbed skillfulness and empathic wonder, from the most ecstatic to the most horrific and tragic. Shakespeare, the "I have a dream" speech of Martin Luther King, Jr., and Sri Jnaneshvar speak from vishuddha.

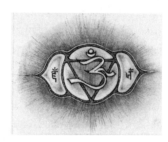

AJNA CHAKRA

Ajna, "the third eye," is where, as the Bible notes, "thine eyes become single," where there is no longer a difference between male and female, and where "the peace that passeth all understanding" dwells. Erotic mystery persists as the continuous, inexplicable unfolding of the eternal moment. Tranquil dispassion has culminated in *vairagha*, the wisdom of nonattachment. Now the unwavering light of true wisdom sends whispers even to those so-knowing missives of vishuddha, for ajna is of *mahat-Tattwa*, utter refinement. From within these gates of heaven, Solomon and all prophets and saints and the many unknown heroes of our daily lives receive their inspirations, beyond all conjecturing. Here Siva, the lord of yogis, presides. He can only bless with dispassion, and he blesses all alike.

Certain uncompromising devotees of the penultimate ajna prefer to bypass the many substeps and complexities of tantric sublimation that I have described. Following the precepts of traditional monasticism, they attempt, in one leap, to attune to ajna, perhaps including vishuddha (practice of constant, repetitive prayers) and anahata (selfless surrender via service or ecstatic devotion). Couples' practices and even the concept of energetic transformation are dismissed or left unexplored. For some of these devotees, celibacy is either easy and spontaneous or a concerted discipline without recourse to any yogic techniques. I find this stark approach to be ominous.

SAHASRARA CHAKRA

The seventh or crown chakra, sahasrara is of such a spiritual nature that restrictions of time, space, and mortality are completely transcended. Sahasrara is the thousand-petaled lotus of holy effulgence, experienced as the light of ten million suns; "like mercury light kept in a vessel of silver. The thousands of convolutions of the brain appear like the luminous petals of a lotus," says the inwardly sighted yogi Vyas Dev.

Reverent awe, unremitting joy, and spiritual freedom are the qualities of the mystery in sahasrara, beyond even the highest of elements. The writings of the great mystics and saints describe and celebrate this realm of the erotic expanse where orgasm-as-adjective reaches the superlative, as in this passage by Allama Prabhu, in Ramanujan, *Speaking of Siva (1973)*:

> Looking for your light,
> I went out:
>
>> it was like the sudden dawn
>> of a million million suns,
>>
>> a ganglion of lightnings
>> for my wonder.
>>
>> O Lord of Caves,
>> if you are light,
>> there can be no metaphor.
>
> (p. 168)

KAIVALYA

When the nondual consciousness of ajna is sustained in sabija-samadhi and then nirbija-samadhi, the crowning birth of kaivalya dawns in sahasrara. In the full liberation of kaivalya, the erotic mysteries of and after death open, as immortality takes on an awesome, crystalline reality.

Thus we have mapped the transformations of passion and consciousness from bodily maintenance and survival to divine rapture. Next we will discuss the "body-ecology" basis of brahmacharya; the energetic initiation of *shakti-pata;* and aspects of the yogic "second puberty" of *khechari mudra, urdhva-reta* along with, finally, *divya sharira,* the "divine body," which some authorities grant an even higher significance than kaivalya, for it denotes literal bodily regeneration.

The Body-Ecology of Brahmacharya

According to *ayurveda,* yogic medical physiology:

> The food we eat is transformed into the seven body constituents (dhatus) by an involved step-by-step transformation process. The digested food is successively converted into lymph, blood, tissue, fat, bone, marrow, sexual secretions, and an eighth constituent called ojas—subtle light energy. The ojas, the most refined essence of the sexual secretions, in turn permeates and nourishes every cell of the body. With an increase in ojas there is a marked increase in well-being at all levels. With a loss of ojas everything deteriorates. The development of every body constituent is directly influenced by the one preceding it. Therefore, if an excessive amount of sexual energy is lost (loss of sexual energy happens mainly through sexual activity) the production of ojas suffers. . . . There is an excess of sexual secretions produced each month to allow for one monthly intercourse without detriment to physical, mental, emotional and spiritual well-being.
>
> (Dass and Aparna, 1978, p. 66)

This observation provides one of the important bases for brahmacharya. Instead of being some sort of moralistic repression of sex, brahmacharya reflects the inexorable yogic rhythms of our anabolic biochemistry and fertility cycles (for both men and women). The quota of one orgasm per month does appear repressive when compared with the statistical averages in the United States, where sex or masturbation is often a daily practice. The question is, are we over-consuming our own sexual drives? Do our outer societal sexual dilemmas reflect internal "eco-sexual" imbalances? Maybe there are sublimative rhythms in addition to those of desire and even fertility that, when added into our sexual equation, effect deep erotic harmonies and balance.

Shakti-pata-diksha, the Phenomenon of Energetic Initiation

Through the energy-transfer initiation known as *shakti-pata-diksha,* the yogic transformations described in this book can be given a strong jump start. Here the role of the trusted teacher or guru must be considered. Although the reputations of certain spiritual teachers have been marred in recent times, studying with a respected guru and receiving his or her energetic initiation—via a mantra, touch, eye contact, or other means—can prove invaluable and, at advanced stages, a necessity. The experience, love, and support of such a person can add so much inspiration to one's life and practice that a gratitude of the highest order often emerges. All the technical knowledge and long-sought attainments can pale in comparison with such feelings. Yet the guru desires our growth, so the thanks he or she prefers is our dedication to these ways of living.

The Bodily Transformations

In the upward flow of urdhva-reta, the glowing beauty of ojas being sublimated in manipura can awaken and attract the "sleeping kundalini" in muladhara to ascend with it toward the summit in ajna. This movement begins to stimulate all the chakras.

The combined awakening of muladhara, vishuddha, and ajna will gradually affect the pineal and pituitary glands as well, inducing in them what could be called a second puberty, given the dramatic changes that ensue throughout the body. One very advanced phenomenon of this sublimative puberty is khechari mudra, in which a passion reaching up from the entrails and the tongue achieves a kind of tumescence in dialogue with the now arousable midbrain glands.

In this most mysterious unfoldment—literally, "taking a stand in the spaciousness of ultimate openness"—the tongue weaves back into the throat in response to, and in warm hopes of, making contact with the moonlike allure of the pineal gland (which corresponds to ajna chakra, the site of the third eye). Through a serene suspension of breathing, a warmth is generated to the point of an "alchemical" awakening in various glands and chakras. After many years of development, khechari mudra will culminate in the secretion of *amrita,* or "nectar," a kind of rejuvenating and even mildly psychedelic essence perhaps akin to the mood-enhancing endorphins.

Altogether, these post-genital processes of sublimation and psychosexual development support the almost magical phenomenon of the formation of the divya sharira, the variously known divine, diamond, yogic, or eternal body. According to Jnaneshvar's commentary on the *Bhagavad-Gita* (Jnaneshvar was a South Indian poet whose commentary incorporates the perspective of kundalini yoga), it has been approximately seven hundred years since anyone has experienced this complete bodily maturation and transformation:

> XIV. Serene and fearless, firm in the vow of celibacy, subdued in mind, let him sit, harmonized, his mind turned to Me and intent on Me alone. . . .
>
> 259. So appears the body (of the yogi) when Kundalini has drunk of the nectar, and even the god of death is afraid to look at it.
>
> 260. Old age vanishes, the knot of youth is loosened, and the lost bloom of childhood reappears.
>
> 261. Whatever his age, the word "youth" should be interpreted as "strength," such is his incomparable fortitude.
>
> 262. Just as the ever new jewel-buds open on the boughs of a tree of gold, fine new finger-nails grow;
>
> 263. new teeth appear, very small, set like rows of diamonds on each side.
>
> 264. Over the whole body tiny new hairs spring forth like small splinters of rubies.
>
> 265. The palms of the hands and feet are red as lotus flowers and in the eyes there shines an indescribable lustre.
>
> 266. As the shell of an oyster no longer holds the pearl when it is fully developed and it bursts open at the joint with the force of its growth,
>
> 267. so the sight, which strives to pass outwards when it cannot be held within the eyelids, embraces the whole heavens, even with half-opened eyes. . . .
>
> 272. She [Kundalini] is the Mother of the worlds, the glory of the empire of the soul, who gives shelter to tender sprouts of the seed of the universe,

273. the phallic symbol of the formless Brahma, the containing vessel of Shiva, the supreme soul, and the true source of the life
breath. . . .

291. 'One body devours another.' This is the secret of the teaching of
Natha, but it has now been revealed by Sri Vishnu.

(*Jnaneshvari,* 1987, pp. 129, 132–33)

These are some, but not all, of the most secret teachings of yoga. Some
rest partially hidden in the metaphors in the above *sutras.* Others are sur-
rounded by a protective secrecy inherent to ars erotica pedagogy; certain
teachings, we are told, cannot be revealed except when the aspirant is fully
ready and in need of them. Sir John Woodroffe (1978), an early translator
of yogic texts, recounts:

Copies of the complete tantra are rare enough. . . . I came across a
complete manuscript some two years ago in the possession of a Nepalese
Pandit. He would, however, only permit me to make a copy of his
manuscript on the condition that the Shatkarma Mantras were not
published. . . . I was unable to persuade him [otherwise]. (p. xiii)

Such protection is not unwarranted, as yogic terms such as *kundalini* or
samadhi often become diluted after entering popular Western usage. In this
singular way, an intimacy surrounds certain erotic truths with living trust.
Others are quite simply ineffable.

6

YOGA PRACTICE
AS ARS EROTICA

◆

*In the erotic art, truth is drawn from pleasure itself, under-
stood as a practice and accumulated as experience; pleasure
is not considered in relation to an absolute law of the per-
mitted and the forbidden, nor by reference to a criterion of
utility, but first and foremost in relation to itself; it is experienced as pleasure, evaluated in terms of its intensity, its
specific quality, its duration, its reverberations in the body
and the soul. Moreover, this knowledge must be deflected
back into the sexual practice itself, in order to shape it as
though from within and amplify its effects. In this way, there
is formed a knowledge that must remain secret, not because
of an element of infamy that might attach to its object, but
because of the need to hold it in the greatest reserve, since
according to tradition, it would lose its effectiveness and its
virtue by being divulged. . . . The effects of this masterful
art, which are considerably more generous than the spare-
ness of its prescriptions would lead one to imagine, are said
to transfigure the one fortunate enough to receive its privi-
leges: an absolute mastery of the body, a singular bliss, oblivi-
ousness to time and limits, the elixir of life, the exile of death
and its threats.*

Michel Foucault
The History of Sexuality, pp. 57–58

Hatha yoga practices have been available in our culture for some time
now primarily as a form of gentle exercise or perhaps as physical disciplines
that purify and prepare the body for meditation. To consider them as erotic

Yoga Practice as Ars Erotica

practices is perhaps a semantical stretch, but only if we are too bound up in the conventional understandings of eros. For what we discover is that the postures, breathing practices, and meditations are all ways to plumb the depths of erotic mystery within our multidimensional bodies and open us to a deeper sensitivity to others.

We are searching for how to animate our yogic practices, solitary or partnered, with the energy of sublimative passion. When we pay attention to subtleties and nuances of movement and feeling, the body language of mystery, we begin to transform the more formalistic exercises into an ars erotica. Yet yoga is rarely taught within this context. We usually learn poses as stretching exercises to hold and perfect, rather than as a repertoire of intimate and passionate gestures of self-expression that inherently perfect themselves. The spirit or quality of passion that we bring to these practices is as significant as the practices themselves. How, then, to find this passion?

The purist approach consists of meditating in stillness until your body begins to move on its own, however long that might take, sometimes called "awaiting the beloved." This approach simulates how many yoga postures originated, in a spontaneity similar to one's first stretchings in bed while barely awake. Here the stillness of meditation allows *prana*, the vital energy of pranamaya kosha, to build to a certain pitch, and then, guided by its inner intelligence, prana moves the body exactly as it needs to be moved to release tensions and blocked emotions, transmute desires, open *nadis* (subtle channels), and stimulate the chakras. We are assured of entrance into sublimative passion through the spontaneity of movement, beyond egoic choosing or desiring. The yogic movements feel like acts of surrendered worship and each asana a bodily form of prayer. However, not everyone can arouse prana through meditation to such a degree that spontaneous, or *sahaja*, yoga results.

There are several ways the breath can be willfully managed in the beginning as an entrance to the more spontaneous movements. Perhaps the easiest way is to move very slowly into a series of asanas, or yoga positions, while breathing just as slowly as you are moving. Synchronizing breath, movement, and concentration engages prana as well, and at some point you will feel as if you are no longer willfully moving but are being moved by prana itself. As you penetrate mundane thinking by mentally merging with the nuances of bodily sensation, you will slip unobtrusively into a meditative state. In this way, postures and variations unfold in the moment as a flow from one asana to another known in yoga as *vinyasa* (posture flow).

A third way to discover sublimative passion is through building up prana through vigorous yogic breathing such as *kapala-bhati* or *bhastrika* as described below. After completing a series of these energizing breaths, you will feel a strong charge of energy or a dominant emotion and can begin moving with these feelings into various asanas until the spontaneity of movement is triggered.

Sometimes *kumbhaka*, the prolonged suspension of the breath, or merely sighing very deeply with each exhalation can rouse this passion. Another way is to use specific exercises that systematically stimulate the five fields of pranas—head (*udana*), chest (*prana*), mid-torso (*samana*), abdomen (*apana*), and circulatory (*vyana*)—and various nadis and chakras through a precise sequence of yoga practices as in the "experienced" routine (pages 107–109.)

Another way to arouse prana is by holding a posture in increasingly more accurate alignment. Here, perfecting an asana is like perfectly attuning an instrument to a certain key. When the pitch becomes perfect, strong vibrations of energy can be felt, and one asana follows another, according to our specific needs. Holding a posture beyond the first limits of discomfort can trigger the yogic passion and spontaneous asanas and pranayamas, and even dance movements. We must give ourselves permission to move, even with the scantiest of internal guidance.

Occasionally, sublimative passion is able to move us through asanas far beyond the reach of any willful attempts. It is as if our body needs to be in a specific asana for a specific amount of time to generate exactly the effects required for our development. You might find that chronic tension is actually held in place by your identifying with it and gripping your muscles from within in a habitual fashion. Giving up the tensions feels frightening, when actually it is more problematic to hold on to them. You can gradually discover how you are gripping your own body internally and how this self-grip releases during yoga stretches.

Other more subtle contractions of the abdominal muscles draw sexual energy to manipura, an important site of transmutation, and also can cause the intercostal muscles to flex with subtle pleasures, propelling energies farther into the nadis in the thorax. Various pumping motions in the throat, rib cage, sacrum, lumbar, and perineum, along with micromotion of the eyelids, nasal muscles, fingers, toes, head, and even the scalp, carry the sublimated energies throughout the whole body. Again, it is the nuances that bring a depth of feeling and expression to each movement, revealing its pleasures and meanings.

Finally, it becomes clear that you are moving from one practice to another, expressing sublimative passion in your own perfect way. Rotating the neck while drawing the breath in, then exhaling the humming sound of "hmmmm" in your throat, which vibrates into a smile as you release the breath and stretch forward on the floor into the cobra posture, then drawing your legs up under you to sit up, cross-legged in stillness; followed by an elaborate series of finger and hand movements, or *mudras,* in which moods change with every tilt of each finger, myriad variations, each unique to the moment. Thus some yoga texts claim that there are 840,000 yoga asanas.

Gradually we achieve a bodily openness and a rechanneling of erotic pleasures that transform our practiced sublimation into a natural brahmacharya. We feel more desireless because we feel more fullness in ourselves, and we are more appreciative of what we are already receiving from others.

THE PRACTICES

50. Though he performs all actions, he is not bound by them, as a lotus leaf in the water is not touched by it.

51. That is called action of the body in which reason takes no part and which does not originate as an idea springing in the mind.

52. To speak simply, yogis perform actions with their bodies, like the movements of children. . . .

(*Jnaneshvari,* 1987, p. 102)

I have grouped practices for beginners, the experienced, partners, and those who are physically limited, along with suggestions for families, children, and groups. I particularly encourage beginners to take a formal class. Although the ars erotica aspect would likely remain unexplored, the class will help bring the asanas to life and encourage your practice. I also recommend the following books: the *Ashtanga Yoga Primer* by Baba Hari Dass, *Kripalu Yoga* by Yogi Amrit Desai, *The Complete Illustrated Book of Yoga* by Swami Vishnudevananda, *Devatma Shakti* by Swami Vishnu Tirtha, and *Light on Yoga* and *Light on Pranayama* by B. K. Iyengar. People with special health conditions should consult a physician regarding specific practices and can refer to the above texts for contraindications for these and many other yoga practices.

Every practice should be entered in the spirit of ars erotica, with slow, graceful movement and with attention to any nuances of movement that sublimative passion calls forth.

The Bandhas

Bandhas (locks) are muscle contractions that seal off specific areas of the body, thus enabling energies to go more deeply into our organs and subtle bodies. Watch for the subtle blissful feelings generated by any of the bandhas and discover other subtle internal contractions that further awaken such sensations. Bandhas are performed in seated postures or as directed. The breath is held on inhalation (kumbhaka, KI) or exhalation (kumbhaka, KO) as noted.

MULA BANDHA

Contract and lift inward the anal sphincter on an inhalation; hold (KI) for as long as comfortable, and release on the exhalation. This seals in the abdominal energy known as *apana pran* and conducts it upward toward manipura chakra, the site of transmutation; it is similar to Kegel exercises.

JALANDHARA BANDHA

Press the chin into the hollow at the collarbone on an inhalation and hold (KI) as long as comfortable to seal energy within the thorax and to preserve a subtle revitalizing nectar that flows down from the sahasrara. Release chin-pressing during exhalation.

UDDIYANA BANDHA

Exhale completely, draw the stomach muscles inward, and hold as long as is comfortable; then slowly release the stomach muscles and the breath.

Maha Mudra

This practice employs all the above bandhas. Sit with the right leg out straight and the left leg bent so that the sole touches the inner right thigh and the left heel presses the perineum. Stretch the arms up, then lower arms forward to clasp the right toe with both hands by the thumbs and index fingers. Maintain concentration on ajna chakra. Begin mula bandha during the inhalation, and hold the breath (KI) with jalandhara and uddiyana bandhas. After exhalation, release mula, jalandhara, and uddiyana bandhas and then reapply uddiyana bandha, holding (KO) as long as is comfortable. Then inhale, release your hands, and repeat, reversing leg positions. Begin with two rounds and increase to ten.

Nabhan-mudra

Curl the tongue back so the tip touches the soft palate; this can be maintained with many asanas and the bandhas to preserve subtle nectars and awaken the higher chakras.

Pranayamas

These breathing practices are done sitting upright, cross-legged or in a chair, with proper ventilation and preferably on an empty stomach.

KAPALA-BHATI

Use the in-drawn abdominal muscles to pump air out of the lungs forcefully, and passively release the abdomen to draw air in.

NADI SHODHANA SAHITA KUMBHAKA

This is an alternate nostril breath and is the single most important practice for brahmacharya. Use the right thumb to open and close the right nostril and the right ring and little fingers to open and close the left. Maintain a ratio of 1:4:2 for the duration of each inhalation, hold (KI), and exhalation, beginning with 4 seconds to inhale, 16 seconds to hold, and 8 seconds to exhale. Begin inhaling left, with the right nostril closed by the thumb, hold the breath, applying the mula bandha and jalandhara bandha while holding the breath in. Then exhale through the right, closing the left nostril, and relax the locks when the breath is empty, for one second. Then inhale through the right nostril and hold the breath while applying the locks. Then exhale left, and so on. A twenty-minute session is usually sufficient to balance various polarities and to stimulate the central nadis in and around the spine. This pranayama balances energies that might have been excited through more vigorous practices. As ars erotica, nadi shodhana is a dialogue toward oneness between the polarities of our being: left-right, yin-yang, female-male, moon-sun, *ida-pingala*.

Asanas

All asanas will further the sublimative process. Choose the ones your particular body needs. Those that follow are especially helpful in brahmacharya. Center yourself with a few slow breaths, and move slowly to your capacity, wherever that may be.

VIPARITA KARANI MUDRA (REVERSE POSE)

Lie on your back. While inhaling, raise your legs to a vertical position and, with your elbows on the floor, support your hips with your hands and hold as long as is comfortable, breathing normally. Lower slowly on exhalation. In the shoulder stand (*sarvanga-asana*), at right, continue raising your upper back off the floor and use your hands to support your raised back, balanced comfortably on your shoulders. Hold. Lower your back slowly, using your hands as a brace.

HALA-ASANA (PLOW POSE)

From the reverse pose, exhale slowly and lower your legs down over your head. Keep your knees straight, and straighten your arms flat onto the floor, parallel with your body. Continue lowering your legs until your toes touch the floor. Hold this position and breathe slowly. Reverse the movement to come out of the pose.

SHIRSA-ASANA (HEADSTAND)

Unless you are already competent in this especially useful pose, I strongly recommend learning it with an instructor.

PASCHIMOTTANA-ASANA
(SEATED HEAD-TO-KNEE, BACK-STRETCHING POSE)

This one is also known as *brahmacharya-asana*. Sitting on the floor with your legs straight out, inhale while raising your arms up; stretch and hold; then exhale while reaching out and forward, lowering your torso and head to legs, clasp your big toes with your index finger and thumb. Perform uddiyana bandha (page 99) and hold the pose. Inhale while raising and stretching up, then lower your arms as you exhale.

BHADRA-ASANA (NOBILITY POSE)

Sitting upright, press the soles of your feet together, and hold your feet with your hands, drawing them close to your body; inhale and press your knees toward the floor, and hold.

PADMA-ASANA (LOTUS POSE)

Sit on the floor with your legs crossed. Lift your left foot onto your right thigh, placing it as near to your hip as possible without straining; lift your right foot onto your left thigh. Rest your hands on your knees, keeping your back straight. Women should reverse the leg position, placing the left foot on top.

SIDDHA-ASANA (ADEPT POSE)

This a basic meditation pose. Women: Bend your left leg so that your left heel presses your anus and perineum; then bend your right leg, placing your right foot on top of the left foot, pressing your genitals. Men: Follow the instructions for women, but reverse left and right leg positions, placing your right heel against your pubic bone.

YOGA MUDRA (GESTURE OF UNION)

Kneeling or in lotus pose, inhale as your arms float behind your back; clasp your hands and raise your arms behind you from the shoulders, stretching; exhale and lower your torso and head to the floor in front of you (KO). Rest, then inhale, raising your torso fully, and release your arms.

SARA HASTA BHUJANGA-ASANA (KING COBRA)

Lying flat on your stomach in the push-up position, inhale, raising first only your head, then your shoulders; then, pressing your hands into the floor, raise your torso with as much arching up and back as comfortably as possible while keeping your pelvis pressed into the floor. Stretch your eyes by looking up, and hold, and exhale while slowly lowering. In the cobra (bhujanga-asana), raise your torso three-quarters of the way up.

Beginner to Intermediate Asana Series

The basic twenty postures, as well as the postures for the more experienced, were given to me through the grace and good wishes of yogis in the lineage of Swami Kripalvananda. Both series systematically strengthen the bodily domains of each chakra by employing specific pranayamas (kumbhaka held out [KO] or held in [KI]) and chakra concentrations for each asana.

Each asana should be practiced two to five times or held for one to five minutes, as indicated on the chart. In repeated asanas, inhale while completing the expansive movement and hold with kumbhaka in (KI). Then exhale on lowering movements for each posture and hold the breath out (KO).

Where KI-KO is noted for asanas that are held for one to five minutes, breathe in the completed pose, employing kumbhakas at both the fully inhaled and fully exhaled points of each breath; "normal breath" during a held asana means just that. Begin coming out of the asana on an inhalation, as you move into the next with as few transitional movements or breaths as possible.

During the first six months, the series should be practiced without the chakra concentrations. Thereafter, attention should be paid to the concentration points and to any spontaneously arising bandhas or pranayamas. After approximately one year of daily or twice daily practice, the series can be done in an unbroken sequence, using only one breath during the transition from one posture to the next. If the lotus is uncomfortable, you may adapt a simple cross-legged position where indicated.

BASIC TWENTY POSTURES

ASANA	CHAKRA	DURATION	KUMBHAKA
yoga mudra in lotus	muladhara	2–5x	KI, KO
back-stretching (*pashchimottana-asana*)	muladhara	2–5x	KI, KO
spinal twist (*ardha-matsyendra-asana*)	svadhisthana	1–5 min each side	normal breath
mountain pose (*buddha-padma-asana*)	svadhisthana	2–5x	KO
lotus-swing (*lola-asana*)	manipura	2–5x	KI
lotus-balance chin lock (*dola-asana*)	manipura	1–5 min	KI, KO
lotus lying on back (*ardha-supta-padma-asana*)	manipura	1–5 min	KI, KO
fish (*matsyana-asana*)	anahata	1–5 min	KI, KO
reverse pose, lotus (*viparita karani-padma-asana*)	anahata	1–5 min	normal breath
plow (*hala-asana*)	vishuddha	1–5 min	normal breath
knee-ear (*karani pida-asana*)	vishuddha	1–5 min	normal breath
shoulder stand (*sarvanga-asana*)	vishuddha	1–5 min	normal breath
reverse, legs inclined posterior (*viparita karani*)	vishuddha	1–5 min	KI, KO

Asana	Chakra	Duration	Kumbhaka
gas release pose (*mukta pavana-asana*)	vishuddha	1–5 min	KI
bridge (*setu-asana*)	ajna	2–5x	KI
cobra, legs apart toes curled under (*bhujanga-asana*)	ajna	2–5x	KI
locust (*salabha-asana*)	ajna	2–5x	KI
bow (*dhanura-asana*)	ajna	2–5x	KI, KO
headstand (*sirsa-asana*)	sahasrara	1–5 min	normal breath
relaxation (*sava-asana*)	vishuddha	1–5 min breath	normal

FOR THE MORE EXPERIENCED

Asana	Chakra	Duration	Kumbhaka
head-to-knee, standing (*pada hasta-asana*)	manipura	2–5x	KO
back-stretching (*pashchimottana-asana*)	manipura	2–5x	KI, KO
spinal twist left, right (*ardha matsyendra-asana*)	manipura	1–3 min each side	normal breath
yoga mudra in lotus (*yoga mudra*)	muladhara	2–5x	KI, KO
lotus balance chin lock (*dola-asana*)	manipura	1–5 min	KI, KO
fish in lotus (*padma matsya-asana*)	anahata	5x	KI
reverse pose, lotus (*viparita karani padma-asana*)	vishuddha	5x	KI, KO
fold down in lotus (*chirsprishta-asana*)	vishuddha	5x	normal breath
knee-ear (*karani pida-asana*)	vishuddha	1–5 min	normal breath

Asana	Chakra	Duration	Kumbhaka
plow (*hala-asana*)	ajna	1–5 min	normal breath
shoulder stand (*sarvanga-asana*)	ajna	2–5 min	KI, KO
reverse pose (*viparita karani mudra*)	vishuddha	1–3 min	KI, KO
gas-release pose (*mukta pavana-asana*)	manipura	5x	KI
navel-gaze pose, lying on back (*nabhidara shana-asana*)	manipura	1–3 min	KI
relaxation pose (*sava-asana*)	vishuddha	1 min	normal breath
king cobra, legs apart, toes curled under (*sara hasta bhujanga-asana*)	manipura	5x	KI, KO
cobra, legs apart, toes curled under (*bhujanga-asana*)	ajna	5x	KI, KO
locust (*salabha-asana*)	manipura	5x	KI, KO
bow (*dhanura-asana*)	manipura	5x	KI, KO
headstand (*sirsa-asana*)	sahasrara	1–5 min	normal breath
relaxation pose (*sava-asana*)	vishuddha	1 min	normal breath

Another Advanced Series

Following is a set of advanced pranayama and purification practices that balance the sub-pranas and stimulate the nadis and chakras in a close sequence in preparation for meditation. These practices will be more useful for those with at least one year of yoga experience.

GHARSHANA PRANAYAMA

Inhale nasally from the chest and exhale by drawing the stomach muscles in, controlling the breath with the glottis (*ujjayi* breath), which produces a soothing, hissing-sighing sound in the throat. Do ten breaths, then do ten rounds of alternate nostril breathing without retention (kumbhaka). Repeat this sequence again. Then,

CHATUR BHUJA PRANAYAMA

Do ten rounds of alternate nostril breathing, of equal duration on inhaling and exhaling and holding out the breath (kumbhaka, KI, KO) each time for the count of ten. Then,

MAHA MUDRA, AGNISARA DHAUTI, MAHA VEDHA MUDRA

(This is an excellent series for sublimation.) Do maha mudra (page 99–100) to the right outstretched leg, holding inhalation (KI); then move to the lotus, exhaling, and hold the breath out (KO) for one breath while pumping the stomach muscles in and out repeatedly. This is agnisara dhauti. Then inhale in lotus, and use your hands against the floor to each side of you to raise your body off the floor, holding the inhalation (KI), and apply mula bandha and jalandhara bandha to your limit, and lower, exhaling. This is maha vedha mudra. Repeat maha mudra to the left leg, and go through the same sequence. Repeat the whole sequence two to five times, ending with maha mudra to the right leg. Then,

ASVINI MUDRA

In siddha-asana, contract and relax the anal sphincter, as in mula bandha, fifty times on an inheld breath (KI). Then,

YONI MUDRA

Using your thumbs, index fingers, middle, ring, and little fingers to close your ears, eyelids, nostrils, and upper and lower lips, take in a slow full breath and hold, pressing very gently against the eyelids on the lower edge of the bony socket (not on the cornea) to release eye tension in a flourish of colors and patterns. Watch them in meditative wonder. This completes the yoni mudra. Then, on the next inhalation,

CHAKRA ACTIVATION

Begin concentrating upon a point outside your body below the base of your spine, and internally say the mantra "humg" (ending with a nasal "mg") while bringing your attention to muladhara chakra; enter into the center

Yoni mudra

of the chakra with the mantra "hamg" (ending with a nasal "mg") and feel the blossoming of the chakra open with the mantra "sahhh." Repeat the combination of mantras and concentration exercises at each chakra, concluding with ajna chakra. Then return to muladhara chakra to repeat the whole sequence again.

BHASTRIKA
Perform a slow, full, deep inhalation with the silent mantra of "swaaa" and an exhalation with the silent "haaa." Ten rounds. Then,

NADI SHODHANA SAHITA KUMBHAKA
Alternate nostril breath with locks and retention, 1:4:2 ratio. Do four to

ten rounds. Conclude with your favorite meditation practice or meditate on the inner spontaneous sound known as *nada.*

Meditations for All

Meditation upon ajna chakra balances all other chakras by attuning them to the nondual poise of this center. Svadhisthana, the sexual center, comes more into balance in this attunement. Hold the nabhan-mudra (page 100) and occasionally the mula bandha (page 99).

Meditate upon the deity as the essence of mother, father, spouse, sister, brother, daughter, son, friend, lover, foe, teacher, student. Meditate upon the serene radiance of the moon as a source of coolly reflected sunlight, the essence of the unexplored forest, the blue of a cloudless sky, the flowing invisibility of crystal-water, the tranquil desirelessness of an unwavering flame, the milky, golden richness of a flowing nectar, the first rays of a sunrise and last rays of a sunset, the subtle movements of a sleeping animal or infant, the cosmic rhythms beyond choices and desires.

The Not-Enough-Time Routine

Practice daily is the golden rule of yoga. So to keep things rolling when you are in a pinch, here is a suggested fifteen-minute routine: Sit down and forget the rush. Do one hundred rounds of kapala-bhati (page 100) in sets of ten or more, according to your comfort, holding the breath out for a few seconds after each set, with the mula and jalandhara bandhas, and then holding the last breath in for a longer time, with the locks. Then do two different asanas, holding each posture for about three minutes, with a rest in between. For the rest of the time, five to eight minutes, do very relaxed, nadi shodhana sahita kumbhaka pranayama (page 100).

I suggest, generally, one hour of daily practice. Two hours per day is a minimum if you would like to see the effects that are possible if yoga becomes a central factor in your life. Of course, there are lesser known tips, like doing one round of alternate nostril breathing at red lights or during commercials (or even during regular TV for the more ascetic types), doing inner mantra meditation while waiting in lines, and so forth. Meditative awareness can also be practiced during the day by tuning in to the subtleties of the colors, sounds, interpersonal communications, and so forth of the external world.

The more formal daily practices should also be done—*should,* the most maligned guidepost of modern times. Can we be disciplined and regular without getting compulsive? Can we employ techniques yet stay open to the mercurial and serendipitous mystery?

Partner-Assisted Practices

Enjoy the close nonverbal rapport of sensing physical limitations while providing gentle support to maintain and deepen any stretch. Breathe and even sigh with each other, and sense the release of tensions during the holding of any position. In balance poses, use the breath to lighten yourselves, and focus your gaze on a stable point several yards away from you. Conclude a series of asanas by resting a comfortable degree of your full chest weight on the back of your partner, who is in child-pose (kneeling with the head resting face down on the floor and arms extending alongside the legs with the palms facing up). Please note that the partner-assisted practices in this section are contemporary adaptations of yogic and other stretching practices.

CORNUCOPIA

Sit on the floor facing your partner with your legs spread wide, holding your partner's legs apart with the edge of your feet on her knees or ankles; reach out and clasp hands to the wrists. As one of you slowly leans backward, the other comes forward; slowly move this leaning into a rotating movement, from the torso. Circle to the left and to the right. Breathe deeply, slowly, and rhythmically, concentrating on manipura when you are leaning back and on anahata when you are upright. Make the sound "mmmm" when leaning back and "aaahhhhh" when coming upright.

You might be able to feel a radiant field of pulsation around each other's genitals. You can discern how sublimative passion permeates this radiance with a natural rapport of desireless blending, while sex-desire passion will make you feel you are lacking something and need to get closer in order to end the longing. It might feel like a rhythm of its own, hidden within your first sensings of the radiance around each other's genitals and svadhisthana chakra areas.

Allow this union to keep spreading throughout your bodies and into the subtle and profound. This will add a gracefulness to your rowing movements and may make them utterly effortless and mysteriously erotic, yet without desire. You might be able to distinguish the procreative passion that pulses within your bodies in synchrony with ovulation-menstrual, lunar, and spermatogenic cycles.

These shared feelings and stretches can permeate chronic tension of back muscles, sometimes called sexual tension, and cause a pleasant release. Just give in to the stretch and gradually let go of the back pain and rigidity. The sublimative passion between the two of you will give you a key to this release. Womb, ovaries, and testicles also benefit through the relaxed stretchings and movements.

HEARTS AND BACKS

Standing back to back with your partner, reach your arms up and have your partner reach up and clasp you at the elbows or wrists, whichever is easier. Before lifting your partner completely onto your back, test his weight to assure your capacity to hold and balance him in the full position. You will then bend forward very slowly on an exhalation, lifting your partner onto your back and onto his toes, slightly, stretching open his chest. The underneath person can hold the exhalation out (KO) and perform stomach lifts, uddiyana bandha (page 99). The raised person will feel an opening of his chest around the heart. Sigh with any sensations of stretching in this area, and feel the vibrations of your sighing ripple through your heart area. The sighing can become more and more expressive of feelings from your heart as they spread into your throat and down into your belly. Your partner will feel the vibrations of any sighing and might join in.

Hold in this stretch, concentrating on anahata and feeling the connection of hearts, from back to back. You can also stretch your held arms slightly open to the sides, and then back toward the center, with the breath. Breathe with the sound "lllllllllllmmmmmmmmmm," from time to time, relaxing your throats and voices. Also, be aware of the contact points at the buttocks and back of the head.

After one to five minutes, exchange positions by rolling slowly up.

CRESCENT MOON

Begin the same as in Hearts and Backs, but stretch slowly and laterally to the left, then to the right, from the torso, in synchrony with the breath. Feel contact points at coccyx, back of heart area, and heads. Converse silently with energy and feeling through these points. Rock slowly and laterally from left to right to left, and become increasingly aware of manipura. Apply the anal lock (mula bandha, page 99) at each extreme of the stretch, and release the lock as you come to center. The stretch is in the sides; the activation point of movement is at the navel. As you find a rhythm to this lateral, swaying movement, feel a balancing of yin and yang, female and male, left and right, moon and sun, objects and space. With each sweep, feel sublimative passion swelling into desirelessness, out of any desirous passion, until your movements have become childlike and playful.

DUAL YOGA MUDRA, STANDING

Stand facing each other, feet shoulder-width apart, at such a distance that when you bend forward at the waist toward each other, your heads nearly touch. While erect, inhale very slowly as you float your hands behind your own backs; clasp your hands behind you, concentrate on muladhara, and slowly bend forward on the exhalation, bringing your head down toward your knees. Then reach your hands up and across to grasp each other at the wrists or forearms, and hold in this position, gently stretching down with your head and neck, and gently pulling at each other's wrists or arms. Feel the presence of your partner's head near your own and the field of space that you share surrounding your heads. Feel the sensations of energy flowing in your spine and perhaps even in your partner's spine. Feel the blood flowing into your head, and scan your legs and feet.

You can experiment with holding your breaths out (KO) and applying the three locks (see Bandhas, page 99), sensing any responses in muladhara. Feel the vibrations of energy at those times radiating up each other's arms as you hold your breath out. Come up slowly, when you want to, on an inhalation, first releasing your partner's wrists, and then exhale as you approach standing position, while your arms float around to your sides.

TWIN COBRAS

You will be doing the cobra facing opposite directions and away from each other, with one person's legs outside of the other's and resting on top of the inside partner's legs to hold them down. Raise your torsos up slowly, together, on an inhalation, and concentrate on svadhisthana on the way up, pressing your pelvises into the floor. You will feel your genitals, womb, or ovaries pressing down into the earth at this time. Feel the earth's energy and massive security holding the two of you in a rapport of giving and receiving through your pelvises. When you have raised your torsos and are each supporting your weight with your arms in the full cobra, move your concentration to ajna. Forget your partner completely. Just concentrate on ajna, with your eyes rolled up, open or closed. Hold and hold (KI). Then, lower on an exhalation, and repeat three to ten times, alternating your leg position with that of your partner. You can also raise in the twisting cobra, by shifting your head and shoulders left, snakelike, then right, then left, all the way up into the completed cobra pose.

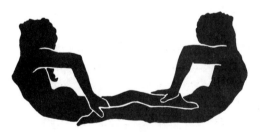

TWIN BOATS

This is similar to the twin cobras, but instead of supporting yourself on your hands, reach your hands behind you to the top of your partner's heels. As you come up on the inhalation (KI), hold onto each other's heels and pull slightly. You can each bend your legs slightly at the knee to draw your partner up a little more, if the extra stretch is needed. You can even start closer together, and then bending the knees to give additional stretching to the arms and legs will be easier. Concentration is on manipura.

SUBLIMATION VEE

Sit on the floor back to back with your legs together and straight out. Hook your arms at the elbow, both of you pressing your hands to the floor. Lean into each other at the head and shoulders, press your palms firmly against the floor, and raise up your legs on a slow inhalation, so you are in a vee pose. (Raising your legs just a few inches is sufficient in the beginning.) Hold, and do thirty rounds of kapala-bhati breath (page 100), then hold the last inhalation (KI) and apply the three locks (see Bandhas, page 99). Bring the energy to manipura and feel the sublimation. Lower on the exhalation and repeat three to twenty times.

This can be done with pillow supports under your raised legs in order to hold the pose longer. If using pillows, raise and lower your legs briefly, bending at the knees if necessary. This is a strenuous practice. Start slowly.

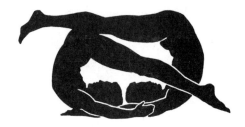

TWIN PLOWS

Lie straight out on your backs, head to head, and reach back to hook arms at the elbows. Raise up into the reverse pose (page 101) and feel the energy and blood supply lower into the abdomen, adrenal glands, kidneys, liver. Let the blood flow out of the legs. Continue to shoulderstand, touching at the ankles for balance, and concentrate on ajna. Then lower your legs back over your head and into the plow (page 101). One partner's legs come to rest on either side of the other's buttocks, and the other rests her legs on her partner's buttocks. Feel the harmony of this balance and the opening of the vertebrae. Breathe and sigh in this pose, gently rocking each other, with micromotions. You can return to a shoulder stand and then lower into the plow again, reversing the position of your legs to give you each a leg-stretch to the floor.

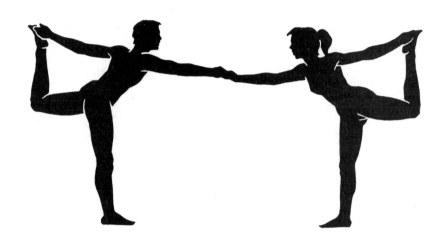

TWIN DANCERS' POSE

Stand facing each other at a distance that allows your outstretched arms to meet in wrist grips. Hold this position, right hand to right hand. Then lift your left leg behind you, bending the knee, and clasp it with your left hand. You will be balancing with each other to accomplish this. Drawing your leg up and up with your arm completes this most aesthetic ars erotica pose.

To help maintain your balance, fix your focus on a spot on the floor or wall until you come down, on an exhalation. Reverse and repeat. You will have to adjust for differences in weight and size, but, theoretically, any two people can come into balance for increasingly longer periods of time once they discover how to work together. Children with adults find this a great practice. In fact, most of these ars erotica practices can be done with all members of the family, over the age of four, without discomfort.

I encourage you to allow the spontaneity of sublimative passion to lead you into further improvisations. Erotic life suffers under constant regimentation.

Chair and Bed Yoga

Age and physical condition need not be limitations to the practice of tantric celibate transmutation. Following are some practices that can be tried:

- Leg lifts, raising slowly on the inhalation, holding with locks, and lowering on the exhalation. Raise your legs a few inches or more but never strain yourself. Holding the ends of a six-foot-long cloth, stretched under your knees, you can raise and lower your legs with the cloth, if necessary. Concentrate on manipura.

- Shoulder, neck, wrist, ankle, and hip rotations, done slowly in synchrony with breathing, and reversing direction of rotation.

- All pranayamas (page 100), adapted to your position.

- Eye rotation exercises and up-and-down rolling of closed eyes while visualizing the sublimative flow of energies throughout the body.

- Squeezing and relaxing fists and feet, with the in and out breaths.

- Undulating the spine with the breath and concentrating on various chakras.

For those unable to move physically, meditation upon the images of asanas, perhaps while viewing a video course, can induce some of the effects of performing the asanas within the causal, mental, vital, and physical bodies. Recommended video courses include *Yoga Journal Video Series* for beginners and intermediates, the *Positively Yoga* video by James Gagner, and the *Forever Flexible* video by Lilias Folan, especially for older yogis. Kripalu Center in Lenox, Massachusetts, also offers a selection of excellent video courses. *Healing Yoga,* an audiotape by Kelly Piper, is another option.

Family Practice Ideas

- Along with grace before meals, try three rounds of rhythmic or alternate nostril breathing.

- Using a children's yoga book as a guide, practice asanas together, with favorite music in the background.

- Have the younger members of the family teach the older ones a new stretch or other practice.

- Massage children, so they learn to receive a variety of types of physical contact.

Prenatal yoga books (and often classes) are available. Practice of asvini mudra (page 108), bhadra-asana (page 103), and nadi shodhana (page 109) are generally helpful to prepare for labor and delivery. This goes for fathers as well as mothers.

7

RELATIONAL WORSHIP

♦

The primary word I-Thou can be spoken only with the
whole being. Concentration and fusion into the whole being can never take place through my agency, nor can it ever
take place without me. I become through my relation to the
Thou; as I become I, I say *Thou.*
All real living is meeting.

Martin Buber
I and Thou

In this chapter, we will speak of going deeper into each other, of being
open to each other, of feelings brought to an exquisite pitch, of a gentle
patience and rhythmic calm. Initially such descriptions might seem purely
metaphoric; with some yogic experiences, however, they will seem literal
yet utterly distinct from sex and apt in their own right.

In these early stages, love, commitment, and passion are expressed
through feeling each other patiently, even confusingly, endeavoring to discover the sublimative tonalities. For what you see is not some perfected
state of tantric nirvana but your utterly human partner entering, just as
you yourself are, an unknown erotic world, while the more familiar one
might still be sending beckoning images. We become partners in this most
uncommon and uncharted exploration of brahmacharya relationship, perhaps also sharing how little we actually know about erotic mystery rather
than how much skill and prowess we have.

That is, we engage in a literal sharing of innocence, wonder, courage, and humility. Sexual thoughts, should they emerge, can seem to be a familiar refuge from this nakedly intimate contact. The early weeks of practice, then, evince a naïve faith. This phase can be short. Appreciate it with the exploratory feel of a second adolescence.

Longings intensify and subside over and over again as various emotional peaks are released in patient hopes of an utterly desireless rapport. Your glands and nerves buzz with energy and arousal while, gradually, the ardor of desirelessness initiates an internal alchemical process, the conversion of bindu into ojas and virya. As the weeks continue, the heightened energies are reabsorbed, allowing your glands and cells to be nourished by this once-enhanced essence.

Therefore, in the months ahead, your glandular arousals will be slightly more fulfilling, charged-up, or desireless than previously. At this incrementally "higher" level of baseline functioning, these newly produced essences will be even more charged than the last, to be raised infinitesimally higher in the months to come.

Over and over again, this hermetic, alchemical passion energizes lachrymose, salivary, genital, pineal, hypothalamus, and pituitary activity as well as the chakras and subtle energies. Amrita, the nectar of human materiality, and its alchemical precursors send their love-intoxicating richness to the roots of our physicality. Here we experience another facet of Natha's secret teaching from Jnaneshvar's commentaries: "One body feeds upon another" (1987, p. 134). In more physiological terms, we initiate the gradual unfoldment of "post-genital puberties."

Subjectively, in the months and years to come, we find sublimation satisfying us, and we release our over-gripping insecurities and under-gripping hopelessnesses. We begin to feel possibility as an essence, a kind of verb that makes things possible, not just as a set of viable, nounlike options. We feel mystery is a new kind of intuitive knowledge. How so? Perhaps the "DNA" of ojas and virya now informs our lives.

The following tantric practices are indications of a certain direction for intimacy and growth. They are not just instructions to be enacted or another set of erotic conventions to be performed and perfected. They are a set of structured suggestions designed to reveal the nuances of sublimative passion. Mystery, subtlety, and discovery take precedence over formality and performance. In tantric sublimation, there are no missionary positions to adhere to or rebel against.

If the yogic practices I describe do not cover your particular innovations and experiences, remember that there are perhaps 840,000 describable yogic practices and not all are requisite for each person. Although each description is a composite of various early, intermediate, and advanced phenomena spanning many months, years, and even decades, I may have missed the ones you are having. Far more than comparative analysis and, certainly, far more than competitive comparison, the spirit of evermore desireless wonder will always be your most reliable thread into the mystery.

THE GREAT GESTURE

Sitting opposite each other, hold hands so that right palms face down and left palms face up. This position is based on the tantric principle that energy enters us through the left hand and is transmitted out through the right. Next, focus your gaze upon each other at the midpoint between the eyebrows. Continue to gaze at each other, going through various phases of recognition, mood, and attention.

Allow your focus to soften so that your vision becomes momentarily blurred, pulsing with your heartbeat. Then, very slowly, refocus. Do this periodically. It will allow your eye muscles to relax and to make possible subtle shifts of perception. Your partner's face will very likely change in appearance, perhaps seeming older or younger, more radiant, or filled with the impressions of past emotion and attitudes. You might also see a sense of his essence, a kind of pervasive quality that permeates all his aspects and actions. In these pulsings, vision reveals a living world. This relaxed vision is an early stage of pratyahara.

Try to find a balance point where you are equally aware of your own presence and the presence of your partner. As you come to hovering at this point of equal internal and external awareness, you will likely feel a kind of spacious opening occur, even a sense of timelessness. Your partner might appear profoundly unique to you in a curiously unsuspected way. As one husband said during his very first try, "I realized for the first time that my wife was giving me the love that I had always been looking for. I had just never really seen who she was before."

It becomes clear, as time passes, that you are each reflecting in your responsive countenance the image of beholding the other. You feel you have known each other for an indeterminate amount of time, perhaps forever. You experience yourselves as the same. You see a deepening beautification surface from each other's depths into the skin, eyes, and spirit, and it seems that this emerging beauty is the living response to your every willingness to see it. Much of what you see that moves you so is your partner's response to you, creating a kind of natural biofeedback that deepens intimacy. The beautification of each other feels to be endless and moving to ever more profound levels of assessment. Early dharana, as the sense of an underlying unity, flutters.

Drink your partner in through your eyes and pores. Each time you lower your eyelids, feel the caressing of his essence with your eyelashes. You will see his eyes moisten ever so slightly, but these secretions transmute from apparent sadness into compassion, shy trepidation, and love. The varieties of tears are legion, revealing a whole expansive world of meanings and submeanings in every radiance. If vision is through tears, which refract the entering light with a prismatic effect, who is to decide whether the dancing rainbows we see are best described as miraculous wonderments or merely as a peripheral and insignificant scientific property of optics?

Shyness and blushing might also emerge, overcoming you with blue-pink whispers of unbearable beauty. For shyness always heralds a greater sense of being seen and known, of seeing and feeling someone seeing and feeling us. We blush in catching another seeing us, for shyness is the innocence that consecrates each birth and revelation of the soul. Shyness is not a problem; it is a precarious mystery tenderly shared.

Perhaps a tear will streak down your cheek, and you realize how much there is to you and your partner, how responsively connected you are to each other. Other tears might follow, yet you feel only momentarily melancholic, then joyous, embarrassed, then wholly softened, for these are the living tears of the present "inner adult" of anahata chakra. If pains and angers from the past emerge, see them wavering, like desert mirages, and then dissolve into the inestimable passions of virya, leaving you in the ever-forgiving vividness of the evanescent present.

In the togetherness now, the experience called Sharing This emerges. Such "suchness" is the furthering of dharana, revealing the near-unbroken flow of mutually absorbed contact. Couples feel, "We are really in it together!"

Perhaps the longing in your genitals, abdomen, heart, and throat, which mounts, subsides, and shifts, now swells into your heart and throat. A subtle salivation, perhaps of a sweetened taste, hints its way into your mouth. In your unguarded state, it seeps out of the corners. You feel utterly innocent and uncontrolled, and your partner appears the same way, in the spell of bodily transformations.

An undisguised openness and steady receptivity begin to unfurl, as heavy and unruffled as a warm flow of sacred oils. A breathless moment. A ringing silence. You both slowly close your eyes. Darkness. One psyche or soul. An ever-growing brightness dawns.

Throughout your whole body an inward caress caresses selflessly; mystics have called it "the inward touch of the divine." You feel a still deeper silence. A wonder arises; it shapes itself and becomes a question: "Is this the soul of me or is it my partner's?" Interrogation reverts to sheer wonder. Dharana, silence, dhyana. Billowing essence of boundaryless love here, there, everywhere. A sound, a smooth sound—breathing; one bloodstream, one pulsebeat, one passageway in: mother-father birth; the in-between; and then, out. Sounds of breathing in and out.

Your sighs of intimacy have now become deeply appreciative. You feel a tingling pass between the palms of your held hands. It traces up your left arm, into your throat, and down into your heart, abdomen, genitals, and spinal base. You begin to experience the subtle body channels, energies, and chakras. You can feel the spontaneous movement of sublimative passion sending currents of pleasure throughout the internal musculature of your body, triggering the bandhas and various mudras. You experience having a human body as a kind of fortuitous stroke of genius on Someone's part, while the buoyancy of desireless attraction to the world around you feels as light and responsive as consciousness itself.

Serenely still, your breathing suspends and suspends. Time withers, place evaporates. Kundalini-shakti stirs. Heat grows stronger and stronger within muladhara, your throat, your heart, in ajna between the eyes, in the midbrain area. Nabhan and khechari mudras stir. Effortlessly, your tongue weaves back into your throat. A glow of electrical heat quivers, connecting the root of your tongue, throat, heart, spine, and perineum. A space of light opens. Time and more time, all is just time. The words pass, it's time, it's time.

You open your eyes slowly to a world of brilliance; the heavy-laden vineyards of the spirit have ripened.

> A fountain of gardens, a well of living waters, and streams from Lebanon.

Awake, O north wind; and come, thou south; blow upon my garden, that the spices thereof may flow out. Let my beloved come into his garden, and eat his pleasant fruits.

(Song of Solomon 4:15–16)

You rest into each other's arms, feeling the heat and energy that is within and between you. Sitting up, you meditate quietly for an indeterminate time, then separate palms and smile, perhaps with some shyness.

NYASA

In *nyasa,* touch enters the concentration of pratyahara and the mood of bhakti, devotional reverence. The subtleties of energetic transfer give it a tantric gist. You will need a vial of scented oil, not for massage or lubrication but as an anointment. It should be special oil; if not, the practice of nyasa will cause it to become special, for nyasa is subtle empowerment through touch, a kind of worship.

Decide who will anoint whom first. Apply some oil to the middle two fingers of each of your right hands. Sitting across from each other, establish contact through gazing.

As the romantic subtleties of pratyahara emerge, slowly begin to raise your right hand in synchrony with the steadiest of inhalations, as if the breath itself raises hand and arm, body, gaze, and all toward the midbrow point of your partner's forehead. If breath should fill, pause; then, exhaling, continue the movement. Continue in this way so slowly that perhaps ten minutes pass before you have neared your partner's forehead. Each moment carries another degree of closeness and is unique. All else has faded into the periphery. Dharana glimmers.

You come closer and closer until the very radiance of your fingers can be felt by your partner. Within inches, another microworld opens up. As in time-lapse photography of an unfurling rose, duration dissolves like salt in the oceans. Nothing is forced. It just happens. Contact is made and a wholeness of selves responds; bodies enliven, chakras whirl, koshas harmonize, sublimative distillates quicken.

Contact continues, essences mix together; the mystery of desireless commitment, of following a mystery, surfaces. Eyes close. Opinions dis-

Nyasa

solve; marriage, no longer an "institution," choice, or task, becomes a living verb, a marrying of the two; gender-sharing becomes a reverence; dharana and dhyana glimmer; samadhi hovers in the far distance; release begins.

Your hand lowers in synchrony with your exhalation until you are at your partner's throat level. Similarly, you approach and finally touch just above the notch of the collarbone, where the windpipe recedes into the neck to carry the life air inward. Another world, different in time (for "time" has passed, "then" is invisibly gone) and being (for vishuddha now shows us other qualities of being), emerges. Other radiances, subtle hopes, and intimacies spark. Inspiration renews itself, the birth of words from ineffable missives.

> . . . yet they went impossibly on with their kneeling, in undistracted attention; so inherently hearers. Not that you could endure the voice of God—far from it. But hark to the suspiration, the uninterrupted news that grows out of silence.
>
> (Rilke, *Duino Elegies*)

Release. Lower your hand all the way and preserve eye contact until you feel like closing your eyes to follow the mystery, intuitively bypassing visual perception completely. Dwell. As you open your eyes, exchange the roles of anointer and anointed.

Although nyasa can empower any of the chakras, the sublimative passion does not prefer svadhisthana as being more erotic than others merely because that chakra is associated with genital arousal. Each chakra has its own characteristic tonality of passion and energy. At certain points it may be unclear who is the initiator of this movement, the anointer or the anointed. Doing this practice with eyes closed creates another sort of spatial context through reaching out to touch the anointed.

MYSTERY OF BALANCE

Sitting cross-legged or in chairs, knee to knee, facing each other, join hands and raise your arms straight up, balancing their weight. Relax all other muscles and focus gently and steadily on your partner at ajna. As your arms get heavier and heavier, notice all the compelling questions you have about what you think you should do, what you think it means to your partner, what you think your partner wants you to do about it, what your proper roles are, and so on.

What is maleness, femaleness, my needs or yours, caretaking, loving too much? What is commitment? All the popular "certainties" that circulate in the great anonymous now circulate in your own mind. Yet the weight continues, even if you cry or yell, "How much longer?" The fight last night

Mystery of Balance

or ten years ago, the little irritations of each other, like flotsam, float through your mind. None of these tirades, diagnoses, or "feelings-gotten-in-touch-with" help for long. In fact, they seem to separate you from something else: what is happening wordlessly, looking and straining and wondering, between the two of you now. *That* is an erotic mystery unfolding.

As you just share the weight, reaching ever more passionately upward, you find the balance Now. Mysteriously, the weight is "gone." On and on the weightlessness of your arms continues, wavers, then returns for five minutes; or perhaps fifteen, twenty, a half hour, or longer. No complaints, criticisms, just the sharing of a difficulty that has, mysteriously, become something profound. Such sharing cannot be explained easily. Your inner adult emerges and grows in faith; the pains of your earlier years, no longer mere wounds, reveal their dignities (as you marvel at the subtle energetics and yogic processes just beneath the obvious, involving the early subtleties of virya).

You lower your arms, roll your eyes in astonishment, for your sharing of the difficulty has transformed it, perhaps waveringly and perhaps not on the first try but never without interesting results. This curious balance is not a goal; it is an inexplicable side effect of mystery shared.

The Mystery of Balance can also be done in a group, with members seated in a circle, each holding up her neighbor's arms and gazing at the others in the circle. The power of the group can often be even more mysterious than that of the couple. Members feel the collective involvement as a sense of loyalty, brother- or sisterhood. The group's purposes and struggles feel shared and uplifting for each individual who is having the same weightiness bearing down on her.

You can use a timer to set the duration of this practice if you wish. Without a timer, another possibility avails.

PRANIC MIRRORING

In this practice, you will be moving as in the slow-motion practice of yoga asanas, synchronizing breath with movement, but you will be doing it while mirroring your partner's simple movement as he mirrors yours. Taking three to five minutes, you might slowly reach across the space to touch hands or perhaps to exchange a rose or a gift. Integrate pratyahara and dharana concentrations into the practice as well.

Dancing, of course, is a perfect activity in which to enjoy various permutations of pranic mirroring. Ecstatic dancing and Sufi whirling are well-known versions of passionate, yet desireless, dancing.

THE SINGULAR CELIBATE KISS

Tantric lovemaking can appear rather predetermined, especially in the first weeks of practice. The single celibate kiss is an example of bringing an ordinary erotic gesture into the celibate context. In conventional sexuality, the genital orgasm is the final gesture of erotic exchange. It is a way of dealing with the endlessness of erotic mystery within the driving currents of desire. That is the temporal function of the orgasm: to bring sex to an obvious and climactic close.

In tantric sublimation, a single kiss can seal the meaning of the moment; for that is what is being called for when eros reaches this pitch: a sign, a ritual, a mudra or gesture that expresses what words cannot say. Then, as this singular communication is completed, we allow the mystery of sublimation to absorb what has just been "said." Usually, we go on seeking more and more sexual arousal through the enactment of escalating sexual desires. In tantric sublimation, we find another sort of erotic "moreness" in the meditative depth of the single kiss.

Remember the first kiss of a relationship? There is nothing to compare it to, and there never will be. There is a whole world of erotic meaning, value, and experience that comes from honoring and preserving the innocence and mystery that is revealed at such times. The first kiss, the singular embrace, deprived of a second, drops our hunger into the chasms of mystery. The eros of nonattachment and subtlety dawns.

BREATHING MYSTERY

After establishing meditative eye contact or after the Great Gesture or nyasa, allow the feelings of *transmuting* passion to become audible sighs. Sharing of these sighs leads to further sharing of them into greater subtleties rather than toward sex.

Allow the mystery of hearing each other's audible transmutation to affect you. This sets up an exchange of feeling that, over and over again, passes through the fires of sublimation. Louder or softer or even into vaguely audible whispers, there is no singular direction, no specific crescendo to aim for.

MANTRA CHANTING

According to the theory of mantra, specific sound vibrations have specific effects on various chakras and emotions. The mantras resonate and stimulate the chakras through this subtle vibrational massage. Melody and rhythm add two other common elements for erotic exchange, yet the medium will once again be voices and feeling. Pratyahara and dharana emerge more easily when we have fed upon the sensations of mantra.

This practice can be engaged in alone, with a partner, or in larger groups with the use of instruments. The chanting can proceed on a steady tempo, or it can be carried away by the escalations of sublimative yearning into faster and faster rhythms, at times surrendering even the formal mantras into laughing, crying, sighing, and so forth.

Several cyclings from slow to faster and climactic tempos can reveal a depth of passsion that has earned bhakti yoga the reputation of being the most profoundly mysterious of yogas, unfolding the entire path to one who merely continues to surrender to its emotional depths. Even spontaneous dancing or impassioned pranayama and asanas can emerge. Thus, chanting is often called the nectar of devotion. The mantras Ram, Om, Hari-om, Namo-shivaya, Sita-Rama, and Om bhur bhuva swaha are some possibilities. If chanting Hindu mantras feels too foreign to you, the sound "ahhh" is in itself exhilarating.

The spiritual side of mantra chanting as a devotional practice can also be explored. As such, the deity enters into the chanting, as in gospel or charismatic hymn singing. In any case, the mantras can be explored for their therapeutic effects upon the emotions and subtle bodies of the practitioners.

RITUAL WORSHIP OF MYSTERY

Rituals reveal feelings of reverence, gratitude, honor, offering, and sanctity that many couples experience toward each other only during their marriage ceremony. Bringing these sentiments to mundane tasks can transform them into tantric practices.

You can create fire, water, earth, and air rituals, group chanting and nyasa practices, anniversary rituals, fertility rituals, menopause rituals, rituals for sharing the vows of brahmacharya, pregnancy, birth, and naming rituals, sunrise and sunset rituals, and home-building rituals.

The use of symbolic ritual objects, gift giving, role reversals, and other dramatizations gives celibate ritual a breadth of possibility similar to what acting out fantasies in conventional sexuality can provide. While enacted fantasies literalize desires, rituals spiritualize our passion, so the two prove to be worlds apart. Rituals, however, are erotic through and through, revealing for a time the hidden powers that surround us, always.

A Sunrise Ritual

Wake up two hours before sunrise; bathe and dress each other. Separate for forty-five minutes of individual yoga practices. Feel both the solitude and the longing for reunion. Reunite at the specified time. Bow before each other. Share nyasa and meditate together with the rising sun, beginning twenty minutes before sunrise. Feel the effects of its slowly building energies. Share the Great Gesture for some minutes after sunrise. Bow and thank each other and the day.

Secret Knowledge Ritual

One of you is the initiate and the other is the initiator in explaining a new aspect of tantric celibate lovemaking. The latter serves by teaching, and the former leads by being curious, and thus the mystery of shared power is revealed, even when it is made clear that one of you "knows" something that the other will learn. The *Tao Te Ching* speaks of the "utmost mystery" as the close mesh between teacher and student, so intimate that an onlooker is unable to discern the roles.

One-Word Ritual

In the Great Gesture, take turns slowly expressing one word or phrase to each other, over and over, for example, "commitment," "yes," "love," "I know only *this*," "together," "deeper," "more."

PROBLEMS, DIFFICULTIES, AND OTHER KNOTS

When it comes to such problems as relationship struggles, slips in one's celibate vows, nocturnal orgasm or emission, or lapses in one's regular yoga practice, we find that tantric sublimation is neither utopian bliss nor an arduous and penitent discipline. Problems of this kind are not a sign that you are sinning, dysfunctional, or inadequate. They can be addressed with the "home remedies" of yogic lore and practices, or they can be explored as immediate springboards into further sublimation; in other words, our problems become viyogic, hidden unions rather than pathologies, potential negative patterns, shortcomings, or embarrassments. Embarrassment or a sense of inadequacy, as we have seen, is merely another tonality of intimate and erotic self-revelation.

Curios

The folk remedies that I have accumulated over the years, like the trade secrets of a small guild of craftspeople whose art has slipped from public interest, are quaint, quick to tell, and probably more curio than cure. They give a little charm to the practice.

The most well known museum piece is the cold shower: useful but jolting. Sharing a pot of sage tea, scullcap tea, valerian root tea, or ginger and cinammon tea is a soothing way to spend an evening telling celibacy stories around a campfire and will have a calming or balancing effect. But the effects of such practices must be considered as limited.

Diet and Sleep

Since svadhisthana is both the sexual and the taste center, some attention to diet can prove useful. Try a lighter diet, less spicy, in moderate portions, eaten earlier in the day, and leaning more toward vegetarian foods and away from heavy animal proteins. The lore of no garlic, onions, or mushrooms (too sexually stimulating, it is said) is worth experimenting with on an individual basis. Occasional fasting can provide a dual recovery of a balanced relationship with food and with sexuality. Some yogis prescribe fasting for one day a week, merely to relax the digestive system. I suggest exploring and sampling what appeals to you and finding out for yourself what you feel has value.

Going to sleep earlier and arising earlier, as in the Franklin adage, can be helpful, given the facts that yogic practices have a greater effect before sunrise and most nocturnal orgasms happen around sunrise. Elimination of wastes before sunrise is important because the rising sun stimulates the bloodstream and our first surges of morning circulation will be purer—a rare point of celibacy trivia!

When Sex Happens

Let's say that you end up engaging in conventional sex in spite of all guidance and vows; you either masturbate or make love with someone. As one of my teachers says, "Do it with awareness." (And remember contraceptive and safe sex guidance!) Observe all the ins and outs of sensuality, of sexual conventionalities, of desire. Take all that you have learned from tantric sublimation about subtlety, sensitivity, lovemaking, energy, and intimacy into your activity.

If you can recover the nuance of sublimation, you might find yourselves drawing away from the conventional sexual behaviors that lead to orgasm and becoming quiet with each other. Tune in to your partner and yourself at the most subtle levels of sensation and allow your experiences to move in the direction of meditation.

Shift your bodily focus toward the base of your spine, heart, throat, or ajna chakra. Feel energy moving into your spine and within the chakras. You might find an energetic route different from the sexologist's path to the orgasmic point of no return. If you have proceeded blissfully toward the release and reflexes of orgasm, just enjoy it and take it all in. Later, you can make your way back to the passions of sublimation. But at such times it is best to be with each other in the passions of desire.

You can think of breaks in your sublimation as the result of overcharging the annamaya and pranamaya koshas, the physical and vital energy bodies. This buildup through overstimulation can become more than the subtle bodies can handle through sublimation. Thus, be thoughtful about partaking of situations that you consider arousing, without repressing yourself. Such are the finer points of tantric practice and decision making.

All of this takes time, patience, and commitment. By staying close to the "middle way," you will preserve the direction of sublimation, without resenting what it takes to get there. Breaks can be an opportunity for unconditional self-acceptance and for accepting your partner, freed from perfectionist ideals. As Mike and Nancy discovered, celibacy brings to the surface many of the same struggles that conventionally sexual couples face.

Mike and Nancy broke their vow of brahmacharya after seeing a movie—only R-rated at that. They were afraid to stop midway in their conventional lovemaking because they each felt that it was the other who "needed to be sexual." Neither wanted to "hurt" the other by frustrating or judging him or her. Yet they both hoped that the other would somehow draw away from sex, toward a tantric practice.

Their sexual exchange felt to be part erotic mystery and love and part automatic habits. They fought about who was more disappointed by this slip, who really wanted to try sublimation more, and whose fault it was. They began apologizing as they felt how big erotic mystery really is, how, at times, it is even beyond our best intentions. They smiled and admitted liking having sex with each other.

They recovered their connection to tantric sublimation as a commitment to as yet unknown possibilities through this spoken passion. They decided that for a while at least, they would forego movies that might overcharge them in the conventional way.

They went over the details of how they moved into sex and uncovered certain sly feelings of each wanting to be irresistible to the other, as if one's power was heightened by being able to draw the other off the vow. It was the same way Mike would typically feel when he started going out with Nancy, and with women in general. He felt he had to and wanted to impress them. Mike was seduced into this slip by this hopeful image of himself as seductive.

Nancy had long believed that her femininity was related to her sexual effect on men. She remembered how satisfying it would be just to see men, out of the corner of her eye, turn their heads as she passed. This subtle need for attention, and the enjoyable desire to affect men, seemed to have opened her to the slip.

She and Mike meditated in the Great Gesture and spoke slowly to each other of how much beauty and erotic power they each saw in the other. They saw the limited nature of their explanations for "how it happened." Beyond blame and even explanation, the mystery of shared gender washed away their theories and opinions.

Desire and Sublimation Reconciled

Relating to a much larger social world that is pursuing the ways of sex-desire presents the tantric sublimator with the danger of becoming judgmental of others. Why be celibate if it isn't "superior" to sex, one might ask. A tempting question, with a potentially heavy price to be paid if one tries to answer it, particularly while in a competitive mood.

Pursuing sublimation and loving celibately while derogating sex-desire diminishes one's innocence. Such has been called "spiritual materialism": using meditative and other practices to feel superior to others. What good is any form of spiritual practice if it contributes to alienation or a condescending elitism? Any form of erotic mystery will always shrink from those who judge or shame it. Avoid the literalness of the above question. Remaining in wonder, experience the celibate's "chaste love" for the world of sex-desire as being just more of the mystery.

I have described the tantric path in as orderly a fashion as possible, but do not be misled. The way is not easy. The tonalities of desire are always nearby, but so are those of sublimation.

Staying Loose, Playing, and Humor

> I say unto you: one must still have chaos in oneself to be able
> to give birth to a dancing star.
>
> (Nietzsche, 1970, p. 129)

Sex is one arena of life in which spontaneity comes out from hiding behind adult decorum and we let our hair down, for reasonless, spontaneous play is an extension of the child's innocent erotic life. With all the preparatory rituals, the structurings of position, breath, concentration, focus upon sublimation and subtlety, how can we ever just "be" with each other?

Playful contact, affection, comforting each other, and even massage are all forms of nonsexual touch. "What about this kind of play? this kind of touch?" To find our answer, the judging or cynical mind, our own or that of others, must wait outside. "What is essential is often invisible to the eye," saith our foxy master. Ultimately, a trusting innocence will need to prevail.

For the too serious sublimator, the annals of celibate conduct note the rare practice of whipped-cream nyasa or the occasional yoga routine to the Rolling Stones. There are even a few celibacy jokes, all of them very bad, such as this: What is the clapping sound of one celibate screwing in a light bulb? Answer: Celibates don't _____ in light bulbs, don't you know!

Without needing to obsessively split hairs, we can discern the difference between playing lightheartedly in one's celibacy and toying with it. There will be a quiet or, at times, more obvious difference between affectionately teasing your partner and "getting at" him. In different contexts, the same comment can be funny or not funny at all. Eros is always a matter of innuendo, and playful eros can become quite rough and in need of a little lightening up. Perhaps a simple apology and forgiveness will reveal the more freeing kind of play in no time. Remember to leave some nonexacting room for the dancing chaos.

Also, be aware of the tendency toward "preciousness." All the subtleties of sublimation can get to you. There is no reason to stop being earthy, juicy, and ordinary just because you are on the sublimative way.

Support for Celibate Traditions in Modern Times

Except for those living on Mount Athos or elsewhere cloistered, modern monastics and celibate clergy are subjected to all manner of modern stimulations that can place great stress on their vows. Such simple and nonsectarian practices as alternate nostril breathing or yoni mudra (page 108) can prove helpful in gathering one's energies.

Gradual Celibacy

To make the path to sublimative passion more accessible to a greater number of people who might otherwise remain unattracted to its mysteries, I offer a "gradual celibacy," a two-step approach to its precincts.

In the first step, all manner of conventional sexual activity can be explored, but the partners (or the individual) must try to delete the endpoint known as genital orgasm from the exploration. A sort of endlessness can emerge, since this phase does not exhaust the partners in orgasm. Lovemaking can last many hours, with periods of meditation, breathing practices, and stretching included. If orgasm should occur, just let go of what it might "mean." Avoid the allure of cynicism and guilt. Merely proceed in continuing your practice toward subtlety, helping yourself and your partner. Remember, a monthly orgasmic exchange still fits the yogic sexual ecology of brahmacharya.

Gradually, in the second phase, more and more of the sublimative practices are added to the lovemaking until the greater amount of time is spent with the rituals and meditations of the tantric practice. The transition might be hardly noticeable; you suddenly find yourselves celibate. If you start missing sex, try just missing it. Feel the longing until it spreads into suggestive innuendos, then evanescent subtleties, and then desireless passion. If desire returns, you might be able to miss the wonder of sublimation. Miss this wonder, feel the longing for it, until the longing spreads into innuendos and subtleties and then desirelessness. And so on.

8

GROUNDING
IN THE ORDINARY:
TANTRIC RELATING IN
EVERYDAY LIFE

◆

What about all the verbal struggles of love? What about the day-to-day trying to "make it work"? We have covered the heights of subtlety; what about the nitty-gritty of the more ordinary when we say to each other "I need to talk"?

SPOKEN PASSION

Speaking with tongues is fiery speech, speech as a sexual act, a firebird or phoenix.

(N. Brown, 1966, p. 251)

Verbal intercourse is the process of coming to understandings: the first words exchanged by intrigued strangers at a party; the auspicious closing words of a first real date; the first fight and all further difficult and passionate communications of apology, forgiveness, accusation, demands, ultimatums, confessions, and resolution; the heightened moments of avowal, gratitude, praise; the innocence of kidding and playing; poetic characterizations of love; proposals to live together, marry, conceive a child, separate, end separation. Such are the more momentous erotic communications, each generating a unique spectrum of emotions, "orgasms," possibilities, and sense of mystery.

As an erotic medium, language is alive with suggestiveness, and even our most black-and-white statements are replete with innuendos, mutability, and implication. All take place in time, thus all bloom and wither in evanescent emotional subtleties. Within the domains of mystery, verbal communication must honor what cannot be said at the present time, what remains implied and ambiguous—between the lines, cleavages, and passages of language itself.

In support of the current psychological interest in clear and direct communication skills, I add my concern for the subtler aspects of nuance, the inscrutable but irrepressible value of the unspoken and untranslatable textures of different silences and gestures. Both precisely hewn clarity and unspeakable poignancy have their place in spoken passion.

What lives in poignancy flickers within the impossible becoming possible, like a child's first steps, like the profusely meaningful warbling in one's voice while proposing marriage or the rise of one's anger already softening before the contrition in the eyes of the accused. The openness of our perception and the living responsiveness of the mercurial perceived are always at stake, for what we miss in any moment shrinks our world into one of ever-grosser generalizations and lifeless approximations.

We must remain meditatively sensitive to the flowering of emotional subtleties that moment to moment rectifies the past. An ear tuned to mystery reveals innuendos of apology for the harm done in every sarcasm; nuances of trepid hope to be accepted in each defensive remark; a backhanded well-wishing in each shaming slur—in the other's or our own voice.

We continue in this section by redefining the primary word of the erotic vocabulary of relationship, *commitment,* and its epiphenomena or "side effects" of marriage, fidelity, and separation in terms of mystery rather than desire. Then we discuss *viyoga* and *spoken passion*—the erotic nature of struggling with the problems within a relationship. Next, we consider the erotic freedom of *belonging,* in contrast to that of license and desire-fulfillment. These explorations set a context of daily living in which the *dharmas,* or ways, of family life or solitary life can unfold tantrically.

COMMITMENT AND MARRIAGE WHEN EROS IS MYSTERY

In the erotic world, our promises and vows are to possibilities and potentialities laboring into birth in the suspenseful moments we share, more than to certainties and preconceived expectations. How, then, does commitment fare in these Heraclitean waters? Let us approach this fundamental word from its underbelly: our fear of love and relationship.

How inadequate, even hopeless, we so often feel because we cannot live up to each other's, or our own, expectations. But this feeling of inadequacy is a tip-off: It reveals the limits of erotic pleasure in a predictable, demystified universe. Who would exchange a relationship in which we live out the unfolding and uncertain mystery of our plans and dreams for one in which our pleasure is in the dutiful achievement of our expectations, pledges, and commitments? As Walt Whitman confessed concerning his life struggles in "Song of the Open Road" (shyly protected in parentheses):

> (Still here I carry my old delicious burdens,
> I carry them, men and women, I carry them with me
> wherever I go,
> I swear it is impossible for me to get rid of them
> I am fill'd with them; and I will fill them in return.)

The deeper value of discovering our inadequacy in this latter way of making erotic commitments to each other is not in motivating us to do better next time. That might be the case in legalistic and business commitments, models that have taken control of marriage in practice and through their well-managed vocabularies. But applying such formalized forms of commitment to erotic relationship can lead to severe distortions.

In a similar fashion, popular psychology converts commitment into an activity to be "worked on." It has become the hoop that a lover tries to get his partner (or himself) to jump through. But in the world of eros-as-mystery, commitment can no longer be used only as a contract, a stabilizing expectation, or a sign of "progress" in one's relationship. We know far less about commitment than what is implied by such definitions. In a typical situation, Mary and Bill become isolated from the invigorating resources of erotic mystery by adhering to their well-defined goals.

Mary is thirty-eight and wants Bill, thirty-one, to "get committed," to choose marriage, children, and a home. Bill says he isn't ready, he wants to travel, he isn't sure. Two years go by. Mary is forty, and Bill is thirty-three: no house, no marriage or children, and no travel.

Their "commitment" has been to expectations as ideas and place-markers for the future. The *idea* of "family" intimidates Bill and gives Mary a sense of certainty in what she wants, while Bill's "traveling" intimidates Mary and gives Bill a place-marker for his future. They are very aware of their "patterns" and interlocking "games."

This dance of expectations and even the detailed analyses of their game-playing displace the sense of mystery that would lure them into life with its uncertainties. Only awe of the mystery of fertility, family, and home-building can nourish Mary's and Bill's commitment toward its fruition; only the romantic allure of travel can move this couple into action. But awe of the possible has become fear of the expected; mystery has been buried under certainties, expectations, and psychological analysis.

The extramarital affair of Carol and Ed reveals its own elusive gamble with mystery and certainty. Carol and Ed are in different marriages. Their affair with each other feels "filled with possibilities" and is a relief from the grind of expectations in their respective marriages. In six months they have divorced their spouses and are living with each other, and in two more months they are pregnant.

We understand their feeling of the magic of possibilities born during their affair, but we wonder whether they will be able to stay committed to possibilities or whether a life of expectations will reemerge. Will the spiritual ambiguities and paradoxes of finitude and infinitude that were awakened in their affair be shared with awe in their marriage, or will these profundities be trivialized in the anxieties of daily life?

Commitment as something that is made or worked on is the trivialized "commodification" of erotic bonding. Real erotic commitment is something our emotions tell us about the very nature of human relationships, "the incredible lightness of being." Our commitment to one another begins in the sheer act of perceiving one another. Commitment, then, is an active meditation on the possible.

The deeper the perception, the deeper the commitment, which is to say the less it can be ended by any event. The most daring perception, being the innocence of the embodied soul, awakens devotional commitment. Such depth allures us with its loyalty and comforts as much as its silent foreshadowing of our own mortality awes and frightens us. Our *effort,* then, is in seeing commitment where it hides, in being so moved, and then following it into word and action—more than in "making one" and "living up to it."

Relational commitment is the natural result of sensing and engaging with both actualized and hidden potentials between lovers. Commitment is to possibilities that can never be recast into expectations without deleterious consequences.

The unknown future, not our expectations, pledges, or verbalized commitments, draws us into keeping our erotic commitments. The mystery of it all draws us on suspensefully. If we camouflage the sense of the unknown future by premeditating a life of expectations to be achieved, then we can lose touch with the magnetism of this mystery. Fear and suspense are precarious erotic allies, not enemies, which indicate that the erotic mystery of the unknown future is alive to us. All relational planning for the future must make room for such erotic fear and not try to plan it out of existence.

Each step along the way, from the first moments of attraction to the decision to live together or marry, is guided by a mystery whose possibilities need and allure our attention. When we plant a seed, we do not water it merely because of a stated agreement but because the mysterious potential within its fertility calls us to water it. When the watering is a chore, our union with the seed is viyogic, or hidden from us, and when joyful, it is yogic, or revealed to us.

In both states we relate to the seed as the mystery of hidden potential that it is and as the mystery of care that we are. Both resentment and enjoyment can lead us to the romanticism of the mystery. Losing the sense of erotic mystery, however, can easily lead to a withering neglect, usually leaving a trail of last-ditch efforts of guilt-inducing expectations, ultimatums, and spelled-out "commitments." To keep commitment alive, perceive the ongoing mystery of things, speak it into words, act it into deeds.

In erotic mystery, we exchange the weight of commitment and the debate of whether or not there is enough of it in a relationship for the more subtle and dynamic task of being loyal to what is mysterious in each other as the source of possibilities. Conclusive, judgmental, past-oriented, or critical thinking that covers erotic mystery with its projective determinations must again and again give way to the hope beneath the dashed hopes, the suspense of our own continuations.

Too commonly, perceptions of what is possible in the other but not yet actual are converted into guilt-inducing expectations and accusations— "You could be doing so much better! But instead you're . . ."—weakening commitment and nurturing the hopes of a greener pasture elsewhere.

So-called fear of commitment is really "awe of the possible" after being crushed under the constraining weight of a contractual ideal of commitment defined by expectations. Here is the source of nearly all diversions from mystery, such as manipulation, abuse, lying, neglect: mistaking the awe of the possible for the fear of the previously expected.

The mistake throws us backward, and we, tragically, wobble, then run, in that direction, looking for explanations (which serve as a kind of ex post facto expectation, as in "I should have *known* it wouldn't work"). Too typically, the relationship becomes primarily an analytic game between two amateur psychotherapists. They miss the current callings of erotic mystery as their analytic machinery sends them whirring into the past, seeking causal-explanatory certainties for the difficulty. "Awesome mystery of marriage? Oh, sure! With my childhood, it's no wonder; and now *this* difference between us! This whole thing is one big mistake!" was Martin's disparaging statement on the stressful eve of his own wedding. But, truly, hasn't each move, from the first date to tuxedo rentals, been an awesome mystery followed forward?

Awe or fear, a nuance within a nuance. But the difference made in choosing between these two word-cousins to describe erotic matters could be all the difference in the world. We hear such a quiet tone-setting in the nuances that distinguish "possibility" from "expectation," that is, between the allure of an awesome mystery and the eager hopefulness of a well-defined demand.

While being clear about one's expectations uses the power of explicitness to mobilize a couple, awe of the possible more enigmatically nourishes every step of the way for those committed to eros as mystery—even the more dire possibilities such as loss, catastrophe, or death. Ann and Mike discover that coming to know each other's expectations has almost covered over the sense of possibility that made such knowledge so important to them.

Ann and Mike improve their communication skills through therapy and by reading several books. They both find it much easier to express clearly their expectations of each other. When they begin to understand the spiritual context of erotic mystery, their recently improved skills reveal the deeper meaning of their efforts.

Their efforts to work on their communication are expressions of that magical feeling, "all is possible for us," that they felt when they first fell in love. More than their acquired skills, these are the feelings that nourish their relationship and are what they really want to communicate about and share. This magical mood makes them feel "more alive" and aware that in real life, their time "here" is limited. But even the sense of a limited lifetime only serves to add a hallowing tint to their sharings.

The side effect of a prolonged commitment to a relationship as an unfolding mystery is doubly awesome. First, we must not be afraid to call such commitment by its towering name: evermore unconditional love. Second, we must not be too trepid to say that we have learned to need and be needed by a particular and noninterchangeable other. And recall, "need" is something we feel and share, more than fill or get met, for sustained need individualizes us with its unifying and deepening passion.

Lifelong Commitment: The Crux of Finitude

As the organic wholeness or grace of the finite, singular lifetime is grasped one way and then another over the years and decades of our lives, it provides a fundamental sense of the range of human possibilities and can stimulate our involvement. Again, eros and thanatos, suspenseful mystery and destinal unknown, are approached and reapproached. Such is the way of maturation. The anxious image of a ticking reproductive clock; fearful signs of midlife crises; concerns about money for now and later; and regressively hopeful preoccupations with the metaphor of the "lost inner child" are all modern, troubled reactions to the forward movement of life.

Deep rhythms vibrate through us whenever we grasp the truths of life and align with them. The sense of a finite, aging lifetime is one such truth, an embodied, erotic truth. Perhaps as we die, at whatever age, we receive a last awakening, remarking to ourselves, "So *that* was what a lifetime is all about!"

The twenty-year project of raising a family (or the forty-year project of a grand-family) is another organic time span that suggests lifelong marriage. As one Chinese proverb has it, marriage is complete on the birth of the first grandchild.

Soon into family life, the finite resources of tasks per day, dollars per year, topics per discussion begin aligning with one economic interpretation of the erotic mystery or another. In a demystified world, a materialistic interpretation often prevails, and nothing mysterious any longer informs life's difficulties with layers of wonder. Yes, Freud tried to unveil the more mysterious meaning of family life but typically went only as far as sex. We need to go further.

Time, money, and speech should be demi-gods of sorts, that is, permeated with a challenge to feel their awe. A counseling client looks in his wallet to pay me. His hushing silence and trepid movements make me feel he is entering a chapel. His payment to me is a painful, sacrificial offering, and, suddenly faith-shaken, he is unclear about what he is receiving from me in return. Beneath perfunctory nods of "thank you," "you're welcome," a mystery of doubt, faith, hope, and survival passes, some calmness surfaces.

Fights about money, about getting the toy everybody else has, or about what was or wasn't said that flare so often in family life—what surrounds such passions? The poignancies of an impermanent mystery fading into the edges of the infinite.

Marriage, monogamy, and lifelong commitment are not goals or securities but rather the natural results of you and your partner sensing the depths of the possibilities within each other. As we see another deeply enough to perceive her glowing mystery, we find that we need the time of a lifetime to fulfill all that is suggested by what we see and how we feel in being so seen. Fear of and attraction to lifelong monogamy are reflections of the awe of the possibilities between any two people who see each other this deeply, for in having a need for the time of the rest of our lives, the finitude of it all quickens. Such is the fructifying nature of need.

Before breaking up, people often say they are "dying" in their relationships. Confusingly, in such situations one is hard pressed to determine how much of this feeling of dying is being induced by one's considered withdrawal from the relationship, by some deficiency in the relationship, or merely by an unavoidable inkling of one's own mortal nature.

To Stay or to Leave?

"Should I get out or should I stay?" Once raised, the question seeks an answer while also pervading our relationship with precariousness and impossibility, even from the earliest moments: "He was late, *obviously* irresponsible!" "She was impatient, I don't need *that!*" Some partners fall into a chronic mode of seeing the other as if through the lens of a high-powered psychological microscope and then wonder why their beloveds look so ill at ease. Of course, it takes some time for them to see themselves as peering at their partners in this hypercritical way and to wonder if such peering induced the immaturity or insecurity that they so perspicaciously identified.

Like many soldiers, they can adapt to these battle-alert conditions and find a certain cynical enjoyment in how well they see each other's faults and how good it feels to point them out and have them pointed out. It feels so good because now the sweetness of righteous anger or even passive-aggressivity can be wielded by these partners, each waiting in ambush for the other to commit an error that can be pointed out, that supports their developing theory, and so on, mounting expectantly to the dark orgasm of an enraged breakup. This is the shadowy side of the erotic mystery of shared gender, the sharing of the desperate powers of destruction and threatened survival.

Through serial relationships and all that we may have learned from friends, experts, or our parents' martial-marital skillfulness (and they from their friends, and so on), we begin to accumulate our own questionable skillfulness in raising this question, "stay-go," and in assessing the "work-ability" of a relationship. All such accumulated skills, especially when silently wielded, gnaw away at the possibilities within each other.

Only renewed innocence can approach mystery and fully imbibe of its nourishing allure. But innocence is infinitely renewable, and thus we are rightfully afraid of its power to make things work out. We are returning to that which we, in our critical moments, were so sure was a kind of hell, and no doubt we are still deathly afraid of a resolution that would be "too good to be true." If we believed in such a possibility, we would only go back to our partner again, innocently hoping for the best—a foolish move, says our more clever and "experienced" voice. We become caught in a paradox created by too much "knowledge" and not enough innocence.

As a defensive maneuver, we might find ways to diminish our partner's unique value to us (or to diminish our imagined, unique value to him, in order to minimize the cost of any potential loss in the future—often before the relationship has even "begun"). Ironically, this might occur just as his value begins to touch the highest levels we've ever allowed ourselves to feel for anyone. We cannot imagine valuing anyone *that* much, or that "it" (that feeling

of total possibility) could ever last for very long. We can even mistake evanescent subtlety for cynical "proof" that it won't last. "It" never does.

Thus, we hover before the Burning Bush of each other's mercurial, inestimable mystery, taking in as much of this radiance as our faith (or our
various fears of "dependency"—ours or his) permits. We dare to value each
other just enough to stay but not so much as to be overly threatened by
the spectre of his or our leaving. The one heartens, the other looks away;
the other reconsiders, the one has just given up. Thus, the depths of erotic
sharing recede from us, for how can we worship what we will not allow to
move us to the point of irreversible devotion?

Innocence is far more powerful than knowledge born of our fear of
past difficulties repeating themselves into the future. Innocence is more creative
than any well-reasoned justifications or ideas on how to make things work.
It is what gives inspiration to such ideas in the first place. Thus, in the realms
of erotic mystery, the question "Should I go or stay?" transforms into a
koan, and, like the well-known enigma of "the sound of one hand clapping," has no literal answer.

As we wonder "How could this be?" with ever-deepening innocence,
our feelings of blame, anger, endangered hope, and hurt become more shar-
able and less a matter of accusations and rebuttals. When we feel a sense
of wonder slip into our worries and problems, we lighten up, we "enlighten."
The energy we were spending worrying about the "right" choice is returned
to our awareness as a feeling of freedom. We see possibilities where we
once thought there were none, either in staying or in leaving. This is not
a mind trick; it is the mystery of our ineluctable freedom.

If we leave in this less-reasoned way, we will carry far less emotional
baggage. We will not need to believe that we have been driven out by our
problems and the weakness they imply about our or her "capacity for relationship." Thus, we preserve our innocence from drowning in a sea of
psychological terminology or vengeful characterizations.

In the currents of erotic mystery there may be *more* uncertainty about
what to do in a relationship, about what you "really" want. No one knows
the answer to the difficult question of going or staying. In matters of erotic
commitment the question is always the same: *Are we attending to the fruition of the possibilities in this relationship or not?* For we cannot know
what change of heart could happen in the next moment.

Whether 'tis nobler to stay or to go is beyond psychological analysis.
The strange simplicity of choosing and continuing to attend to what we've

chosen is what baffles. Such choosing may be a matter of destiny, where the final possibility ordains all precedents with their truest meaning.

Hidden Unions, Viyoga, and Spoken Passion

> Better than meeting
> and mating all the time
> is the pleasure of mating once
> after being far apart.
>
> When he's away
> I cannot wait
> to get a glimpse of him.
>
> Friend, when will I have it
> both ways,
> be with Him
> yet not with Him,
> my lord white as jasmine?
>
> (Mahadeviyakka,
> in Ramanujan, *Speaking
> of Siva*, 1973, p. 140)

Viyoga refers to that well-veiled class of erotic unions that are lost to some more obvious experience of apparent separation. It includes those feelings of missing each other and longing to meet each other. It also includes the run of angers, frustrations, shames, guilts, hurts, fears, and "problems" that obscure the felt sense of union. Through the unreasonable faithfulness interior to viyoga, all such feelings disguise a hidden union and, within mystery, an erotic one.

The feeling of missing each other is usually thought of as merely the pain of separation, while it is actually the felt sense of being in hidden union with someone distant from us. It is the felt cord of emotional connection that transcends spatial proximity and empirical proofs. There is no need to resent missing each other, as any romantic can attest.

Yet most of us must learn and perfect the romantic art of "missing" as a throbbing anticipation and not tighten its difficulty into blame and resentment. In viyoga, calls made to another while apart *express* missing, rather than aiming to ending it. As that expert on such matters, Saint-Exupéry's fox, explained:

> "It would have been better to come back at the same hour," said the fox. "If, for example, you come at four o'clock in the afternoon, then at three o'clock I shall begin to be happy. I shall feel happier and happier as the hour advances. At four o'clock, I shall already be worrying and jumping about. I shall show you how happy I am!" (p. 84)

Viyoga becomes a velvety array of erotic feelings and communications to be shared, perhaps invisibly, with each other. Synchronous experiences—phone calls, shared nocturnal dreams, and other psychic phenomena—rest within this occult dimension of relationship. Viyoga denotes an evermore unconditional relatedness, reaching beyond time, space, and perhaps even the veils of death.

Sharing is the unavoidable basis of the erotic relationship; thus a loss of a sense of sharing is a primal deprivation, experienced as a missing. The short route back to sharing is to share missing directly, which, seen in each other's eyes, transmutes to a wavering longing and reuniting, for the truth of sharing is already occurring. The apologies, forgivenesses, logistics, and details of the problem can then be worked out together.

In the long or incomplete route, each uses evidence and opinions about the other, about the other's or one's own childhood, and tries to explain why the breakdown has occurred. These explanations can take the form of vengeful blamings and cross-blamings, studied analyses, or some combination of the two. A sense of understanding occurs, perhaps apology and forgiveness and reconciliation, but not even then is sharing necessarily revived. And if it is, the inspiring sense of sharing "the exact-same missing" of the one relationship that they are both in very likely remains hidden. The spiritual sense of the One Relationship known to lovers of ajna remains even more hidden.

Knowing about these more subtle levels of relationship is important, so that we can start missing them and thus spread the depths of human longing onto the whole range of our being. Meditation is the attention-captured, falling in love with these levels, known first as "impossible ideals" or memories of the best of times, and then as an innuendo happening right now. Then, from the detected nuance of some gesture or quivering inflection, in floods an obviously heart-felt reunion. "He got so shy, and I saw who he really is; my forgiveness just came." "Her voice got so soft; suddenly I knew that I had been missing her greatly." Without access to moments of such a devotional attention directed toward each other, how can these turning points occur? Thus the special potency (and beauty) of tantric meditative lovemaking practices in the viyogic arts.

As the reunion occurs, a paradox emerges: All that was "negative" a moment ago is now positive proof of the tensile strength of the partners' sharing. What they have just weathered is now becoming an inspirational memory and not a despondent one, as was almost the case.

We must always struggle to grasp the erotic magnitude of each single confession, each act of forgiveness, each act of giving or receiving, and each moment of hurt, shame, or anger. Larry, Jill, and Ruth discovered the intimacy within viyoga.

Larry was making a birthday party for Jill, the twelve-year-old daughter of his girlfriend, Ruth. Larry promised that Jill could invite any eight people to the party. But then a fight occured between Jill and her mom, and Jill told Larry she didn't want her mom at the party, "and you said I could invite *my* choice. . . ." Then Ruth was mad at Larry, too, for being "manipulated" by Jill and for not being invited. Larry agreed and felt caught in the middle.

They had spent some hours yelling about their repetitious patterns when Jill apologized to Larry for having manipulated him so as to get back at her mom. Ruth apologized for trying to build a "case" against Larry. Larry agreed with Jill that he should have confronted her with being manipulative and not let her get away with it. They all felt closer, having shared their shame, anger, accusations, apologies, and forgiveness.

Unexpressed gratitude, admiration, and respect are other submerged viyogic unions repeatedly deferred by the habitual conversations of daily life. Sometimes partners will spare their mates their difficulty in receiving compliments by withholding them. Or the recipient shrugs off a compliment with "Oh, it was nothing." Paradoxically, hidden within these perfunctory shrugs are shy waves of gratitude for being acknowledged, arousals of the sublimative sort.

As these communications occur, they provoke unpredictably passionate responses, for shy gratitudes and blushing admirations are the greatest of celibate aphrodisiacs. Such are the glimmers of the soul and the momentarily deeper penetration of the body with their radiant vitality. Often, all that is needed is to begin a sentence with the words "I really admired you when . . . ," which is responded to by the simple words "Thank you." Or, more fully, "The glowing blush you now see on my face is from receiving your gratitude. This is how much your admiration means to me." Then the other, too, begins to brim up, look to, and then look away. Too often it seems easier to feel miffed at something lacking than to walk on these quivering viyogic waters toward each other.

Should we listen to each other (and ourselves) with viyogic artfulness, we can trace envy and jealousy back to admiration and worship; sadness and pity back to compassion; fear, doubt, and suspicion back to the awe of great powers within us and others; longing, yearning, loneliness, desiring, and missing back to the viyogic unions during separation; anger, resentment, grief, disappointment, and hate back to the anguish of ruptured hopefulness; and shame as a mockingly inverse form of praise; while embarrassment and shyness can be understood as sudden awakenings to one's own visibility and an even greater sense of one's existence.

The Erotic Freedom of Belonging

In our psychologically sophisticated culture, we are witnessing an overdifferentiation and overdemystification of erotic phenomena that has become xenophobia: the significance of erotic differences made so great as to induce a fearful, confusing, or even hostile sense of foreignness. Even our sexual icons have exaggerated desire's mystery into a clashing harshness that causes even the most liberated to shudder. The ever-converging way in which I have defined the terms of the erotic vocabulary—"eros" as mystery, "commitment" as the allured response to deeply sensed mystery, "gender" as immediately shared, "longing" as the essence of union, "life-long marriage" and "monogamy" as inherent to the arc of a single lifetime—perhaps can have a rectifying effect. The simplifying convergence helps to unite us in a humbling uncertainty to which we, as humans, all belong.

This erotic humility gathers together all forms of "otherness"—genders, erotic preference groups, ethnicities, sexo-political factions. It reveals that deeper than our differentiating certainties is that which draws us together, fearfully or alluringly, because, finally, eros is so mysterious. This humility suggests that deeper than desire's freedom of unbridled choices is the seemingly more restricted, but actually more liberating, ecological freedom of belonging to something vast.

In many ways, the freedom of belonging is the highest and most difficult social or world-embracing enjoyment of the erotic mystery. Love becomes the one-embodied-flesh; it is the all-forgiving, long-enduring, and at times excruciating perception of the world as one huge family, where everyone and everything belongs, for no other reason than the fact that we are all here in the same mystery, facing the same unknown.

Creating New Life: The Passions of Fertility

Unseen buds, infinite, hidden well,
Under the snow and ice, under the darkness, in every square
or cubic inch.
Germinal, exquisite, in delicate lace, microscopic, unborn,
Like babes in wombs, latent, folded, compact, sleeping;
Billions of billions, and trillions of trillions of them waiting,
(On earth and in the sea—the universe—the stars there are
in the heavens,)
Urging slowly, surely forward, forming endless,
And waiting ever more, forever more behind.

(Walt Whitman, "Unseen Buds")

Reproductive Intentions

The passions of fertility awaken during genital puberty and continue afterward in the approximately monthly cycles of ovulation and spermatogenesis. Throughout most of the rest of nature, the rhythms of these passions orchestrate all sexual behaviors, with many species following cycles or subcycles of the seasons and others in intricate rapport with their own community's fluctuating population densities.

In human societies, fertility and viability have been subjected to all manner of interventions and intentions, ranging from colonization and international wars to tribal fertility rituals, infanticides, and abortions; from arranged marriages and mail-order marriages to shotgun weddings and "love marriages"; from the planned parenthood of responsible contraception to arduous efforts to conceive via surrogates, sperm banks, and artificial insemination.

These intentions have shaped procreative mystery into a "lineage responsibility," an "overpopulation problem," a "biogenetic phenomenon," a "rite of passage into adulthood," a "gender-political problem," an "unintended side effect" or an "intended choice," or the "divine purpose of sex and marriage." The power of well-intended shapings of procreativity reached its modern technological zenith in this prediction:

> It is quite possible that within the next decade the surrogate mother can be circumvented entirely by the development of an artificial uterus that maintains the developing embryo-fetus in an incubator-like environment, hooked up to an artificial placenta that functions not unlike a kidney dialysis machine. While some may be horrified at first by this notion (they'll miss the emotional experience of being pregnant and the joy of delivering their own child, critics will undoubtedly object), several surveys conducted to date have found that as many as 40 percent of women in their twenties would choose to have children only in this manner. (Masters, Johnson, and Kolodny, 1985, p. 558)

In such a future, the sense of a procreative mystery might be felt only by its absence or as translated bizarrely into the "marvel" of technology.

Procreative Wonders

In this chapter we will be searching in a direction quite different from any of those mentioned above. We will be asking, What is the actual mystery of our incarnate beginning before any religio-political or scientific theorizings or findings or personal decidings? Instead of a literal answer to our question, however, we hope to recover the actual sense of wonder and awe involved in this mystery.

For what seethes within our bodies, although we rarely experience it as such, is the coiled beginning of all future human possibilities. And at some point deep within fertility, all forms of conceptive hopefulness dissolve into a humbling yet exhilarating powerlessness to which only we can give expression.

The term itself, *procreation,* speaks to the ominous simplicity of conception as a creation—*pro,* on behalf of the divine—not as a biotechnical re-"production" nor as a mere personal intention or social expectation but as an innocent miracle. For procreative choice cannot be reduced to the lone matter of intention to have or not have a child. It is the entrance into the power and wonder of creating life and the uncanny rhythms in which it abides.

Such perceptions are possible only when the specific passions of fertility have been revived, for now fertility is determined largely in deference to the passions of sex-desire. Estral cues have all but vanished, while spermatogenesis, or male fertility cycles, remains unexplored; fertility rhythms themselves are, ironically, thought of as either "good" (infertile) or "bad" (fertile) times for sex. Within modern sexual life, fertility has become something we try to "do" when we want to conceive.

Simply stated, conception is always an innocent miracle. Even the most well-planned conception or totally controlled artificial insemination does not disguise the fact that we are dealing in mystery and miracle and that participants' intentions circulate at some distance from the realities of conception, gestation, and birth.

Why do people have children? Underneath all the passionate and thoughtful answers, innocent fertility reminds us that there is no answer. The interrogative should not trick us into seeking the wherefore to this deep why. The matter is a wonder, and conception itself the primal gateway through which all human wondering proceeds. Thus, we will speak less of an intentional conception than of a conscious conception; we search less for a planned parenthood than for an innocent parenthood.

During the cyclical peakings of our fertility (the female and the less visible male cycles), we are brought to the very core of the passions of fertility. To share in tantric celibate lovemaking at this time is to sustain the fullness that has been approaching all month in the many subtle nuances of impending ripeness.

Perhaps the partners will be especially drawn toward each other and their sublimations will be not only of sex-desire but also of the very energies and images of fertility itself. What is "unsafe time" in the eyes of conventional sex-desire appears as awesome possibility in tantric sublimation. Conscious procreativity and parenthood hover within the relationship during those days and in varying nuances of possibility throughout the fertility cycle, as discovered by Lisa and Rob.

Lisa and Rob had been practicing tantric celibacy for four years. About a year ago, they began to experience the passions of fertility as gradual changes in Lisa's complexion and in a subtle "tang" in the odor of their perspirations. Then, during an evening ritual, Rob was receiving nyasa and began to see a kind of infinite regression of feminine subtleties in Lisa. He felt a slowly turning field of radiance moving around her that made him think of a cornucopia, an endlessly receding vortex that just kept drawing him into her.

Lisa felt her ovaries and womb quivering from time to time, and when she looked into Rob's eyes, her own breath momentarily stopped. She saw an intentness in his eyes, a captivated look that made her feel that "the time" had arrived. As Rob exchanged nyasa with Lisa, he felt a veil slip away in his contact with her. She rather suddenly became more vivid to him, visually, in her scent, and to his touch. Being practiced in sublimation, they allowed their genital arousals to shift through many phases over the following twenty minutes.

During this time, they had a constant, silent experience of embracing each other's thoughts, which were like folds of concern and wonder that kept leading them into quieter depths of each other. Then they heard a buzzing sound, which Rob thought sounded like "the engines of the universe."

Later, when they talked, they wondered if this sound was the buzzing of fertility itself that waxed and waned during the lunar cyclings of fertility. While they had previously feared that conceiving and raising a child would be "too difficult" for financial and other practical reasons, now they didn't really know what to do. To follow this experience of their shared fertility seemed worth any expense.

As each month went by, the whole fertility cycle kept inspiring them with its mystery, and all their reasonings and analyses about readiness became inconsequential. They almost broke their celibacy on one occasion because the draw toward this fertility was so great; but the bliss and wonder of the sublimation was equally great, and they continued their meditations instead. They decided to approach the procreative mystery together but only in meditative silence.

They then began to feel how little it was up to them yet it was completely up to them. The mystery was dizzying, no longer a thing to merely talk about. There was no decisive way to know beforehand whether or when to leave their celibacy for the draw of the passions of fertility.

Not until they had shared numerous tantric encounters with the passions of fertility did the following occur: In the middle of a tantric ritual involving the exchange of flowers, they fell into a "pranic mirroring" with each other and began taking off each other's clothes. It felt to them like the "very first time" that not only they but *anyone* had ever joined genitals.

The sensations were exquisite, no doubt enhanced by the three-year hiatus in genital contact. Every movement was so fresh and alive. They shared the sublimation of several waves of desire, but the stronger images were of fertility and the immediacy of their contact. They felt each other as "mother of all beings," as "father of all children." Their own fertility seemed to echo inward toward that of their children and their children's children, and on and on. In another way, they felt a proud connection with their parents, grandparents, and a chorus of ancestors who seemed to be smiling delightedly as if some angelic obstetrician had just come into their "waiting room" with the momentous announcement.

They felt on the verge of creation, with everything else in the universe doing this same thing, silently, invisibly, all matter and all spirit, dwelling on the edge of an upcoming thrill. The sexual pleasures came to a resounding pitch and then relaxed into a feeling that whatever happened was totally fine.

Curiously, they did not become pregnant that month. This only served to humble them, to suggest to them that conception was beyond their wildest dreams, intentions, and premonitions. Several months later, however, they did become pregnant. Lisa felt it as a twinge that raced up from her womb, through her solar plexus, and into her heart, like a determined "that's it."

Rob didn't feel anything distinct until one week later, when he found himself utterly content, "like a contented cow," as he put it. Both their bodies had a subtle buzzing, which they had heard many months before, but now it felt as though it were coming from every cell. During the months that followed they described two levels to the pregnancy: the throbbing internal gestation and its magnetic, nest-building effect on their home and relationship.

In the innocence that develops through such repeated tantric sublimative exchanges while following the passions of fertility, the possibility for innocent, conscious conception—neither intended and planned nor unintended and accidental—can occur. What can be said about this event that is beyond the probabilities of any fertility calculations, any hopes, avoidances, or fears of conception, any thoughts or plans? I suggest the following: In some unfathomable depths a rhythm of destiny awaits the synchronous and choiceless touch of our human hands.

Procreation and the Shared-Gender Mystery

The shared-gender mystery is nowhere more obvious than in procreative sexuality, for we see that egg and sperm require each other and that no woman ever became a mother without simultaneously a man becoming a father, technological interventions notwithstanding; that women and men confer parenthood on each other— with the help of the child, of course.

What obstetrician Thomas Verny, author of *The Secret Life of the Unborn Child,* and others have revealed and conjectured concerning the psychic relationship between a mother and the unborn child's "secret life" must be extended to include, equally but more subtly, the psychic role of fathers. Just as fathers have been invited into the delivery room only recently, our map of procreativity must restore them more fully into the whole of gestation.

Perhaps the loss of truly felt access to this psychic level of procreative rapport has contributed to our sense of pregnancy as being so difficult and isolating that the artificial womb is a serious alternative. We know in the biblical myth that the arising of a certain type of desire in the archetypal couple resulted in difficulties between the sexes and laborious childbearing processes. The breakdown of an erotically fulfilling sense of immediate rapport between the sexes may be ancient, yet through tantric sensitivities its recovery is within our reach.

Pregnancy might not necessarily get easier, but it might be experienced as more fully shared. As one of my interview couples stated, procreative sex was wonderfully different from conventional sex. It continued until the pregnancy test came back from the lab. They enjoyed an unexpectedly mysterious connection for all those days, which has, upon the birth of their daughter, become a substantive part of their felt relationship with each other.

We cannot easily say how any of the stressfulness of pregnancy could be experienced by partners who consider their pregnancy as an equally, although differentially, shared phenomenon. The psychosomatic interactivity of two persons is a profound mystery. My most impressive clinical experience was with a couple whose emotional impasse with each other was resolved when they shared, for the first time, the buried grief of an abortion that had occurred approximately nine months previously. Coincidentally (!) the wife was headed for a hysterectomy within the next weeks because she had endometriosis. After the tearful session in which this couple finally shared their grief, the wife's next gynecological exam revealed a complete remission of symptoms, and the surgery was canceled.

Tantric celibate lovemaking during pregnancy can be a way to share the special wonder of gestation and family creation. Over and over, fear of what is expected is displaced by awe of what is possible, and separations are transformed into viyogic unions. Yet we must beware of demystified expectations that seek "the perfect conception and pregnancy," "the perfect parenting," or "the perfect child." We must beware of fearing that which is inherently awesome. Instead, follow a mystery, for anything is possible.

Sharing a Home with Mystery

Adult fertility reaches from this world into the world yet unborn while children reach out from the invisible world into this more visible one. The contact of all adults and all children is based on this natural reaching toward one another's different worlds. The child's admiration and trust of the big adult and the adult's protective and nurturing feelings toward the child constitute the mysterious allure of their relationship. Sex-desire and most of sublimation are irrelevant.

There is no sexological goal or specific psychosexual developmental path that anchors the child's smile, coy looks, or even bodily explorations to some quickening end. It is pure, reasonless play, free of language and theory. Even the child's "self-play" is pointless and utterly dissimilar from adult masturbation. Scientia sexualis concepts, so heavily embedded in their own sexo-political agendas, simply don't apply. The moralist's fears of a "dangerous eros" are equally inappropriate.

Furthermore, late childhood is not best described as "sexually confusing." It is a time of intimate contact with the inherently mysterious passions of an emerging fertility and the possibilities within sex-desire (and sublimation) while leaving one's own procreative origins of conception and birth far behind. No amount of "sex education" will ever explain away the sense of mystery as fertility, sexual desire, and sublimative passions converge within the (pre)adolescent, nor should such a goal be attempted. Efforts to preserve the awe and wonder of those times would, however, be a worthy endeavor.

The family is the procreative tree of life, not the oedipal hothouse that Freud "uncovered" nor the training ground that the moralist has mandated. Instead, the family can be a home for mystery, and tantric sublimation a family-centered, community-building approach to its precincts. Communication is raised to the level of spoken passion, while tantric family rituals bring eros out from behind closed doors and into more shareable family life.

Learning the "facts of life" becomes the teenager's careful learning to discern and respect the nuances of fertility, sex-desire, and sublimation within himself, not just instruction to be contraceptively responsible, to wait for the right person, or to "have fun—but don't get (anyone) pregnant!" Celebrating and ritualizing the onset of puberty for each child might prove to be an emotionally rich family event, as Julie, twenty-five, recounts:

> *When I was twelve, I had my first period, and we had this special dinner with my family, for me. My mother gave me six red roses and six white ones. My father gave me a pendant, which I still wear, with an infinity sign with two pearls in it. The pearls were like two souls meeting. My brother, I guess he was fifteen, gave me one of his bronze baby shoes. Two years earlier, I had given him a journaling book for his passage.*
>
> *Over the years, this has had a great effect on me. I always can feel that world of fertility, passion, and magic, and it always adds something that I can share with just a few of my girlfriends and guys that I have been with.*

Such are the ways of the passions of innocence in a family following a mystery, supportive of any future erotic pathway that one might choose. Tantric sublimation will, however, lose its allure if it is converted into a parental imposition that offspring "must follow."

THE WAY OF SOLITARY CELIBACY

On that joyous night,
In secret, seen by no one,
Nor with anything in sight,
I had no other light or mark,
Than the one burning in my heart.

(Saint John of the Cross,
The Dark Night of the Soul,
in de Nicolas, p. 103)

A solitary celibate is someone whose brahmacharya has released the desire for a mate through a growing merger with the world as a whole, with life as one family. No longer rebelling against the feeling of aloneness, she embraces its particular potentials and limitations as her home.

As though coming out of a deep sleep filled with dreams of romance, intrigue, ups and downs, the solitary celibate is captivated by her awakening to the reality where nothing further is needed. The anchorite of classical monasticism, the hermit of mythic lore, the crone of wiccadom, the sadhu of yoga are among its archetypes. The Great Alone, avadhut, Sada-Shiva Mahadeva are its profound call notes. Breathless, compassionate, ashen, completed. Secrecy of all secrecies. Wordless. Done.

These are the more dramatic images of the solitary celibate, yet our modern culture has little understanding of them. For most people, the notion of the world being one great family is at best a distant ideal, at worst a hopeless delusion. Perhaps in a biogenetic sense, the world might *be* one family; certainly, we are all here together, trying to make the best of things, with estranged, disowned, and close relatives everywhere.

Within this expansive embrace, the solitary celibate encounters Martin Buber's challenge, the "dreadful point" of loving everyone, with all the suffering, confusion, fear, and struggling that is in our world. She just loves it now, just the way it is, in a perhaps difficult but compassionate sense, and does not need to wait for the world to get better or more utopian before she can love it. In other words, she considers her life situation as her mate and lives her commitments to herself and others at the level equivalent to that of a lifelong marriage.

Jungian psychology presented the idea of the internal or alchemical marriage to the modern audience as resting upon the possibility that all polarities are within each of us. We can achieve the union of various polarities in the outer theater of relationships or in the inner theater of personal phenomenology. Literal withdrawal from society is not necessary (nor is it proscribed), but the sense of looking or waiting for Ms. or Mr. Right is reinterpreted as the longing for constant remembrance of the unitive Self, the longing for the inner marriage.

The experience of the inner marriage is easy enough to reconstruct. It is the swell of poignant possibility that ripples through friends and family at that singular moment of a wedding when the betrothed marry spiritually. The moment itself is quite obvious. Perhaps it happens as the couple first meets at the altar, or when a certain vow is exchanged, the rings, the kiss. And those given to tears, and even those not so given, find their tears welling up. The more philosophical wedding guests sense the profundity of the moment, so filled with human commitment and faith. Children grow silent; infants sometimes cry out or fall asleep. Even the cynical turn in their seats. A rainstorm begins suddenly or ends, or perhaps an animal wanders into the space. Likewise, the poignant essence of betrothal and this phenomenon of spiritual marriage sustains the solitary celibate who endeavors to marry herself to love and through this inner union to become love itself.

A central passion for the solitary brahmacharin is that of alluring aloneness. Should you be interested in pursuing this way of celibacy, even for a set duration of months or years, you will uncover the vast transmutations of feelings of the alone, the lonely, the desolate, the singular. A rare passion resides therein, an embracing surrender to every hinted sense of being alone.

These feelings are not enemies that we must combat with an arsenal of friendships and involvements. These are the passions that house a welcoming spaciousness for all those who dwell simply, and more simply. Aloneness or even loneliness, when loved, proves the dearest of friends. When such moods open their hearts to one who has pursued and loved them well, a gust of the cosmos rushes into that one's being. Rare and difficult to find, the sublimative orgasm of unbound aloneness marries one to the universe, for when embraced as a whole, the universe is a single totality and thus singularly alone.

For the solitary yogini, sadhana or yogic practice (upwards of five to eight hours a day) can become the beloved, for it reveals the endless mystery and allures her into utter fidelity. The practices of yoga reward her fidelity with many faith-strengthening experiences and attainments. Thus, like a person in a good marriage, she feels that she is "the luckiest person in the world" to have found such a fascinating life path. She feels she is missing out on nothing. For the karma yogini, her service is the beloved; for the bhakti yogini, the deity is the spouse. All these yogis and yoginis cannot wait until it is time for sadhana, service, or worship. Renunciation of certain aspects of life such as a spouse, money, and personal possessions or even a personal home can only be understood in response to such a passionate sadhana.

Everything—the homebound hordes of rush-hour traffic, a swaying cobweb, a child's cry—reminds her of the longing for union until she even forgets herself, and all that remains is the Union-of-It-All. This is nirbija-samadhi, jivan-mukti, moksha: absolute liberation. All fragmentary attachments are dissolved in an undescribable simplicity, that is, an exceedingly intricate complexity that flashes into a oneness. Those who understand find tears in their eyes and a pang of awe in their hearts, for it is another marriage, an eternal one. The children of such a marriage ripple through the entire world family, for they are the mystics of all times, and all the untold, inconspicuous others who think of this attainment and all the yoga and devotion that has preceded it and are inspired and filled.

These are the more romantic images of the solitary celibate. Daily life presents her with the more subtle struggles with fidelity to one's inner marriage. While appreciation of more conventional lives is natural, the vicarious enjoyment of the lifestyles of others can be a quiet breach of the inner marriage. The question of self-deprivation, like the charm of another person's spouse, can tempt one into other infidelities. "What am I really looking for, and why don't I think I have access to it now?" is the question that guides the solitary celibate. Meditation, yoga, service, devotional acts, friendships, recreation—all such elements of life must be considered, yet with an ear tuned to the quiet winnowing of one's more superficial attachments.

As the years roll on, the consequences of this inner marriage rise farther above the horizon that obscured them in earlier years. Growing old in this aloneness, the solitary celibate sees life and death with few obstructions. Tens of thousands of hours have been spent in total silence in a darkened meditation room, bypassing many more worldly delights.

Is it worth it? This question that emerges for the married couple also emerges for the solitary brahmacharin. Is it worth it? The question becomes a meditation, a koan, that reveals the voice that queries. The voice has no reality; it is just wind bouncing off the eternal limitations of human existence. Then the doors of an inner sanctum open and another more ancient draft blows a gust. The awesome truth is as unspeakable as it is unquestionable.

Epilogue:
An Open Ending

---◆---

One night I had the following dream: I was hiking in the wilds in pitch darkness. It was so dark that I decided to hike with my eyes closed. I walked slowly and cautiously as the terrain beneath my feet steepened. My arms and legs swung in slow motion, and although my eyes were closed, I could somehow sense that I was beginning to scale a mountain and that tens of thousands of others all around me were silently and perseveringly making their way up the same heights. Some walked in pairs, others were in larger groups, some pressed on alone. Chattel lay discarded and windblown at various points, first the heavier things like books and tools and, later, currencies and sacred objects. Finally, even ideas and words were left to the sides as the climbers forged on silently.

Trailing down the craggy escarpment was an occasional rope made of twisted vines. Some were using these ropes to pull themselves up and to guide themselves in the dark. Often the ropes would come to an abrupt end. Some of my companions then struggled in confusion; others created small dwelling places at that point; still others made their way free-climbing until, perhaps, another rope appeared.

It was obvious that previous travelers had braided these ropes and tossed them down for those who might follow, hoping they would be of use. But there was no way of knowing whether the rope tossed down was from some-

164

one who had made it to the top or from some straggler who had wandered haplessly into a conundrum. Who the first climber ever was, why she climbed, to where, and why she threw ropes down were questions from which many legends, like the ropes themselves, were fashioned. The "dwellers" would, for example, sit around their fires and retell the legends about vast panoramas visible from the peaks of the surrounding mountains and of the mythic heros (known as the "climbers") who lived there still. Occasionally, one would slip away into the night, thinking the legends to be real, and begin his ascent using the lengths of sinewy ropes hanging beyond the dweller's pale.

From uncertain heights as the dawn broke, innumerable glistening ropes could be seen quivering over the rocks. Glowing encampments of thousands of dwellers dotted the mountainside below, beneath the tossing strands. Before my groping hands, two ropes appeared. One was sleek and obvious and the other, weathered and more hidden.

We are each on our own path, formed by our beliefs, dreams, pleasures, and fears. Some of those before us have tested a certain path, a sublimative path that at some points breaks down into indecipherable free-climbs and scattered, twisted ropes. In this book, I have described the path leading to the rarest and most hidden yogic practices and concepts, and I have tried them. Should you shift your weight onto their support, from the indeterminate heights, they will pull taut. They will hold.

APPENDIX 1

WHAT EVERY TEENAGER SHOULD KNOW ABOUT TANTRIC SUBLIMATION

---◆---

Some adults will admit that they don't know about some things, but not many will admit that they don't know much about sex. Yet anyone can see that adults are confused about sex. They worry about the right things to do so you won't become sexually repressed, but they also hope that you can tell the difference between love and sexual attraction. They worry about you getting AIDS or herpes. They fear that you will have babies by accident or that after you are older you won't have any, that you will get all hung up on "boys" or "girls" and you won't finish your education. Or that you'll get interested in the wrong kids, period.

You know it all by now, all the things that parents and other adults worry about when they think about sexuality. It's not their fault. They really have no alternative. The only choice they have is to be either hip parents or firm parents—or some combination of the two. I assume that everyone is trying to do the best they can, parents included. I just have another approach to sex for you to think about.

There isn't even an English word for what I want you to think about, so I'll use the one that comes from India, *brahmacharya* (pronounced: bra-ma-char-ee-ya), and means a way to live to know your absolute potential through your own experience of your mind and body.

This is where meditation and yoga come in. Meditation can give you a sense of satisfaction that is all your own, that no one and no thing can take away. Brahmacharya gives your meditation the best fuel imaginable: your sexual energy. Yoga exercises work like a nuclear reactor to convert this energy into potent forces that fill and nourish you. In order to have this sexual energy, you will need to let it sublimate—that is, to meditate and do yoga and breathing exercises instead of letting it out in sex (including masturbation).

I'm not asking you to consider brahmacharya because sex is something bad that you should give up. I am simply suggesting a completely different way for you to grow to adulthood. If you save up some cash, you get to decide how you want to spend it. I am suggesting that you have a lot of various energies "saved up" within you, and you have some choice about whether to spend it in brahmacharya or in sex. Given some months of practice, you might find that you like what brahmacharya enables you to buy: a sense of vibrancy, a closeness with others, an inspired creativity.

After many years, should you continue, brahmacharya can give you a deep calm and serve as a basis for natural, higher states of consciousness. Drugs imitate these states, but they are both illegal and dangerous. Yoga is neither of those things and works with your own energies. It may be slower and less dramatic, but it will eventually exceed any chemically induced experiences.

If you try brahmacharya for a while, you can decide for yourself what to do; you may need a little firsthand experience. I suggest that you try it for fifteen months—that will give you enough time to assess the results.

If you are going out with someone, there are plenty of ways to get close to that person through *tantric* (which means "to weave truth into your daily life") brahmacharya. The practices are described in this book. Some of them are more emotional, and others are more physical. The key is to learn how to share your feelings for each other directly rather than through sex-desire. If you are not involved with anyone at the moment, you can do many of the practices alone.

THE CORE OF YOUR BODY:
THE YOGIC SPINAL PATHWAY

In yoga it is said that there is a hollow pathway in the center of one's spinal cord so small that not even the strongest electron microscope could see it. Since it cannot be seen, science doesn't believe this pathway exists. Nevertheless, the yogis (people who practice yoga) say that if we practice brahmacharya, meditation, and yoga (which have been practiced for thousands of years), we can help our energy to go up this pathway. Sending energy up this pathway awakens all sorts of hidden potentials in our minds, bodies, and spirits. Sex takes a lot of that energy and sends it into our genitals. Having sex more than once a month at the most, expends that energy, and it can then barely trickle into this pathway.

The two practices described below are part of the foundation of yoga and are particularly useful in brahmacharya. I recommend taking a class in yoga postures, as well; consider spending at least half an hour each day practicing yogic techniques. Perhaps some of your friends will be interested in doing them with you.

Yourself Breathing

This is easy. Each time you breathe in, say your first name or your nickname. When you breathe out, say your last name. Say everything very, very slowly during the whole time you breathe out for your first name, likethis:RRRRROOOOOGGGGGGGGGGEEEERRRRR or LLLLLIIIIIIIINNNNNNNNNDDDDDDDAAAAAAA. Feel how unique you are, that there is only one you in the entire universe and there will always be just one you in the entire universe. Let the sound of your name go through your whole body and feel and appreciate your whole being. Start with ten minutes and then increase to twenty minutes.

You can do this alone or with a friend. With someone else, you can say each other's name aloud to each other, as well as other things that you feel about each other, slowly, very slowly as you exhale. Just feel what it is like. You can hold hands when you do this, and you will feel an electrical current flowing between the two of you.

The current is the energy of your relationship, and you can feel it coursing all through your bodies. If you want to feel this energy quickly, just shake both your hands vigorously at the wrist for twenty seconds, then stop and stir the tingle of one hand with a finger of your other hand without touching it. Or have your partner stir your palm, without touching it, with his or her finger. You will feel the stirring on your open palm even though there is no physical contact.

If you are with your girlfriend or boyfriend and have sexual ideas about each other, just feel the feelings and breathe with those feelings while facing each other and holding hands. Just gaze at each other for two or three minutes and then close your eyes and be very still but relaxed in all your muscles.

Any thoughts you have will dissolve into the sensations, and the sensations will be more pleasurable than the thoughts. If you were to be sexual at this time, as most people would be, you would act on those thoughts and feelings. In brahmacharya, you find out that not acting on them allows the desire to *sublimate,* that is, to flow into the spinal pathway and diffuse throughout your body, leaving you feeling great.

Alternate Breathing

Use your right hand to close and open one nostril at a time so that you can inhale and exhale alternately through the left and right nostrils like this: Sitting up straight, breathe in the left while the right is closed with your thumb; then breathe out of your right nostril while your fingers close the left. Then breathe in the right and out the left, in the left and out the right, and so forth. You can do Yourself Breathing at the same time, with each breath.

These breathing practices will help you discover meditation, which is your own mind before you get caught up in words and thoughts. By balancing the breath coming in each nostril, you balance both sides of your brain and the whole of your nervous system.

In this balanced condition, with your eyes closed, you can feel your own being, without any words. It is you, just you, directly. It feels great, and you can do it for ten or twenty minutes to relax or to prepare for schoolwork, sports, or almost any project. It centers you back into yourself, smoothing away any annoying distractions.

BRAHMACHARYA AND
EMOTIONAL AND SPIRITUAL GROWTH

In brahmacharya you discover an essential feeling of love and understanding buried in each sexual desire and longing. You learn how to further sensitize yourself to the underlying creative forces in the universe. If you try this, you will see that sex is not just sex, it is the beginning of an enormous growth process, a big mystery that goes through many possible changes.

Of course, many people would tell you that you need sex to reach your potential. Certainly you can get an immense amount of value through sex, but it isn't necessary. You can always try sex, before or after you have tried brahmacharya.

So you can do all the other things you like to do. Just remember these yogic teachings, follow them, and see what happens.

APPENDIX 2

THE FUTURE OF
A MYSTERY:
TOWARD AN ECOLOGY
OF THE EROTIC

———————◆———————

"Men," said the little prince, "set out on their way in express trains, but they do not know what they are looking for. They rush about, and get excited, and turn round and round. . . ."

Antoine de Saint-Exupéry
The Little Prince

Why now? Why might tantric sublimation, or any alternative formulation of the erotic mystery, be of interest to us at this point in the history of erotic life? Perhaps because the maps we have been using to navigate these terrains of bodies, pleasures, and relationships are showing their limitations, and our struggles are forcing us to look elsewhere for answers.

In the first part of this appendix, I present observations that support the above hypothesis. In the second part, I present a new mapping of the mystery that could help us restore some measure of ecological balance to these intricate terrains. Our practical discourse of the main text now moves toward the more theoretical interests of erotic map-makers and "ecologists," which should include just about everyone.

THE CONTEMPORARY SEXUAL SCENE

We must admit that from all angles the sexual revolution is showing the signs of midlife crisis. The youthful vigor that motivated the carefree promiscuity of the sixties and seventies has matured into a more thoughtful concern for intimacy and enduring relationship. That adolescent feeling of sexual omnipotence has been disrupted repeatedly by the unwieldiness of free sex, most confusingly in our inability to contracept effectively.

We see this in a national abortion rate of over 33 percent, with as many as thirty million abortions in the past twenty years; unintentional pregnancy rates, aborted or not, are reported to be as high as 85–90 percent. The Pill is pathogenic to many, the foams, IUDs, sponges, and douches are irritating to others, and condoms and diaphragms are like canes—they get you there, but awkwardly.

We have increasing reports of sexual abuse, date rape, and sexual harassment, indicating both dark confusions in our intimate relationships and a greater willingness to report such violations. The consequences of AIDS alone are inestimable. We seem to be caught between the desire for sex and all the liberational values that support it, and some severely limiting factors in such pursuits.

To help us with some of the limitations, medical science has gone beyond merely remedying sexually related problems to literally creating bodies for us that are consistent with our sex-desire. Breast implants (many found to be toxic), penile prostheses, and liposuction techniques have become common procedures, with advertisements for some appearing in the general media. Surgical sterilization now surpasses all other forms of contraception, with more than twenty million Americans relying on it.

The sexual therapies for impotency and inorgasmia (said to affect from 40 percent to 70 percent of all men and women at various times) are well established in our culture. The most recent maladies to afflict us, despite all healing efforts, are "disorders of sexual desire"—not wanting sex enough (how much are we supposed to want?), for which specific therapies have been devised.

With all this dependence on doctoring, and with new and old problems mounting, perhaps modern sexuality is beyond a "mid-life" crisis. Isn't it more like that of a bedridden old grandfather who, hobbling about, still insists adamantly that he'll live another fifty years? Yet, in another way, it is like a helpless child, hoping that the authorities will come to the rescue with medical, educational, and legal solutions.

Is it enough to see these dilemmas as problems to be solved? For decades, medieval astronomers adjusted for troublesome observations that contradicted their geocentric solar system by adding more and more cumbersome orbital patterns to their celestial maps. Thus, data was forced to match the existing map, rather than forcing the existing map to reveal its inaccuracies. Fortunately for our understanding of the cosmos, Copernicus saw it differently, although he waited over thirty-five years to publicly state his findings, for fear of rejection and ridicule:

> When I considered in my own mind how absurd a performance it must seem to those who know that judgement of many centuries has approved the view that the Earth remains fixed as center in the midst of the heavens, if I should, on the contrary, assert that the Earth moves; I was for a long time at a loss to know whether I should publish the commentaries which I have written in proof of its motion, or whether it were not better to follow the example of the Pythagoreans and of some others, who were accustomed to transmit the secrets of Philosophy not in writing but orally, and only to their relatives and friends. . . . When I considered this carefully, the contempt which I feared because of the novelty and apparent absurdity of my view, nearly induced me to abandon utterly the work I had begun.
>
> (*De Revolutinibus*, pp. 52–53)

No doubt every age believes itself to possess final mappings of certain domains of existence and resists alterations. While our age has decided to claim, among others, the final chartings of the erotic universe, the times are obviously changing again.

As an example of a "final erotic truth" that has been rendered questionable within the space of five years, compare these two observations on incest:

> When we examine a cross-section of the population, as we did in the Kinsey Report . . . we find many beautiful and mutually satisfying relationships between fathers and daughters. These may be transient or ongoing, but they have no harmful effects. (Wardell

Pomeroy, pioneering sexologist of the Kinsey team, 1976, quoted in Russell, 1986, p. 3)

For those who aspire to an image of free womanhood, incest is as destructive to women as genital mutilation or the binding of feet. (Judith Herman, feminist psychiatrist, 1981, quoted in Russell, 1986, p. 3)

The conclusion of the Kinsey team is rendered more than just questionable; its not-so-hidden "liberational" and "normalizing" intentions to have all sexual phenomena fit their desire-centered erotic map become quite visible. Thus Diana Russell, who in 1986 paired these two quotes in her incest study, *The Secret Trauma*, suggests a correlation between some sexual liberation values and recent incidents of incest. With such "normalizing" and "liberating" strategies (or the "abnormalizing warnings" of moral mappings regarding other erotic phenomena) so obviously at work, how can the mappings of our sexuality "cartographers"—Freud, Kinsey, Masters and Johnson, Hite, and others—be taken as "final truth"?

What if many of our problems indicate potentially dangerous limitations inherent in our current map of the erotic universe? If this is the case, navigating with such a faulty map could result in our crashing into more uncharted hazards and unpredictable black holes in the future. If the pattern of problems we now encounter circulates around our loyalty to a sexocentric erotic map, then these problems might very well spin on as long as our sexological loyalties remain unquestioned. As Foucault (1980) maintains, the various "deployers" of this map of "sexual liberation" have already gone too far:

The Faustian pact, whose temptation has been instilled in us by the deployment of sexuality, is now as follows: to exchange life in its entirety for sex itself. . . .

By creating the imaginary element that is "sex," the deployment of sexuality established one of its most essential internal operating principles: the desire for sex—the desire to have it, to have access to it, to discover it, to liberate it, to articulate it into discourse, to formulate it in truth. . . it is this desirability that makes us think we are affirming the rights of our sex against all power, when in fact we are fastened to the deployment of sexuality that has lifted

up from deep within us a sort of mirage in which we think we see
ourselves reflected—the dark shimmer of sex. (pp. 156–157)

If the medical, legal, and commercial "deployers of sex" have gone
too far in their "certainties" about sex and its "liberation," then we must
face some frightening possibilities that only our hopeful naïveté has pre-
vented us from considering: that since sex is capable of transmitting diseases as well as loving feelings, AIDS might not be the last of the tragic
wild cards to enter the sexual deck; that yet another new sexual turn-on
might be incapable of supplying the depth of connection we are hungering
for in our love relationships; that all the deeper issues of abortion and
unintentional pregnancy can never be reconciled in a courtroom or by
administering courses in contraceptive education to ever-younger children;
that defining infant pleasures and body explorations as a "budding sexuality" or an "early danger sign" will neither liberate nor save them, and
both characterizations might be completely inaccurate; that teaching five-
and six-year-olds how to protect themselves from the sexual advances of
adults is telling, tragic, and very likely to induce severe side-effects for adults
and children alike. Such "solutions" will continue to bequeath us new and
perhaps more insidious problems in the future.

We needn't believe that somewhere there exists a utopian sexuality
based upon final truths. This, perhaps, has been the greatest naïveté of modern
sexuality: that it *should* work easily and without difficult challenges. We
have come to expect so very much from sex. Perhaps it is the overburdened,
middle-aged experiment called the sexual liberation movement that is finally asking us for some caring attention, if we can hear it.

Only a certain "innocence of desire" and an almost petulant sense of
natural entitlement to a problem-free sexuality keep us from such suspi-
cions. Being concerned about safe sex methods, improving the sexiness of
our relationships, abortion and sex harassment legalities, and contraceptive and incest-prevention education might not address our erotic problems
fundamentally enough. What we really need is a far more accurate erotic
map.

The surface of our current erotic map bears delineations, or shall we
say scars, that correspond more to the sexo-politics of the heatedly entwined
liberal-conservative debates than to the natural contours of eros. That this
is so becomes clear when we realize that nearly all our sexual problems
are embedded in partisan political ideologies.

One cannot wonder for long what conception might be. One is compelled to be either for or against the legality of abortion, and these political positions shape all the phenomena of conception and gestation to fit their respective requirements. We are not amazed at the bodily play of the infant, we use our moralities and sexologies to "decode" its meaning and thus inform us on what to do about it.

A teenager is not encouraged to marvel at her own blossoming fertility but instead is told she or he must take "responsibility" for it—that is, "be good, or at least be careful." Marvel, we believe, would be "too dangerous." One does not wonder at the mystery of homosexuality, or heterosexuality, for that matter, one is either for or against it, and "them." Wonder, we fear, might lead to self-doubt (not to the greater Mystery) for the gay or the straight individual.

Sex and celibate sublimation are not conceived of as equally attractive erotic possibilities. They are seen as freedom and repression, have and have not. Even the papacy has taken a stand against the spiritual possibilities of yogic practices.

The politics of our map, whether conservative or liberal, prohibit us from probing into the depths of erotic mysteries. If mathematics were subjected to such political considerations, Jerry Falwell would add a set of numbers one way, while Shere Hite would add the same figures another way. We have yet to create an erotic map as politically neutral as simple arithmetic.

TOWARD AN ECOLOGY OF THE EROTIC

Wilderness was not just one of, say, a dozen wholly different responses here on earth. The silent green world from which we so recently evolved was a precisely balanced organism making fullest use of the available resources compatible with long term existence. . . . For proof of this, look around you; everything out of step with those systems is already in trouble.

(Wells, 1980, p. 218)

As a theory with politically vested interests becomes a widely used map, how we see and what we do with the terrain changes accordingly. As Lao

Tzu stated, "If desire always within us be, its outer fringe is all that we shall see" (1962, p. 47). A map with a hidden agenda of getting the traveler to a certain destination will lead him, just as blinders would, to that very destination—as any advertising executive can tell you.

A geological resource map placed in a developer's hands leads to mining, welling, and lumbering, but how far can we go? As far as our desire leads us? Desire, unfortunately, is typically too self-obsessed to track the *consequences* of pursuing our desires. Desire only knows how to want more. Thus, where we have ore deposits, we also have strip-mining disasters; where oil might reside, we have had precarious oil-drilling sites; and where we find vast forests, our lumbering industry threatens massive deforestations. And what of the "ultimate desire"—sex?

The cartographers of our liberalized sexuality map, particularly Havelock Ellis, Wilhelm Reich, Alfred Kinsey, and A. S. Neill, looked out on the virginal erotic expanse as a vast, semi-political resource for achieving world utopia through mass proliferation of loving sexual activity. However, while the terrains of desire are rich, exciting, and deserving of much liberation, they are also treacherously vulnerable to any map-maker's unquestioned assumptions or short-sightedness.

Their maps can lead to activities and technologies that disrupt the subtle ecology of erotic structures that lie deeper than their purview—a purview that is exactly limited by its hidden or not-so-hidden agendas. This is equally true of the conservative mappings, with their views of "sinful pleasure" and the "deplorable weaknesses" of the flesh. We have yet to consider the terrains of eros ecologically, as a broad system in which neither sex-desire nor sexual fear (or their respective erotic maps and myopic strategies) can reign supreme but must bow to the elusive contours of erotic mystery.

Although we have achieved great gains in individual sexual rights, education, and research, sex has not become the panacea of world tensions, marital strife, and personal neurosis. This observation, like the emperor's new clothes, involves less embarrassment in the admission as time goes on. And a backlash, repression of sex, as we might guess, provides few answers, either.

We must certainly avoid Western sexology's seductive error of thinking of ourselves as arriving at a final erotic truth. In a universe of eternal time and erotic mystery, final truths are only temporary. As temporal beings, we are *always* verging on something in the process of revealing itself, and we are always arriving at this horizon: the mystery of human history itself. As Martin Heidegger's expositor, Reiner Schurmann, pondered:

As an epoch comes to an end, its principle withers away. The principle of an epoch gives it cohesion, a coherence which, for a time, holds unchallenged. At the end of an epoch, however, it becomes possible to question such coherence. As long as its economy dominates, and as long as its order disposes the paths that life and thought follow, one speaks otherwise than when its hold loosens, giving way to the establishment of a new order. . . . Ultimate reasons are unquestionable, but only temporarily so. They have their genealogy and their necrology. . . . They establish themselves without a blueprint and collapse without warning. (1987, p. 25)

By creating a new map that follows the phenomenological terrains of erotic mystery and abandoning the near-collapsing erotic map based on the principle of "sex-desire,"a rebalancing of our overtaxed erotic ecology might result, at least temporarily. By focusing upon eros as a mystery that allures, rather than as a well-defined desire to liberate or to control, its elements can cohere in a new gestalt.

THE FOURFOLD MAPPING
OF THE EROTIC MYSTERY

The ars erotica of tantric sublimation was not devised as a remedy to any of the particular problems we face in contemporary sexuality. But by pursuing the same ever-deepening pleasures that the yogis have long pursued, we find that many of those problems are, almost as a side effect, rendered vestigial. They remain as vestiges of a different, scientia sexualis approach to the mystery, as that approach attained predominance in these past decades.

In our tantric ars erotica, we have revived eros as a mystery, instead of the restrictive overdeterminations of scientia sexualis, psychoanalytic and sexological concepts, moralistic codes, or confessionals; liberational political mass-movements; educational preventions; legal supports, proscriptions, and remedies; and technological, psychological, and medical interventions.

We might ask how this ars erotica, as difficult as it might be initially to practice, comes to obviating so many contemporary sexual problems. I believe this is due to its reviving a devalued tonality in the erotic scale, that of sublimation, which brings more harmony to the whole. Reviving this nondesirous tonality alleviates the desperation that its devaluation in the age of scientia sexualis has bred. For the emotional vacancy left in us by having pathologized so much of sublimation was further deformed into various negative motivating forces—stigmatizing shame for being a virgin, fears of states of consciousness in which the ego plays no part, and, of course, the fear of possible "repression," thought to be the foundation of many mental illnesses—that, according to the formula, only a satisfied sex-desire could truly remedy.

A revival of sublimation brings out the relative, rather than ultimate, importance of the tonality of sex-desire, as well as differentiating and strengthening two other erotic tonalities—those of fertility and child play eros—often lumped together within the throbs of the desire. Clearly, reviving and differentiating each of these erotic tonalities can bring greater balance to the conventionally sexual person who otherwise takes only a passing interest in the pathways of sublimation.

In this section I will sketch what appears to me to be the four inherent tonalities of erotic mystery and the four distinct domains of erotic life into which they radiate their passions. They are sex-desire, sublimation, procreativity, and child and adult play. Like the four cycling seasons, each is empowered with specific vital potencies, thus each can innocently manifest—that is, manifest in a spontaneous, natural way—one discrete span of the whole erotic spectrum. When these domains are in balance, our erotic ecology is as well. This erotic balancing act is accomplished in two parts: (1) discernment of the tonalities, and (2) preserving their integrity. (See Figure 2.)

Discernment

First, all four tonalities must be discerned, for sex-desire has come to so predominate the other three that they almost seem not to exist in their own right. This discernment is made more complex by the fact that the same body parts are awakened by each of the four tonalities of passion, and that the tonalities usually reverberate with one another in actual life.

Additionally, how we view puberty (as the culmination of a slowly developing sex drive into adult desire) disguises the pure-play aspect of childhood eros and its continuity as such into its various adult forms. "Polymorphous perversity" was Freud's strange name for his sexualized observations of a child's play. Yet such play is even less determined than he surmised. Complicating matters further, in both the pre- and post-pubescent phases, erotic "play" can be lighthearted or more teasing, and even darkly competitive, seriously contentious, or cruel.

Certainly we face an initial struggle in extricating our bodies and minds from the "grip," as Foucault called it, of scientia sexualis principles. We must shake off the singular spell of sex-desire and the modern mandate to have it or grow ill. We must become free from the demystification of reproduction as merely a kind of "intention" or "responsibility," instead of a bodily and spiritual erotic mystery.

Preservation

In order to preserve the integrity of each tonality, we must grant them equal stature and erotic allure, in an operational sense. That is, whichever tonality now guides our life, we must grant an equal erotic potency and validity to the other three. We must strive to feel that each holds the potential to allure and provide us with its particular range of erotic satisfactions, whether we explore it for very long or not.

Each tonality tells us what it "means" and, thus, "what to do" to follow it into its specific expanse of mystery. Yet the clarifying *logos* of each tonality "speaks" of a mystery, not with demystifying certainty: the allure of desire, the miracles of fertility, the wonder of sublimation, the indeterminacy of play. Thus logos and eros must sustain their own cognitive balance of clarity and awe.

For further protection, we must not reduce the terms of one tonality to those of another. Sex is not fallen sublimation, nor is sublimation a derivative of the sex drive. Child play is not a miniature, developing sex drive, sublimative drive, or procreative urge. Procreation is not the "real purpose" of erotic attractions, nor does sex-desire explain the matter conclusively.

As a result of this new erotic economy, sex-desire no longer has to feign omnipotence in providing us all erotic pleasures, nor omniscience in knowing the "real meaning" of all erotic gestures, dreams, and ambiguities, as Freud and his followers believed. Sex-desire can relax and allow the other three tonalities to pull their own weight in fulfilling and guiding us.

I must add that the fourfold mapping is merely one possible constellation of eros that can emerge from an ars erotica approach. Other mappings are quite possible.

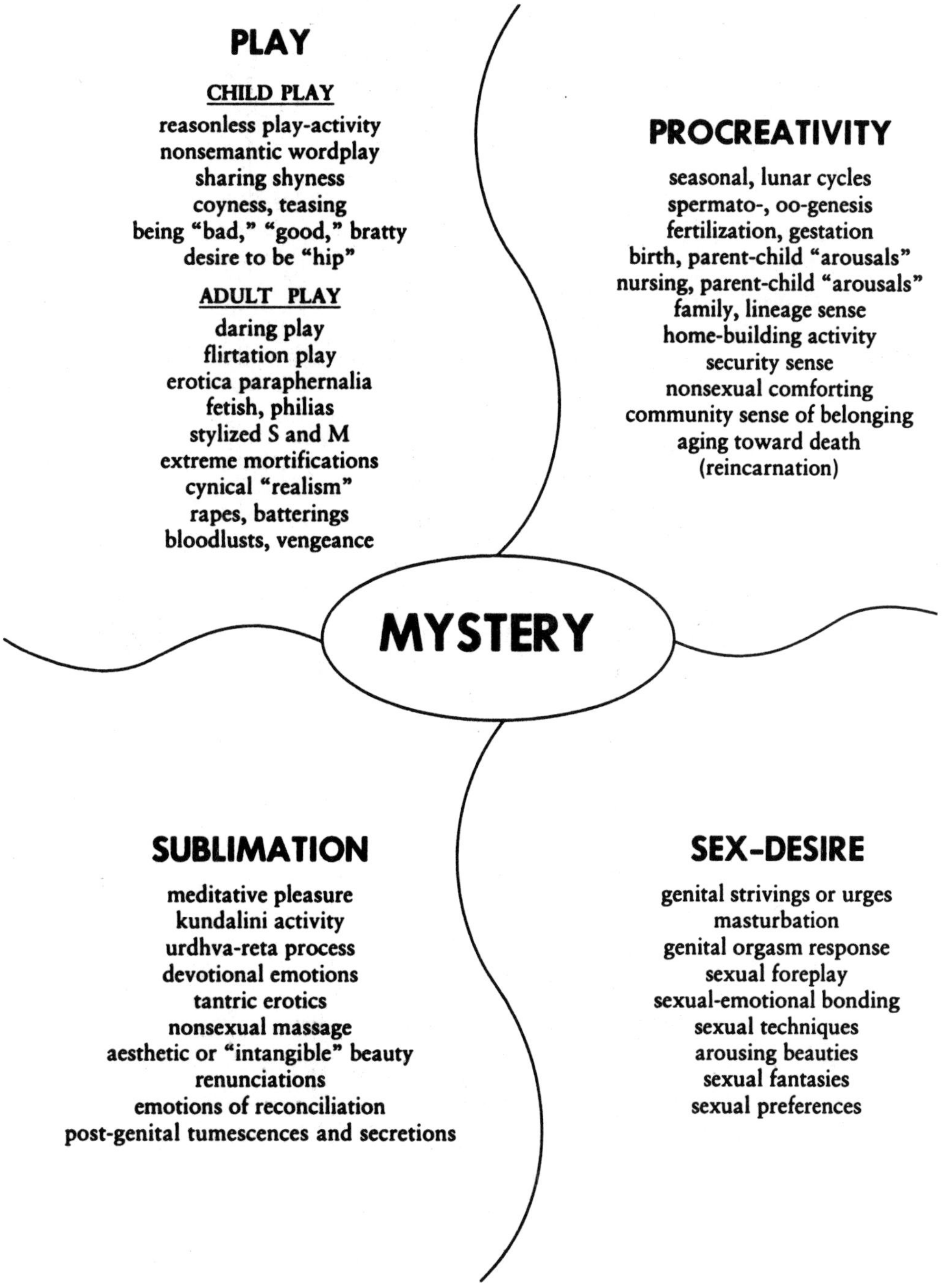

PLAY

CHILD PLAY

reasonless play-activity
nonsemantic wordplay
sharing shyness
coyness, teasing
being "bad," "good," bratty
desire to be "hip"

ADULT PLAY

daring play
flirtation play
erotica paraphernalia
fetish, philias
stylized S and M
extreme mortifications
cynical "realism"
rapes, batterings
bloodlusts, vengeance

PROCREATIVITY

seasonal, lunar cycles
spermato-, oo-genesis
fertilization, gestation
birth, parent-child "arousals"
nursing, parent-child "arousals"
family, lineage sense
home-building activity
security sense
nonsexual comforting
community sense of belonging
aging toward death
(reincarnation)

MYSTERY

SUBLIMATION

meditative pleasure
kundalini activity
urdhva-reta process
devotional emotions
tantric erotics
nonsexual massage
aesthetic or "intangible" beauty
renunciations
emotions of reconciliation
post-genital tumescences and secretions

SEX–DESIRE

genital strivings or urges
masturbation
genital orgasm response
sexual foreplay
sexual-emotional bonding
sexual techniques
arousing beauties
sexual fantasies
sexual preferences

Figure 2: Four Tonalities of Erotic Mystery

Beginning the Discernment

We begin by considering bodily, erotic sensations as preludes to mystery. Thus, discerning different tonalities of suspensefulness furthers our study. What is this erotic suspense about? is our guiding question. By following this suspensefulness as it fans out into life, we begin to discern the four-fold terrains of eros. "What should we/I do next with *this feeling?*" This is the suspenseful bottom-line question. It leads us into action, relationship, consequences, and counter-consequences.

SEX-DESIRE

Consider erotic mystery, feel it in your body and mind and in the larger world. The allure begins. The suspense. It becomes more urgent, a sense of need, particularized as a desire being allured forward. Genital sensations and inviting sexual images predominate and thus are given priority: the way into this growing suspense of "a mystery going on" is to be found in en-acting the images of these "genital strivings." Every gesture, however subtle, is thought to be a covert cueing toward possible sex: a "yes," a "no," a "maybe."

Good sex (that is, sex that is itself guided by the suspenseful pull of other, "more emotional" hopes and needs) and orgasm bring the suspense to a peak and a close—providing the basis for cycles of suspenseful sex-desire and the fulfillment of good sex. Our needing, choosing, and loving of each other is expressed through the enactment of sex-desire. The boldness of our desire leads our shyness suspensefully into the mystery of bodies, relationships, loves, and pleasures.

SUBLIMATION

Consider erotic mystery, again. Feel the allure, the suspense. In feeling it more and more, the sense of mystery renders sexual ways of ending the suspense evermore uncertain. The suspense continues for many months, even years. Every day we feel it, are consumed by it to the point of meditative absorption until it becomes an ongoing awareness of mystery, the ek-static allure of flowing impermanence. "What do I/we do next?" We feel the wonder in the question and share it as possibility, as union.

We begin, then, to experience the body as filled with arousals that have nothing to do with sex-desire and orgasm. *Chi,* kundalini, charismatic stirrings, "orgonomic streaming" (what Wilhelm Reich himself concluded went beyond sex-desire)—such are the names for sublimative energies within.

The tongue arouses, and we think, nabhan mudra, and later, khechari mudra. We feel tingles up the spine, and we wonder, pranic activity, urdhva-reta, kundalini. Even genital arousals mean to us the invigorations of sub-limation. How so? We feel a diffusing tonality of sensation that is devoid of desirous urgency and provokes no sexual fantasies, only a kind of won-der or a sense of the eternal. Here we "need" each other erotically for no other purpose than to awaken further desireless awe and to share it in the spirituality of life.

PROCREATIVITY

A third time, consider erotic mystery. Feel the allure, the suspense. Over time, notice its cyclings, without acting to end or heighten the suspense. Feel a waxing and waning of suspense each month. Feel your own aging process as a waxing and waning; the urges that are stirred by this suspense-fulness feel to be a kind of living-and-aging biological clock.

If you tune in to this tonality of suspenseful allure for a sufficient length of time, it will induce imaginations and desires of conceiving a child (or of being glad you already have, or glad you have not, or of grieving that you have not). Within this tonality we feel a need for each other in order to create family and new human life. Visit a couple with their newborn baby and feel this tonality stir. When stirred, our shy hopes become bold, and we enter this particular domain of mystery, revealing fertility, conception, gestation, birth, familyhood, aging, and death lineage successors.

Here lives the contentment of pregnant fullness, the pleasures of nursing, the challenges of home and hearth building (what is often called "commit-ment"), the felt sense of community, parental pride and the love of the child's special beauty, the longing to be with (aging) family members (or the grievous lack of such longings). Or you might merely get that comfortable slippers-and-robe-urge to return to the coziness of your own home. You buy life insurance for the first time in your life, for in grounding and rooting you feel your limits, as well.

As this warm, steadying, and awesome tonality fans out into our bodies and our lives, we find that all the elements of sex—the body parts, sensa-tions, substances, relationships, desires—must be reinterpreted in terms of the erotic mysteries inherent in fertility, conception, and family life. Their erotic meanings and agendas change abruptly or even reverse, verifying that they cohere as a natural domain of erotic meaning, distinct from other domains that have their own codes of meaning.

"Bad" (for sex-desire), "unsafe," fertile times are suddenly favored over "good," "safe" infertile times; an infertile couple with a wonderful "sex life" who now wants to have children suddenly has a problem. Homosexuals seek out surrogates or donors from the other gender. Sperm banks and adoption centers suddenly become crucially important.

Provocative and exciting *tits* become the more serene breasts that might now be exposed discreetly during nursing—but with a sense of erotic beauty informed by the mysteries of fertility and lactation rather than desire. Testicles produce wonderfully viable or hopelessly nonviable sperm cells rather than the desire-eroticized, infertile, or dangerously fertile *cum*.

Sublimating couples encounter images of conception and family in their celibate lovemaking and find a different order of erotic mysteries (than those of sex-desire) suspensefully alluring them. Ojas transmutations are now far less important than the possible meeting of sperm with ovum through pro-creative sex.

Likewise, the newborn boy's not uncommon erection is a phenomenon of childhood procreative innocence and has nothing meaningfully in common with desirous or even sublimative adult arousals; nor should the newborn girl's lubrications or clitoral tumescences be considered "pre-sexual." Similarly, the nursling's genital arousals are procreatively, not desirously, based.

Contraceptives and legal abortion, which might have been necessary, even fought for, as supports for sexual activity in the domain of desire, no longer pertain. Since it is now conception and live birth that is being sought by the same people engaging in nearly identical sexual activities, these "valued supports" are now personally irrelevant and may seem at least somewhat unpleasant. The radiant new mother and the giddy new father represent the glow and afterglow of the "orgasm" of this domain: birth. Being a parent is itself a lifelong "psycho-procreational" rather than a "psychosexual" maturational process.

CHILD PLAY AND ADULT PLAY

Childhood eros is difficult to recover because we have been taught by sexology and moralists to view childhood erotics as a miniature version of adult sex-desire. But this teaching is a well-intended error generated by sexology's efforts to legitimate and "liberate" adult sex-desire by trying to find its "natural precursor" in childhood. From the moralist, we have the equally intrusive interpretations of the dangers of masturbation and the "innocent" child's possible "corruption." The childhood observations of both, as well as their guidance to parents on sex education, prove to be the sexo-political projections of their respective ideologies.

In all actuality, however, childhood eros is very simple to recover, so simple we adults sometimes overlook it. Recall being four years old. Feel the suspensefulness of mystery. Isn't it funny? Scary? You don't want to just sit here, do you? You want to play, to play with anything, a string, your body, to tease and joke. When you were younger, your play was even more pointless and endlessly diverting; you could joyfully pull your pants up and down, or bang a pot. Flirtation? Hardly. Gourmet cooking? What's that? As you had little language, it is hard to say what your play was like. Thus the suspense of early childhood and its pursuits seems to be a kind of original innocence, as when James Joyce called the sound of children playing in the street "God."

A five-year-old literally "plays with" herself and is not performing "immature masturbation." However similar looking to masturbation, it deserves another name. Singing out gleefully, "Pee-pee, fuck, fuck," the child enjoys a playful teasing devoid of either semantic or desirous import. Little girls and boys can be playfully coy, teasing, or cute, but not seductive, for, as Webster notes, the latter, by definition, aims for sexual intercourse.

Here the peek-a-boo game of sharing shyness with baby, as the first encounters with hiddenness, begins the daring pathway of intimacy, a pathway that continues fundamentally unmodified for the rest of our lives. This play is not, as psychoanalysis maintains, the child's learning how to renounce immediate instinctual satisfactions for the sake of "individuation." There is no firm "individuation process"; all matters of erotic "development" are those of an evermore refinable sharing and interrelating. Quiverings of shyness or embarrassment passionately consecrate each wavering increase in awareness of being in the world with others with a remarkable innocence. Such blushing arousals charm and nourish all and yield what individuation hopes to achieve.

Play is a matter of oscillation, capable of escalating by nuances from the harmonious to the contentious. And then, suddenly, a subtle line is crossed and the play is anything but playful. Thus, child's play can also become bratty, rebellious, deceptive, competitive, and even cruel. The vulnerable and hopeful child (and the adult's so-called "inner child) can be, in a strangely natural way, these darker things as well.

These oscillations within and between light and dark moods of play reappear in adulthood in the vast range of embellishments to sexual foreplay and in certain empassioned and too often insidious marital power struggles. "Being bad" becomes, by teasing degrees, fun and "good," then treacherous and heinous; emotional interplay begins as "honesty" but tightens into deadly polarizations; sustained obedience and trust allure with a promise of some ultimate reward, yet also threaten with innuendos of domination, guilt, and servitude.

Rules and limits of play and sheer familiarity imply that hidden beyond them is the untamed, which suggests the more passionate, the even *more* real, the truly sexy. Within such ambiguous certainties and suggestive ambiguities—the "play" of play itself—the sense of mystery peeks out from behind each tabooed hiddenness and thus winkingly, daringly, shyly beckons.

This norm-teasing ambiguity of bad becoming good in conventional or "vanilla" adult erotic play begins with the mild kinkiness of "getting down to it" and goes on to the more serious stylized forms of sadomasochism, known in those circles as "playing." Here pleasure and pain blur, even bleed, into each other, but always governed by agreed-upon rules and procedures. Less a matter of sex-desire, these erotic plays are teasing trust games: Can we trust each other with the most darkly hidden of intimacies, the seemingly most shameful and shameless? A long and winding way from the teasings of peek-a-boo.

Sex-desire is itself overshadowed by this X-rated offshoot of childhood's erotic play, as the broad realm of fetishes and philias attests. Within sublimation such fascinations can lead to mortifications and severe penances that, in the name of purification, can displace the subtleties of sublimation with a thirst for power over all trepidations.

The dance of rules and chaos, of one kind of power with another, can go too far. Vengeance and the blood-lusts of war are the most deadly extreme. The sense of violence and tragedy dormant in the darker sides of mystery suddenly bursts all our innocence. In such shadowy ways, thanatos and eros come to tortuous distortions of the darkly fascinating hiddenness within each other. Yet when skillfully played, as in Edward Albee's *Who's Afraid of Virginia Woolf?*, the game concludes in a dawning resolution of poignant reconciliation. When it is over, a buried love soothes once again.

Same Body Parts, Different Passions: Preserving the Tonalities of Erotic Mystery

Since the same body parts are often stirred by each of the four tonalities (usually, overlappingly), we are presented with a major challenge in preventing our wires from getting crossed and misinterpreting a particular arousal. Of course, relying upon a onefold map may be easier, but all sorts of trespasses and misreadings have been occurring in this undifferentiated, liberated simplicity. Once discerning these four erotic tonalities becomes second nature to us, we can expect matters to improve. Some obvious discernments of tonality have already been made, such as the distinctions between sex and intimacy, but their full implications have not yet been pursued.

For example, the pleasures of a mother's not-uncommon breast and genital arousals as she suckles her infant derive their meaning from the passion of procreation, and we instinctively appreciate the experience with a sense of naturalness rather than seeing it as child sexual abuse. The amorous arousals she experiences in breast-sucking foreplay with her husband will feel characteristically different because they originate from a different nuance of erotic passion, that of sex-desire. As yet, sexology hasn't begun to wonder whether any innocent, paternal, procreative (nondesirous) arousals exist; nor, as we have seen, whether most yogic sublimative arousals have a bonafide existence.

Couples face their own difficulties when one partner wants only to be held and comforted with nothing more in mind and the other misinterprets these nonsexual caresses as the foreplay of sex-desire. Likewise, a masseur enters confusing territory as he moves up his client's legs; the massage will remain nonsexual if his attunement to the client's body remains caring and therapeutic yet nondesirous, and as long as his client remains similarly attuned.

A teenager feels that her uncle's touch is "sort of funny," that is, sexual rather than affectionate; an actor and an actress doing a love scene find they are no longer just acting; Aschenbach, in Thomas Mann's *Death in Venice,* longs for the boy Tadzio with a spiritual, rather than a carnal, love; an opera virtuoso soars into a solo and feels tremendously aroused but is not embarrassed because she knows her passion is sublimative.

Naming the suspenseful prelude to a mystery is thus a world-creating event. It determines "What will I/we do next?" Thus we need a vocabulary of accurate and discerning terms that covers equally and nonreductively all four erotic tonalities:

- "This yearning could be the desire for moonlit, long, and passionate sex!"
- "This longing could be the longing for nyasa."
- "This hoping could be my longing for family."
- "This tingling seems like urdhva-reta."
- "This suspense might be my shy hope to be seen."
- "This desperate churning is my unwillingness to forgive and plays upon me with endless ruminations and dark passions."
- "This undetermined urge is pure foolishness; I think I'll just jump in the air and tickle you!"

The Hope of the Fourfold Erotic Map

The fourfold mapping of erotic mystery offers us a possible exit from the strife-ridden history of Western sexuality. Through carefully won discernments of different tonalities of suspense, we can learn to preserve and explore the varied terrains of the four passions in our lives. If, then, the current storms of our many crises should settle, new and further vistas of erotic liberation might become visible beyond the horizons of our present erotic knowledge.

GLOSSARY

———————◆———————

Phonetic transliterations of Sanskrit terms found in most popular works have been used throughout the text. More academic (without diacritical marks) or other common transliterations appear in this glossary for further reference.

ahamkara   self-sense, or ego, which can be isolated from the more subtle jiva, or soul, and thus becomes bereft of spiritual input and believes itself to be limited to the physical body.

ajna chakra (cakra)   brow center of nondual consciousness, presides over "highest element."

anahata chakra (cakra)   heart center, associated with love and courage, presides over the air element and the pranamaya kosha; seat of jiva and ahamkara.

anandamaya kosha (kosa)   bliss or causal body, where jiva dwells.

annamaya kosha (kosa)   food body; the fleshy, physical body.

apana pran   pranic currents of abdomen concerned with elimination and reproductive/sexual functions.

ars erotica   Michel Foucault's term for erotic knowledge gained through bodily experience and seeking to deepen those experiences, unmodified by overarching social concepts as in scientia sexualis.

asana   a formal position or pose in hatha yoga.

atman   soul.

auras   the quintessential distillate of sublimation, arising from virtuous action (see *virya*).

ayurveda   yogic system of medicine and physiology.

bandhas   muscular holdings, or "locks," that keep subtle energies in a specific area of the body for the purpose of healing and transmutation.

Bhagavad-Gita   "Song of God," sermon on life from Krishna to Arjuna; usually understood as dealing with karma yoga, the ways of dutiful and honorable activity in the world.

bhakti yoga   the yoga based in deepening devotional feelings.

bindu   the essence of the gamete, sexual fluids, seed-force.

brahmacharya (brahmacarya)   living in accord with absolute truths; celibacy.

brahmarandhra   subtle center at the crown of the head attuned to absolute truths and ideals corresponding to ultimate reality.

buddhi   intellectual power of mind.

chakras (cakras)   nonphysical energy centers that regulate the physical and more subtle bodies.

chi   life energy, according to the Chinese system of medicine.

daya   compassion.

decoupled sex   sociobiology's term for the separation of sex-desire from fertility rhythms.

dharana   near to complete unwavering concentration on an object.

dharma   a way, or manner, of life or of acting in a particular situation that is in accord with spiritual principles; virtuous or honorable living.

dhyana   unwavering attention to an object; the beginning of meditation proper.

divya sharira (divya sarira)   divine body attained through lifetimes of yogic development.

ekagrata   one-pointedness of concentration.

guru   "light that dispells darkness"; an accomplished teacher of yoga and dharma.

hatha yoga "forceful"   practices that purify the physical body through balancing polar forces. Esoterically *Ha-tha* is "sun-moon."

hri   humbling shame, modesty.

ida   the main lunar or cooling channel that crosses the central spinal *sushumna* at each of the first six chakras.

intimus   Latin for "within," "most interior"; root of the word "intimacy."

Ishvara (Isvara)   God.

japa   rosary-like chantings of a mantra.

jiva   the being that has the life; the soul of one's being.

jivan-mukti (jiva-mukti)   spiritual liberation of the individual soul in this lifetime.

Jnaneshvari-Gita (Jnanesvari-Gita)   an interpretation of the *Bhagavad-Gita* of particular relevance to kundalini yoga, the yoga of bodily and energetic transformations.

kaivalya   separated from all illusions and resting in the natural state; eternal beatitude.

karma   actions begetting consequences.

khechari mudra (khecari)   advanced stage of urdhva-reta in which the tongue spontaneously moves back toward the palatial cavity of the head, the "reverse" of an early stage of oral, cranial, and lingual embryological development, as the body seeks its own source.

koshas (kosas)   sheaths or gradients of the human being.

kshama (ksama)   forgiveness.

kundalini   intelligent energy that, when awakened, animates all sheaths in accord with highest levels of purification and discrimination; "serpent coiled" energy at the muladhara chakra.

lila   activity of the universe considered as a divine play.

mahat-Tattwa (mahat-tattva)   subtlest and highest matter; cosmic principle.

manipura chakra (cakra)   navel center, governs physical body, presides over fire principle; associated with willful emotionalities.

manomaya kosha   mental-emotional sheath.

mantra   sacred Sanskrit incantation, often producing specific vibrational effects in the physical and subtle bodies.

moksha (moksa)   complete spiritual liberation.

mudra   gesture of spiritual significance; poses that affect kundalini.

muladhara chakra (cakra)   spinal base center, presides over earth element, associated with instincts of physical survival.

nabhan mudra (nabho)   curling the tongue back in the mouth so that the tip touches the soft palate.

nadis   subtle bodily channels, analogous to acupuncture meridians.

nirbija-samadhi   highest meditation, without seeds of future desire, for such are now unnecessary.

niyama   guidances for positive actions and observances.

nyasa   placing of subtle energy, anointment.

ojas   transmuted bindu; radiantly glowing bioenergy.

pingala   solar energy channel corresponding to ida along the spinal sushumna channel and passing through each of the first six chakras.

prana   vital energy of life; vitality in the air, food, and water.

pranamaya kosha (kosa)   vital energy sheath.

prana-pran   currents of prana in chest concerned with breathing.

pranayama   control of breath, or prana; breathing practices.

pranotthana (prana-utthana) intensified pranic activity; a precursor to kundalini awakening.

pratyahara early stage of meditation in which focus is gathered from its more ordinary scatterings through the senses and through "mind chatter."

rajas female sexual fluids.

retas vital juice-current, procreative essence.

sabija-samadhi highest meditative state, with remaining seeds for future desires.

sadhana spiritual practices that gather virtue and energy.

sahasrara chakra (cakra) crown chakra, beyond all elements; awakens into effulgent brilliance and divine knowledge; "thousand-petalled lotus."

samadhi meditation with concentration unwaveringly gathered unto consciousness itself.

samana pran pranic current between navel and heart, concerned with digestion.

shambhavi (sambhavi mudra) seeing of the divine through a gesture of the eyes.

scientia sexualis Michel Foucault's term for erotic knowledge that is conformed to moral codes and scientific or "scientist" principles, political policy, and research methods of garnering reports or data about private erotic experience, including the confessional, the psychoanalytic interview, the laboratory and demographic study, and the diagnostic-nosological method.

shakti (sakti) spiritual force apparently analogous to the charismatic Holy Ghost of Christianity.

shakti-pata-diksha (sakti-pata-diksa) transmission of energy from a guru to an aspirant as an initiation.

shraddha (sraddha) faith.

Shiva (Siva) the Hindu deity who presides over yogis.

shukra (sukra) male sexual fluid.

sushumna (susumna) central spinal channel through which urdhva-reta and kundalini processes proceed.

svadhisthana chakra (svadhishthana cakra)   associated with sexual and reproductive functioning; presides over the water element.

talu (taluka)   subtle energy gateway on soft-palate where the reversed tongue in nabhan and khechari mudras helps preserve amritas, and helps quiet the mind.

tantra   yoga of weaving the spiritual into the physical.

udana pran   pranic currents from the throat to the top of the head; govern swallowing movements of throat and tongue.

urdhva-reta (urdhva-retas)   upward refinement of the juice-current of life, the body's inherent capacity for "inner alchemy," or what is loosely known as *sublimation*.

vairagha (vairagya)   nonattachment arising from contentment and dispassion.

vasana   subtle basis of desires.

vijnanamaya kosha (kosa)   intellect sheath, capable of reflective knowing.

virya (vira)   the quintessential distillate of sublimation, arising from virtuous activity, as noted by Sri Aurobindo.

vishuddha chakra (cakra)   throat center, presides over the etheric element; associated with the spirit of words.

viyoga   the hidden union that occurs when one believes that only separation exists.

vritti (vrtti)   thought waves that interrupt meditation.

vyana-pran   circulatory pranic currents that pervade the whole body.

yama   moral guidances of moderation and restraint.

yoga   ways of union; union.

BIBLIOGRAPHY

Alan Guttmacher Institute. *Teenage Pregnancy: The Problem That Hasn't Gone Away*. New York: A. Guttmacher, 1981.

Albee, Edward. *Who's Afraid of Virginia Woolf?* New York: Atheneum, 1962.

Altman, I. "Report on the Annual Convention of the Society for the Scientific Study of Sex." *San Francisco Bay Guardian,* 28 August 1991.

Ananda, D. [Bubba Free John]. *Love of the Two-Armed Form*. Middletown, Calif.: Dawn Horse, 1978.

———. *What You Need to Know to Be Happy*. Clear Lake, Calif.: Dawn Horse, 1988.

Aranya, S. H. *Yoga Philosophy of Patanjali*. Trans. by P. N. Mukerji. Albany, N. Y.: State Univ. of N. Y. Press, 1983 (original date, 1963).

Aries, P. *Western Attitudes Toward Death From the Middle Ages to the Present*. Translated by Patricia Ranum. Baltimore: Johns Hopkins University, 1974.

Aurobindo, G., and the Mother. *On Love*. Pondicherry, India: Sri Aurobindo Ashram, 1973.

Avalon, A. [John Woodroffe]. *The Serpent Power*. New York: Dover, 1974.

Baker, L. *The Fertility Fallacy*. Philadelphia: Saunders Press, 1981.

Barbach, L. *For Yourself, the Fulfillment of Female Sexuality.* Garden City, N.Y.: Anchor, 1976.

Barrel, J. "Sexual Arousal in the Objectifying Attitude." *Review of Existential Psychology and Psychiatry* 8, no. 1 (1974).

Bass, E., and L. Davis. *The Courage to Heal.* New York: Harper & Row, 1988.

Bergson, H. *A Study in Metaphysics: The Creative Mind.* Translated by Mabelle Andison. Totowa, N.J. : Littlefield and Adams, 1965.

Bhagavad-Gita. Translated by S. Prabhavananda and C. Isherwood. New York: Mentor, 1951.

Boehme, J. *Six Theosophic Points.* Ann Arbor, Mich.: Ann Arbor, 1970.

Boorstein, S. *Transpersonal Psychotherapies.* Palo Alto, Calif.: Science and Behavior Books, 1980.

Bradshaw, J. *Healing the Shame That Binds You.* Deerfield Beach, Fla.: Health Communications, 1988.

———. "KQED presents John Bradshaw" (flier). Oakland, Calif. 23 July 1992.

Brake, M., ed. *Human Sexual Relations.* New York: Pantheon, 1982.

Briggs, G. W. *Gorakhnath and the Kanphata Yogis.* Delhi: Motilal Banarsidass, 1982.

Brown, G. *The New Celibacy.* New York: Ballantine, 1980.

Brown, N. *Love's Body.* New York: Vintage, 1966.

Buber, M. *I and Thou.* Translated by Ronald Smith. New York: Scribner's, 1958.

Buddhananda, C., with S. Satyananda. *Moola Bandha, the Master Key.* Monghr, India: Goenka Bihar School of Yoga, 1978.

Carter, S., and J. Sokol. *Men Who Can't Love.* New York: Berkeley, 1988.

Chamberlain, D. *Consciousness at Birth: A Review of the Empirical Evidence.* San Diego: Chamberlain, 1983.

Chesser, E. *Salvation Through Sex.* New York: W. Morrow, 1973.

Chia, M. *Taoist Secrets of Love, Cultivating Male Sexual Energy.* New York: Aurora, 1984.

Chia, M., and M. Chia. *Healing Love Through the Tao, Cultivating Female Sexual Energy.* Huntington, N.Y.: Healing Tao, 1986.

Clark, K. *An Experience of Celibacy.* Notre Dame: Ave Maria, 1982.

Cole, F. *Early Theories of Sexual Generation.* Oxford, England, 1930.

Copernicus, N. "Dedication of the Revolutions of the Heavanly Bodies." In *Famous Prefaces.* Edited by Charles Eliot. Harvard Classics. New York: P. F. Collier, 1969.

Corless, I., and M. Pittman-Lindeman. *AIDS Principles, Practices and Politics*. Washington, D.C.: Hemisphere, 1988.

Courtois, C. *Healing the Incest Wound*. New York: Norton, 1988.

Coward, R., S. Lipshitz, and E. Cowie. "Psychoanalysis and Patriarchical Structures." In *Conference on Patriarchy*. Women's Publishing Collective, 1976.

Crewdson, J. *By Silence Betrayed*. New York: Harper & Row, 1988.

Darwin, C. *The Origin of Species*. 1859. Reprint. New York: Mentor, 1958.

————. *The Descent of Man and Selection in Relation to Sex*. New York: A. L. Burt, 1874.

Dass, A., and Aparna. *The Marriage and Family Book*. New York: Schocken, 1978.

Dass, B. *Hariakhan Baba, Known, Unknown*. Davis, Calif.: Sri Rama, 1975.

————. *Silence Speaks*. Santa Cruz, Calif.: Sri Rama, 1977.

————. *Ashtanga Yoga Primer*. Santa Cruz, Calif.: Sri Rama, 1981.

Delora J., and C. Warren. *Understanding Sexual Interaction*. Boston: Houghton Mifflin, 1977.

DeMaria, R. *Communal Love at Oneida*. New York: Edwin Mellen, 1978.

de Nicolas, Antonio. *Avatara: The Humanization of Philosophy Through the Bhagvad Gita*. New York: Nicolas Hays, 1976.

————. *St. John of the Cross: Alchemist of the Soul*. New York: Paragon House, 1989.

de Ropp, R. *Sex Energy*. New York: Delta, 1969.

de Rougemont, D. *Love in the Western World*. Translated by M. Belgion. New York: Schocken, 1983.

de Saint Exupéry, A. *The Little Prince*. Translated by Katherine Woods. New York: Harvest/Harcourt Brace Jovanovich, 1971.

Desai, A. *Kripalu Yoga*. Lenox, Mass.: Kripalu Yoga Fellowship, 1985.

Dimock, E. *The Place of the Hidden Moon*. Chicago: University of Chicago Press, 1966.

Douglas, N., and P. Slinger. *Sexual Secrets*. Rochester, Vt.: Destiny Books, 1979.

Dychtwald, K. "Sexuality and the Whole Person." *Journal of Humanistic Psychology* 19, no. 2 (Spring 1979): 47–62.

Eckhart, M. *A Modern Translation*. Translated by R. Blakney. New York: Harper & Row, 1941.

Eisler, R. *The Chalice and the Blade*. New York: Harper & Row, 1987.

Eliade, M. *Patanjali and Yoga.* New York: Schocken, 1976.

Ellis, H. *Psychology of Love.* New York: Mentor, 1933.

Eventz-Wentz, W. *The Tibetan Book of the Dead.* 1927. Reprint. London: Oxford University Press, 1978.

Evola, J. *The Metaphysics of Sex.* Rochester, Vt.: Inner Traditions, 1983.

Feuerstein, G. *Encyclopedic Dictionary of Yoga.* New York: Paragon, 1990.

———. *Enlightened Sexuality.* Freedom, Calif.: Crossing Press, 1989.

———. *Textbook of Yoga.* London: Rider, 1975.

———. *Yoga: The Technology of Ecstasy.* Los Angeles: J. P. Tarcher, 1989 (original date, 1979).

———. *The Yoga-Sutra of Patanjali: A New Translation and Commentary.* Rochester, Vt.: Inner Traditions, 1990.

Ford, C., and F. Beach. *Patterns of Sexual Behavior.* New York: Harper Colophon, 1951.

Forward, S., and C. Buck. *Betrayal of Innocence: Incest and its Devastations.* New York: Penguin, 1976.

Foss, M. *Symbol and Metaphor in Human Experience.* Lincoln, Nebr.: University of Nebraska Press, 1966.

Foucault, M. *An Introduction.* Vol. 1 of *The History of Sexuality.* Translated by Robert Hurley. New York: Vintage, 1980.

———. *The Care of the Self.* Vol. 3 of *The History of Sexuality.* Translated by Robert Hurley. New York: Vintage, 1986.

———. *Technologies of the Self.* Edited by Luther Martin et al. Amherst, Mass.: University of Massachusetts Press, 1988.

———. *The Use of Pleasure.* Vol. 2 of *The History of Sexuality.* Translated by Robert Hurley. New York: Vintage, 1986.

Fracchia, C. *Living Alone Together.* San Francisco: Harper & Row, 1979.

Freedman, J., and E. D'Emilio. *Intimate Matters: A History of Sexuality in America.* New York: Harper & Row, 1988.

Freud, S. *Beyond the Pleasure Principle.* 1920. Reprinted in *The Freud Reader,* Edited by P. Gray. New York: W. W. Norton, 1989.

———. *Civilization and its Discontents.* 1930. Reprint. Translated by J. Strachey. New York: Norton, 1961.

———. *The Future of an Illusion.* 1927. Reprint. Translated by W. Robson-Scott. Garden City, N.Y.: Doubleday, 1961.

———. *The History of the Psychoanalytic Movement.* 1914. Reprinted in *Basic*

Writings of Sigmund Freud. Edited by A. Brill. New York: Modern Library, 1977.

———. *Sexuality and the Psychology of Love.* 1905, 1938. Reprint. Edited by P. Reiff. New York: MacMillan, 1963.

———. *Three Essays on the Theory of Sexuality.* 1905. Reprint. Translated by J. Strachey. New York: Avon, 1971.

Gardner, R. *Sex Abuse Hysteria.* Cresskill, N.J.: Creative Therapeutics, 1991.

Gilligan, C. *In a Different Voice.* Cambridge, Mass.: Harvard University Press, 1982.

Giorgi, A., W. Rischer, and R. von Eckhartsberg, eds. *Duquesne Studies in Phenomenological Psychology.* Vol. 1. Pittsburgh: Duquesne University Press, 1971.

Greer, G. *Sex and Destiny.* New York: Harper & Row, 1984; Harper Colophon Edition, 1985.

Gregor, C. *Working Out Together.* New York: Berkeley, 1983.

Griffin, S. *Rape, the Power of Consciousness.* New York: Harper & Row, 1979.

Haich, E. *Sexual Energy and Yoga.* Translated by D. Q. Stephenson. New York: Asi, 1972.

Hales, D., and R. Hales. "American Health Partners." *San Francisco Chronicle, Our World,* 23 January 1983.

Hardin, G. *Population, Evolution and Birth Control.* San Francisco: W. H. Freeman, 1964.

Hatcher, R., et al. *Contraceptive Technology, 1988–1989.* New York: Irvington, 1988.

Heidegger, M. *An Introduction to Metaphysics.* Translated by R. Manheim. Garden City, N.Y.: Anchor, 1961.

———. *Being and Time.* 1927. Reprint. Translated by John Macquarrie and Edward Robinson. New York: Harper & Row, 1962.

———. *Poetry, Language, Thought.* Translated by Albert Hofstater. New York: Harper Colophon, 1975.

———. *What Is Called Thinking?* Translated by F. Weik and J. Gray. New York: Harper & Row, 1968.

Henderson, J. *The Lover Within: Opening to Energy in Sexual Practice.* Barrytown, N.Y.: Station Hill, 1987.

Himes, N. *Medical History of Contraception.* New York: Schocken, 1938.

Hite, S. *The Hite Report.* New York: Dell, 1976.

———. *Women and Love: A Cultural Revolution in Progress.* New York: Knopf, 1987.

Iyengar, B. K. S. *Light on Pranayama*. New York: Crossroad, 1981.

———. *Light on Yoga*. New York: Schocken, 1976.

Jnaneshvar, S. *Jnaneshvari*. Translated by V. Pradhan. Albany, N.Y.: State University of New York, 1987.

Johari, H. *Chakras, Energy Centers of Transformation*. Rochester, Vt.: Destiny Books, 1987.

Jung, C. *The Basic Writings of C. G. Jung*. Edited by V. DeLaszlo. New York: Modern Library, 1959.

Kadloubovsky, E., and G. Palmer, trans. *Writings From the Philokalia, on Prayer of the Heart*. London: Faber, 1977.

Kagan, J. *Unstable Ideas*. Cambridge, Mass.: Harvard University Press, 1989.

Kale, A., and S. Kale. *Tantra: The Secret Power of Sex*. Bombay: Jaico, 1976.

Kaufmann, W. *Religion in Four Dimensions*. New York: Reader's Digest, 1976.

Keleman, S. *The Human Ground, Sexuality, Self and Survival*. Palo Alto, Calif.: Science and Behavior, 1975.

Kent, M. *How to Marry the Man of Your Choice*. New York: Warner, 1987.

Kierkegaard, S. *The Concept of Dread*. 1844. Reprint. Translated by W. Lowrie. Princeton, N.J.: Princeton University Press, 1973.

———. *The Present Age*. 1846. Reprint. Translated by A. Dru. New York: Harper & Row, 1962.

———. "The Sickness Unto Death." 1849. Reprinted in *A Kierkegaard Anthology*. Edited by R. Bretall. New York: Modern Library, 1946.

———. *Works on Love*. 1847. Reprint. Translated by Howard and Edna Hong. New York: Harper Torchbook, 1962.

Kinsey, A., et al. *Sexual Behavior in the Human Female*. Philadelphia: W. B. Saunders, 1973.

Kinsey, A., W. Pomeroy, and C. Martin. *Sexual Behavior in the Human Male*. Philadelphia: W. B. Saunders, 1948.

Klotz, J. "Love and Transference." Unpublished paper given at San Francisco Society for Lacanian Studies, April 17, 1991.

Koestenbaum, P. *Existential Sexuality*. Englewood Cliffs, N.J.: Prentice-Hall, 1974.

Kripalvananda, S. *Realization of the Mystery: A Commentary on the Hathayogapradipika by Yogiraj Atmarama*. Unpublished manuscript.

Krpalvanad (Kripalvananda), S. *Krpalupanisad*. St. Helena, Calif.: Sanatana, 1979.

———. *Pilgrimage of Love*. Vol. 3. Lenox, Mass.: Kripalu Yoga Fellowship, 1984.

———. *Science of Meditation*. Kayavarohan, India: D. H. Patel, 1977.

———. "Success or Freedom?" *Vishvamitra* 4, no. 1 (January 1977): 1–3.

Krishna, G. *Kundalini: The Evolutionary Energy in Man*. Berkeley: Shambhala, 1971.

Kuhn, T. *The Structure of Scientific Revolutions*. Chicago: University of Chicago Press, 1966; 2nd. ed., 1970.

Ladas, A., and B. Whipple. *The G Spot and Other Recent Discoveries About Human Sexuality*. New York: Harper & Row, 1982.

Laing, R. *The Facts of Life*. London: Penguin, 1976.

———. *Knots*. New York: Pantheon, 1970.

———. *The Voice of Experience*. New York: Pantheon, 1982.

Lao Tzu. *The Tao Te Ching: The Texts of Taoism*. 1891. Reprint. Translated by J. Legge. New York: Dover, 1962.

Lasch, C. *The Culture of Narcissism*. New York: Norton, 1978.

Lati, R., and J. Hopkins. *Death, Intermediate State and Rebirth in Tibetan Buddhism*. Reprint. Valois, N.Y.: Gabriel/Snow Lion, 1979, 1985.

Leibowits, M. *The Chemistry of Love*. Boston: Little, Brown, 1983.

Leonard, G. *The End of Sex*. Los Angeles: Jeremy P. Tarcher, 1983.

Lowen, A. *Love and Orgasm*. New York: New American Library, 1967.

Luker, K. *Taking Chances*. Berkeley, Calif.: University of California Press, 1975.

Maharaj, N. *I Am That*. Vols. 1 and 2. Translated by M. Frydman. Bombay: Chetana, 1979.

Marcuse, H. *Eros and Civilization*. New York: Vintage, 1955.

Masters, W., and V. Johnson. *Human Sexual Response*. Boston: Little, Brown, 1966.

Masters, W., V. Johnson, and R. Kolodny. *Masters and Johnson on Sex and Human Loving*. Boston: Little, Brown, 1985.

Merleau-Ponty, M. *The Essential Writings of Merleau-Ponty*. Edited by A. Fisher. New York: Harcourt, Brace & World, 1969.

Miller, A. *Thou Shalt Not be Aware: Society's Betrayal of the Child*. Harrisonburg, Va.: Meridian, 1986.

Miller, W., and L. Newman, eds. *The First Child and Family Formation*. Chapel Hill, N.C.: Carolina Population Center, University of North Carolina, 1978.

Millet, K. *Sexual Politics*. Garden City, N.Y.: Doubleday, 1970.

Money, J. *Love and Love Sickness*. Baltimore: Johns Hopkins University Press, 1980.

Montague, A. *Sex, Man and Society*. New York: Putnam, 1969.

Mookerjie, A. *The Tantric Way.* Boston: Little, Brown, 1977.

Morris, D. *The Naked Ape.* New York: Dell, 1967.

Moses, P. *The Voice of Neurosis.* New York: Gruen & Stratton, 1954.

Motoyama, H. *The Theory of the Chakras.* Wheaton, Ill.: Quest, 1981.

Muni, R. *Yogic Experiences.* Kayavarohan, India: Patel, 1977.

Neill, A. S. *Summerhill: A Radical Approach to Childrearing.* New York: Hart, 1960.

Newton, N. "Interrelationships Between Sexual Responsiveness, Birth and Breast Feeding," In *Critical Issues in Contemporary Sexual Behavior.* Baltimore: Johns Hopkins University Press, 1981.

Nietzsche, F. *Thus Spake Zarathustra.* Translated by W. Kaufmann. In *The Portable Nietzsche.* New York: Viking, 1970.

Oaklander, N. "Sartre on Sex." In *Philosophy of Sex.* Edited by A. Soble. Totowa, N. J.: Littlefield, Adams, 1980.

Otto, R. *Mysticism East and West.* Wheaton, Ill.: Quest, 1987 (original date, 1932).

Peck, M. *The Road Less Traveled.* New York: Touchstone, 1978.

Phelan, N., and M. Volin. *Sex and Yoga.* New York: Harper & Row, 1967.

Prabhavananda, S., and C. Isherwood. *How to Know God: Yoga Aphorisms of Patanjali.* New York: Signet, 1969.

Quine, W. *Ontological Relativism and Other Essays.* New York: Columbia University Press, 1967.

Radha, S. S. *Kundalini for the West.* Spokane, Wash.: Timeless Books, 1978.

Rama, S., R. Ballantine, and S. Ajaya. *Yoga and Psychotherapy.* Honesdale, Pa.: Himalayan Institute, 1979.

Ramanujan, A., ed. and trans. *Speaking of Siva.* Baltimore: Penguin, 1973.

Raphael, S. *Finding Love.* New York: Jove, 1984.

Rawson, P. *The Indian Cult of Ecstasy: Tantra.* New York: Bounty, 1973.

Reich, W. *The Function of the Orgasm.* Translated by V. Carfagano. New York: Simon & Schuster, 1973.

———. *The Sexual Revolution.* Translated by T. Wolfe. New York: Farrar, Strauss, and Giroux, 1974.

Reik, T. *The Psychology of Sex Relations.* New York: Farrar & Reinhart, 1948.

Resnick, S. "Sex Without Sex." *Self Magazine,* July 1988, 98–103.

Richardson, W. "The Mirrors Inside: The Problem of the Self." In *Review of Existential Psychology and Psychiatry: Heidegger and Psychology.* Edited by K. Hoeller. Seattle, Wash.: Review of Existential Psychology and Psychiatry, 1988.

Rieker, H-U. *The Yoga of Light (Das klassiche Yoga-Lehrbuch Indiens)*. Translated from the German by E. Becherer. Los Angeles: Dawn Horse Press, 1971.

Rilke, R. M. *Duino Elegies*. Translated by J. Leishman and S. Spender. New York: Norton, 1963.

———. *Letters to a Young Poet*. Translated by M. Herter. New York: Norton, 1934.

Roszak, T. *The Making of a Counter Culture*. Garden City, N.Y.: Anchor, 1969.

Russell, D. *The Secret Trauma*. New York: Basic, 1986.

Russianoff, P. *Why Do I Think I Am Nothing Without a Man?* New York: Bantam, 1983.

Saint John of the Cross. *The Dark Night of the Soul*. Translated by K. Reinhardt. New York: Ungar, 1957.

Sannella, L. *The Kundalini Experience*. Lower Lake, Calif.: Integral, 1987.

Sartre, J.-P. *Being and Nothingness: An Essay on Phenomenological Ontology*. Translated by H. Barnes. New York: Philosophical Library, 1956.

Schaef, A. *When Society Becomes the Addict*. New York: Harper & Row, 1987.

Schurmann, R. *Heidegger on Being and Acting: From Principles to Anarchy*. Translated by Christine-Marie Gros. Bloomington, Ind.: Indiana University Press, 1987.

Schutz, A. *Collected Papers*. 3 vols. The Hague: Martinus Nijoff, 1962, 1964.

Scruton, R. *Sexual Desire: A Moral Philosophy of the Erotic*. New York: Free Press, 1986.

Shengold, L. *Soul Murder*. New York: Fawcett, 1991.

Singer, J. *Androgyny: Toward a New Theory of Sexuality*. Garden City, N.Y.: Anchor Doubleday, 1977.

Singh, L. P. *Tantra, Its Mystic and Scientific Basis*. Delhi: Concept Publishing, 1976.

Sivananda, S. *Kundalini Yoga*. Sivanandanagar, India: Divine Light, 1971.

Soble, A., ed. *Philosophy of Sex*. Totowa, N.J.: Littlefield, Adams, 1980.

Sovatsky, S. "Clinical Contemplations on Impermanence: Temporal and Linguistic Factors in Client Hopelessness." In *Review of Existential Psychology and Psychiatry* 21, nos 1, 2, 3; Highland, N. J.: Humanities Press International, 1993, pp. 153–179.

———. "Eros as Mystery: The Shared-Gender Mystery." *Journal of Humanistic Psychology*. Vol. 33, no. 2 (Spring 1993): 72–90.

———. "Eros as Mystery: Toward a Transpersonal Sexology and Procreativity." *Journal of Transpersonal Psychology* 17, no. 1 (1985): 1–32.

———. "Kundalini: Breakthrough or Breakdown?" *Yoga Journal* no. 63 (July 1985): 42–43.

———. "A Phenomenological Exploration of Orgasmic, Tantric, and Brahmacharya Sexualities." Ph.D. dissertation, California Institute of Integral Studies, 1984.

———. "The Pleasures of Celibacy." *Yoga Journal* no. 73 (March 1987): 41.

———. "Tantric Celibacy and Erotic Mystery." In *Enlightened Sexuality*. Edited by G. Feuerstein. Freedom, Calif.: Crossing Press, 1989.

Spinoza, B. *Works of Spinoza*. Translated by R. Elwes. New York: Dover, 1951.

Steinhoff, P. "Premarital Pregnancy and the First Birth." In *The First Child and Family Formation*. Edited by W. Miller and L. Newman. Chapel Hill, N.C.: Carolina Population Center, University of North Carolina, 1978.

Stern, D. *The Interpersonal World of the Infant*. New York: Basic, 1985.

Strasser, S. *Phenomenology and the Human Sciences*. Pittsburgh: Duquesne University, 1963.

Symons, D. *The Evolution of Human Sexuality*. Santa Barbara, Calif.: University of Santa Barbara Press, 1979.

Szasz, T. *Sex by Prescription*. Garden City, N.Y.: Anchor, 1980.

Taimini, I. K. *The Science of Yoga*. Wheaton, Ill.: Quest, 1967.

Tart, C., ed. *Transpersonal Psychologies*. New York: Harper Colophon, 1975.

Tripp, C. *The Homosexual Matrix*. New York: McGraw-Hill, 1975.

Van Kaam, A. "Sex and Existence." In *Readings in Existential Phenomenology*. Edited by L. O'Connor. Englewood Cliffs, N.J.: Prentice-Hall, 1967.

Vasu, R. B. S. C. trans. *The Siva Samhita*. New Delhi: Oriental Book Reprint Co., (no date).

Verny, T., with J. Kelly. *The Secret Life of the Unborn Child*. New York: Dell, 1981.

Vishnudevananda, S. *The Complete Illustrated Book of Yoga*. New York: Julian, 1960.

Vishnu Tirtha, S. *Devatma Shakti*. Delhi: Swami Shivom Tirth, 1948.

Vissell, B., and J. Vissell. *The Shared Heart*. Aptos, Calif.: Ramira, 1984.

von Eckhartsberg, R. "Existential-Phenomenological Knowledge Building and Psychological and Community Research." In *Knowledge Building in Community Psychology*. Edited by E. Susskind and D. Klein. Pittsburgh: Duquesne University Press, 1981.

Vyas Dev, S. *Science of Soul*. Rishikesh, India: Yoga Niketan Trust, 1972.

Wells, M. "Address Before National Technical Conference on Earth Sheltered Building Design Innovations," Oklahoma State University, Oklahoma City. In *The Next Whole Earth Catalog.* Edited by S. Brand. New York: Random House, 1980.

Wilber, K. "Are the Chakras Real?" In *Kundalini, Evolution and Enlightenment.* Edited by J. White. Garden City, N.Y.: Anchor, 1979.

———. *Up From Eden.* Garden City, N.Y.: Anchor Doubleday, 1981.

Wittgenstein, L. *Philosophical Investigations: The English Text of the Third Edition.* Translated by G. E. M. Anscombe. New York: Macmillan, 1968.

Woodroffe, J. *Principles of Tantra.* 1914. Reprint. Madras, India: Ganesh, 1978.

Yogananda, S. *Autobiography of a Yogi.* Los Angeles: Self Realization Fellowship, 1946.

Yu, L. *Taoist Yoga, Alchemy and Immortality.* New York: S. Weiser, 1973.

INDEX

abortion, as contraceptive failure, 70, 153; debate over, 4, 22, 31, 53, 175; frustration with, 63, 158, 172

abuse, sexual, 4, 53, 172, 175

accepting difficulties, by forgiving self/others, 87, 135; as sacred, 5; via self-acceptance, 66; via sheer wonder, 148; via viyoga, 133

addictions, culturally pervasive, 16; sexual, 16, 25, 31, 53

admiration, 152; of children, 159

advertising, as a form of eros, 33

agnisara dhauti, 108

ahamkara, 81. *See also* ego-self

AIDS, conflictual problems of, 4, 48, 175; and homophobia, 53; limiting of sexual freedom, 172

Albee, E. (*Who's Afraid of Virginia Woolf?*), 186

alchemical marriage, in solitary celibacy, 161–63; and urdhva-reta process, 91, 121

aloneness, opening to, 161–63. *See also* solitary practice

Alpert, R. (Ram Dass), 75

allure, 23, 39; of impermanence, 36; of uncertainty, 26, 142–44

ambiguity, in emotions, 140; in erotic difficulties, 69, 151; and erotic innuendo, 32–34, 144; as play, 186; of rules, 186; as signaling the erotic, 19, 29, 32–34; in teasing, 137; of the "too good to be true," 69, 147. *See also* paradoxicality

amrita, preservation methods, 99, 100; and second puberty, 91, 121

androgeny, and shared-gender mystery, 55

anger, as cynical enjoyment, 28, 30, 147; as erotic play, 180, 181 fig. 2, 185–86; as existential frustration, 146; impermanence of, 140; transmutation of, 9–10, 151–52; without vengeance 87; as viyoga, 150. *See also* child play

apology, 69, 135, 140, 151, 181 fig. 2

ars erotica, 12, 35, 94; in gender research, 54

asana, 17, 96–98, 101–7; formal alignment of, 97; and subtle movements, 97–98; as worship, 96. *See also specific asana*

asvini mudra, 108

atman. *See* Self; soul

attractions, 3, 26, 32, 42, 85

"awaiting the beloved," 96

awe, 23, 26, 39; of gender, 54, 56–57; of impermanence, 37; misunderstood as fear, 37,
142–44, 146, 152; of the possible, 38, 69,
144; of tantric path, 79; trivialized, 142. *See
also* Burning Bush, The

balanced awareness, 122
bandhas (locks), 99
beginner's mind, 14, 47
belonging 41. *See also* Freedom of Belonging
bhadra-asana (nobility pose), 103
bhakti, (devotion) 16, 44; in chanting 131; with
diety as spouse, 162
bhastrika (bellows-breath), 96, 109
bhujanga-asana (cobra), 104
bindu (seed force), 16, 121
biological clock, 145, 183
birth, 155, 181 fig. 2; arousals, 184; as "orgasm"
of procreativity, 184
blushing, 38–39, 151–52; childhood, 185; Freudian view of, 9. *See also* shyness; turning away
brahmacharya, ambivalence toward, 64; breaks
in practice, 134–35; compared with sex, 65,
90, 120, 132, 176, 180; early stages of, 120–
21; with partner, 65, 75; and personality
issues, 65; and procreation, 70–71, 159–60;
setting duration, 64–65, 79, 167. *See also*
celibacy; tantric sublimation
Breathing Mystery practice, 130
Brown, G. (*The New Celibacy*), 12
Brown, N. (*Love's Body*), "erotic sense of reality," 49; speech as erotic, 139
Buber, M. (*I and Thou*), I-Thou, 61, 120; universal love, 161
Buddha, enlightenment of, 78
Burning Bush, The, 23, 54, 148. *See also* under
chakras, sahasrara

Catholic clergy, 64, 137
celibacy, breaks in practice, 134–35; and creativity, 66; as frightening, 8, 34, 79; gradual
approach to, 137–38; as misunderstood, 13,
72, 161, 179; and spirituality, 72; types of, 5,
88. *See also* brahmacharya; tantric sublimation
celibate kiss, singular, 130
chakras, 17, 82–89; activation practices for, 104–
110; ajna, 88; anahata, 84–87; manipura,
84, 97, 99; muladhara, 82–83; sahasrara,
89; svadhisthana, 83; vishuddha, 87–88
charismatic stirrings, 182

child play, 181 fig. 2; brattiness, 180, 185–86; as
dissimilar from sex, 159, 175, 179–81, 184–
86; distorted by sexo-politics, 184; and sadomasochism, 185–86. *See also* humor; sadomasochism
commitment, 140–46; commodification of, 142;
hidden forms of, 143; lifelong, 69–70, 145–
46; as loyalty to mystery, 141, 143, 148; to
possibility, 69, 142–44; without preset duration, 65; and suspensefulness, 143; and the
unknown future, 69–70, 142, 153
communication, verbal, 139–41; and evanescence, 140; implied meaning 140. *See also*
language; suggestiveness
communication, nonverbal: of attraction, 26, 48,
32–33; sighing, 130; at "turning away"
points, 9, 37–38; beyond verbal clarity, 38,
140; of one's vulnerability, 9. *See also* ambiguity; awe; shyness; suggestiveness
competitiveness, in erotic play, 185–86; female/
male, 44, 53; with noncelibates, 136; relational, 122
consciousness, and sublimation, 15, 75, 78
contraception, as controling fertility, 154; as
problematic, 7, 63, 70–71, 172, 175; should
sex happen, 134; and teenagers, 159–60
Cornucopia practice, 27, 111
Crescent Moon practice, 113–114
cynicism, 24, 28, 29 fig. 1, 30–31, 54, 147; as
erotic play, 181 fig. 2; regarding tantra, 22,
79; transcending, 75, 87

dancing, 129, 131
Dass, B. (*Ashtanga Yoga Primer*), 98
decoupled sex, 15
demystification of eros, 21, 24, 28, 29 fig. 1, 31–
33, 42, 55; effect on commitment, 141– 42;
in daily life, 142, 146; by pop psychology,
141, 144–45, 147–48; and procreativity, 154–
55; via sexo-politics, 176. *See also* Freud, S.;
moralistic control of eros
Desai, A. (*Kripalu Yoga*), 96, 98
de Saint Exupery, A. (*The Little Prince*), 68, 150
desirelessness, of ajna chakra, 88; in meditative
intimacy, 39; in nirbija-samadhi, 78; as well-
hidden, 34
destiny, 149
devotion, 181 fig. 2; and commitment, 143; in
gender relations, 55, 57–58; irreversible, 148;
in mantra chanting, 131; of meditative concentration, 77

dharana, 75, 77–78, 123, 125, 131
dhyana, 75, 78, 124
diet, 133–34
divya sharira, 90, 92
Dual Yoga Mudra, Standing, 114

earthiness, 83, 115, 137
ego-self, 60–61, 81–82
Eisler, R. (*The Chalice and the Blade*), 55
ek-stasis, 76, 182
Ellis, H. (*Psychology of Love*), 177
embarrassment, 39, 152
emotional transmutations, 152
envy, transmutation of, 152
erotic ecology, of body energies, 90; disturbed, 7, 176–78; and freedom of belonging, 152–53; in gender relations, 52, 55–66; rebalancing, 178–79, 188; rhythms of, 90, 157
erotic mystery, 7, 19–20; and impermanence, 35–39, 76; and intimacy, 76; loss of, 21, 24, 51; misunderstandings of, 20; as suspenseful, 25
eternity of human species, 36, 39, 154
evolution of sex, 15–16
exploitation, sexual, 25
eyes, as doors to the soul, 39

faith, and dharana, 77; in early stage of brahmacharya, 121; in gender worship, 58; within intimus, 39; leap of, 72; and viyoga, 149
family practices, 118–19, 129, 159–60
fantasies, 3, 83, 181 fig. 2; transmutation of, 26, 35, 41, 46
fear of strangers, 48
fertility, 153–59, 181 fig. 2, 183–84; conscious procreation, 155–57; intentional control of, 153–54; and sublimation, 155–57
fickleness, 34
flirtation, 26, 40, 181 fig. 2
Freedom of Belonging, 152–53; and planetary wholeness, 152
Foucault, M. (*History of Sexuality*), 12, 54, 180; "sex" as fictitious, 174–75
forgiveness, 57, 60, 69, 86–87, 123, 135; and shyness, 151
friendship, nonsexual, 67
Freud, S., basis for sexual freedom, 12; genital tyranny, 27; limited views of, 2, 4, 9, 180; polymorphous perversity, 179; sex and family life, 146, 159

Gandhi, M., 18, 66
gender, ecology of, 50, 55; as explanation 54, 56; inequities, 53, 56, 59; as over-differentiating, 51, 53; as shared immersion in mystery 27, 50– 59, 129; spiritual response to, 55–59; as trust, 52
genital tyranny, 27
God/Goddess, 59, 72, 79, 81, 185
grace, 17
gratitude, 69, 91; and shyness, 151
Great Gesture practice, 122–25
Greer, G. (*Sex and Destiny*), 12, 22
grief, 152, 158
group practice, 129, 131; same-gender, 62
guru, 91

hala-asana (plow), 101–2
Hammarskjold, D., 66
harassment, 53, 172
hatha yoga, 94–111; as ars erotica, 94–95; as spontaneous movement, 96–98
heart, seeing with, 68, 86
Hearts and Backs practice, 112–13; and sharing differences, 5–6
Herman, J., 174
hermaphrodism, 55
hiddenness, as essence of the erotic, 19–22; made speakable, 20, 21, 24
home-building, 8, 69, 132, 159–60, 181 fig. 2; and commitment, 183
homophobia, 30, 48, 53, 176
homosexuality, 22, 30, 62, 176, 184
hope, 140, 143–44, 152, 182, 183; procreative, 153
hospice practice, 118
house-holder's path, 70, 145–46
humility, 23, 57, 83; procreativity and, 154, 157; as unifying, 152
humor, 85, 87, 136–37
hyper-repressive desublimation, 49

I-Thou, 120
impermanence, 29 fig. 1, 35–37, 76; confused with abandonment, 37; confused with loss, 148; shared, 38
immortality, 79, 89, 92, 94, 150. *See also* mortality
incest, 53, 173–74
inner adult, 123, 129
inner child, 31, 145, 185
inner marriage. *See* alchemical marriage

innocence, diminished by judgmentalism, 136, 147; as erotic contact, 34; of erotic mystery, 7; and naivete, 47; and sublimative wonder, 25–26; and wildness, 39

intelligence, higher, 77

interpreting erotic feelings, 3, 28, 179–88; linguistic difficulties of, 15; as playful, 136, 159, 175, 179, 180–81; as procreative passion, 154–59, 180–81, 183–84; as sex-desire, 159–60, 180–82; as sublimative passion, 14, 43, 134, 137–38, 159–60, 180–82. *See also* language

interrogation of eros, 24–6, 124

intimacy, 67; and childhood shyness, 185; fear of, 38; as shared impermanence, 36

intimus, 29 fig. 1, 39, 80

Iyengar, B. K. (*Light on Pranayama; Light on Yoga*), 98

jealousy, transmutation of, 152

jiva. *See* Self; soul

jivan-mukti, 163

Jnaneshvari-gita, 79, 88, 92, 98, 121

John of the Cross, Saint (*The Dark Night of the Soul*), 160

Kagan, J. (*Unstable Ideas*), 9

kaivalya, 75, 78–79, 89

kapala-bhati, 96, 100

karma, 64, 66

karma yoga, 66, 162

khechari mudra, 91, 124, 183

Kinsey, A., 4, 173–74, 177

koan, 34

Koestenbaum, P. (*Existential Sexuality*), 11

koshas (subtle bodies), anandamaya, 80, 81, 82; annamaya, 80, 82, 134; manomaya, 80–81; pranamaya, 80, 134; vijnanamaya, 80, 81

Kripalvananda, S., 74, 104

Krishna, G. (*Kundalini: Evolutionary Energy in Man*), 83

kshama, 87. *See also* forgiveness

kundalini, allured upward by ojas, 84, 91; and genius, 83; in Jnaneshvari, 92; and primal creativity, 83; and second puberty, 91; in sublimative passion, 181 fig. 2, 182–83

Laing, R. D. (*The Facts of Life*), 71

labeling, dangers in, child behavior, 185; erotic phenomena, 59–61, 180, 184, 187–88; oneself, 33

language, and creating a world, 61, 144; and humor, 137; and subtle distinctions, 14–15, 87, 144; and suggestiveness, 33, 140

Lao Tzu (*Tao Te Ching*), 35–36, 177

Lawrence, D. H. (*The Plumed Serpent*), 28

Leonard, G. (*The End of Sex*), "high monogamy," 12

longing, being filled by, 14; in bhakti yoga, 44; and viyogic union, 149, 152

love, 17, and the allure of sex, 85, 182; and anahata chakra, 84–87; desireless, 78, 86–88; unconditional, 87, 162, 145; universal, 17, 153, 161. *See also* prema

Luker, K. (*Taking Chances*), 70

Mahadeviyakka, 149

maha mudra, 99

Malebranche, N. de, 79

Mann, T. (*Death in Venice*), 187

mantra chanting, 131; and pratyhara, 76

Marcuse, H. (*Eros and Civilization*), hyper-repressive desublimation, 49

marriage, 69, 145–46

Masters and Johnson, 4; and artificial wombs, 154

masturbation, 181 fig. 2; and child's play, 159, 185; opposing views of, 31; as vestigial 3

meditation, before asana practice, 96; and beautification, 36, 122–23; and creativity, 66; eros-enthralled, 73, 76, 96, 150; objects for, 110; as research method, 7

menopause, 132

"midlife crisis," 145

missing another, 44, 149–52; and sublimation, 138

money, 146

Money, J. (*Love and Love Sickness*), 74

moralistic control of eros, of childhood eros, 159; inducing cynicism, 31; as disturbing erotic ecology 177; as an erotic play, 186; through guilt, 22, 27; and sexo-politics, 21–26. *See also* demystification of eros; sexo-politics

Morris, D. (*The Naked Ape*), 15

mortality, 181 fig. 2; awakened to via solitary celibacy, 163; known via impermanence, 35–36, 38; and the NOW, 29. *See also* immortality

motivations for brahmacharya, 63–72; as adventure, 63; to deepen intimacy 67–68; desire for solitude 66–67, 160–64; to develop nonsexual friendships, 67; to enhance marriage, 69–70; explore spirituality, 72; frustrations with contraception, 63; health, 64, 67; for priests, 64, 137; problematic, 65–66, 160; support for creativity, 66; to transform relational struggles, 68–69

motivations in breaching brahmacharya, 135, 163

mystery, as essence of eros, 19–20; gender as shared, 50–59; pleasure as opening to, 23

Mystery of Balance practice, 44

nabhan mudra, 100, 124, 183

nadi shodhana sahita kumbhaka, 100

Neill, A. S. (*Summerhill: A Radical Approach to Childrearing*), 177

Nicephorus the Solitary, 77; nirbija-samadhi, 75, 78, 89, 162–63

nonattachment, 67, 88. *See also* desirelessness; vairagha

nondualism, 81

nonjudgmental openness, 13, 81, 136

nursing arousals, 181 fig. 2, 183–84, 187

nyasa, 125–27, 156

ojas, as body constituent, 90; as "DNA-like," 16–17; within erotic ecology, 90; and inner alchemy, 121; and manipura chakra, 84; and virya, 86

orgasm, as adjective, 9, 89; of aloneness, 162; of consciousness, 17; genital, 86, 181 fig. 2, 182; in gradual celibacy, 137–38; of released hiddenness, 25

orgonomic streaming, 182

"owning" sexuality, limitations of concept of, 59–61; as recovery word-tool, 59–60

padma-asana (lotus), 103

paradoxicality, of erotic allure, 23; of a holiness hidden everywhere, 59; of mercurial emotions, 69

parental pride, 183

pashchimottana-asana (back-stretching pose), 102

Patanjali (*Yoga Sutras*), 75

perceptual bonding, 15–16

perfectionism, avoiding, 135, 159

pornography, 20, 24

possibility, compared with expectation, 141–45; greater than actuality, 57

post-genital puberty, and psychosexual development, 73; and sensing cosmic rhythms, 37. *See also* urdhva-reta

power struggles, 46, 186

Prabhu, A., 89

prana, apana-pran, 99; sub-pranas, 97

pranayama, bhastrika, 96, 109; chatur bhuja, 108; gharshana, 107; nadi shodhana sahita kumbhaka, 100

Pranic Mirroring practice, 129

pratyahara, and the breath, 76; defined, 75; and evanescent subtlety, 76; and mantra chanting, 76, 131; and the senses, 76; and slow movement, 125; and suggestive ambiguity, 75; and visual acuity, 122

pregnancy, unintended, 7, 70–71, 172

prema, 78, 87. *See also* love

prenatal yoga, 119

pretentiousness, 136, 137

"pre-transpersonal fallacy," 84

procreation, as erotic domain, 181 fig. 2, 183–184; as miracle, 71, 153–59; as temporal urgency, 36–37

puberty, conventional view of, 179; ritual, 159–60

Ramakrishna, 65

recovery, moving beyond, 59–61

Reich, W., 4, 70, 177, 182

religion as *religare,* and meditation, 76

renunciations, 18, 162, 181 fig. 2

repression, 21, 177, 179

respect, 60–61, 151; for all yogis, 79

restricted-movment practice, 118

Rilke, R. M. (*Duino Elegies*), 60, 76, 79–80, 127

ritual worship, 76, 131–32; for families, 159–60

Russell, D. (*The Secret Trauma*), 173–74

sabija-samadhi, 75, 78, 89

sadhana, as formal practice, 18; as love partner, 67, 161–63

sadness, 152

sadomasochism, 147, 181 fig. 2, 186; and ascetic mortification, 186; as trust games, 186

safe sex, 64, 134

sahaja yoga, 96

sara hasta bhujanga-asana (king cobra), 104

sarvanga-asana (shoulder stand), 101

Schurmann, R. (*Heidegger On Being and Acting: From Principles to Anarchy*), 177–78

scientia sexualis, 12, 178, 180; in gender research, 54

secret teachings, 93, 94

Self, 18, 81, 161. *See also* soul

sensate focusing, 74

sensuality, 80

separating, 146–49; and hypercriticism, 147; and sadomasochism, 147; and wonder, 148

sex-desire, 179, 181 fig. 2, 182, 187

sex education, 71, 166; reinterpreted via mystery, 159, 175

sex therapy, 74, 172

sexo-politics, 21–24, 31, 175–76, 185; of "owning one's sexuality," 59–60. *See also* demystification of eros

sexual liberation movement, as aging, 172–76; distortions created by, 9, 184; faulty erotic map of, 4, 173–75, 177–78, 187; as grandiose, 12; imperialism of, 22; limitations of, 4, 8, 11–12, 25, 27, 37, 174–78

sexual images as symbolic, 22, 86

sexual safety, 49

sexually transmitted disease, 7, 64

sexuality, as fictitious notion, 174–75; and the media, 48

shadow, 53

shakti-pata-diksha, 91

shame, 23, 39, 140

sharing, 150; contrasted with "individuation," 185; difficulties, 6, 9–10, 44–45, 52, 62, 120, 127–29, 134–35; forgiveness, 151; mystery, 26, 52; procreation, 158–59; same experience 26, 47; as viyoga, 150

shirsa-asana (headstand), 102

shyness, beauty of, 38–39, 43, 45, 48–49, 55, 180, 183; in childhood, 185; as emotional illuminant 39; and meditation, 75, 123

siddha-asana (adept pose), 103

silence, 39, 43–44, 67, 77, 124, 140

skepticism, 30, 46–47

sleep, 134

solitary practice, 68–69, 160–64; and daily life, 163

Song of Solomon, 34, 124–25

soul, 39, 81; and commitment, 143; devaluation of, 12; and meditation, 78, 124; "murder" 61; resiliency of, 60–61, 87; shyness as a radiance of, 39, 151–52. *See also* Self; shyness

spinal arousals, 13, 168

Spinoza, B. (*Works of Spinoza*), 81

spiritual, needs, 14, 145; aspect of daily life, 5, 7–8; materialism, 136

sublimative passion, 43, 73, 74, 90, 96–98, 187–88; and channeling energy, 3, 17, 45, 54, 124, 168; point of no return, 38–39; and uncertainty, 85; and yogic stretching, 3, 13, 17, 27, 43, 97

Sublimation Vee practice, 116

suchness, 78, 123

suggestiveness, 19, 29; and ambiguity, 29 fig. 1, 32–35, 75

surrender, 43, 46, 57, 62; to aloneness, 162

suspensefulness, 143–44, 182, 187; of play, 185; of procreativity, 183; of sex-desire, 182; of sublimation, 182

Symons, D. (*The Evolution of Human Sexuality*), 15–16

synchronicity, 50, 150, 157

systems theory, 55

tantric sublimation, 5, 120; body-affirming, 5, 136; breaks in practice of, 134–35; compared with sex, 65, 74, 136; and the emotions, 16, 121, 123; and intimacy, 12; and the 1990s, 171–75, 178; and "tantric sex," 17

tantra, in daily life, 7, 8, 10; defined, 7; history of, 16; as paradoxical, 5, 8, 59

tears as erotic secretions, 123

Teresa, Mother, 66, 87

teenagers, 6, 63, 71, 159–60, 166–70; Alternate Breathing practice, 169; couples practices for, 168–69; meditation for, 167–69; parental concerns for, 166; and spirituality, 170; Yourself Breathing practice, 168–69

thanatos, 145, 186

Tirtha, S. V. (*Devatma Shakti*), 98

turning away, 37

Twin Boats practice, 6, 115–16

Twin Cobras practice, 115

Twin Dancers' practice, 117

Twin Plows practice, 116–17

union, with another, 12–13, 44; with life's harmonies, 85, 90

uniqueness, individual, 81, 122

unity, 8, 78, 152–53

unspeakability, 140, 163. *See also* silence

urdhva-reta, defined, 16; as second puberty, 91–

92; as sublimative passion, 181 fig. 2, 183. *See also* post-genital puberty

vairagha, 88. *See also* desirelessness; non-attachment
Verny, T. (*The Secret Life of the Unborn Child*), 158
Victorians, 23
video yoga courses, 118
viparita karani mudra (reverse pose), 101
virya, 17, 86, 123
Vishnudevananda, S. (*The Complete Illustrated Book of Yoga*), 98
viyoga, 68, 133, 143, 149–52
vulnerability, emotional, 9–10
Vyas Dev, S. (*Science of Soul*), 81, 89

war, eroticism of, 186
Wells, M. (*Address . . . 1980*), 176
Whitman, W. *(Leaves of Grass),* 46, 141, 153
wonderment, 7, 25–26, 35, 124; of procreativity, 155
Woodroffe, J. (Avalon, A.), 93
worship, hatha yoga as, 96; in shared-gender mystery, 57–59

xenophobia, 152

YHWH, 78
yoga, defined, 8; schedule of daily practice, 67, 105, 110–11, 162
yoga mudra, 104
yoni mudra, 108–9